THE
MIAMI INDIANS
OF INDIANA:

A Persistent People

1654–1994

THE
MIAMI INDIANS
OF INDIANA:

A Persistent People

1654–1994

■

STEWART RAFERT

Indiana Historical Society Press

1996

©1996 Indiana Historical Society Press. All rights reserved.
Reprinted 1998, 2000, 2003
Printed in the United States of America

This book is a publication of the
Indiana Historical Society Press
450 West Ohio Street
Indianapolis, Indiana 46202-3269 USA
www.indianahistory.org
Telephone orders 1-800-447-1830
Fax orders 317-234-0562
Orders by E-mail shop.indianahistory.org

The paper in this publication meets the minimum requirements of
American National Standard for Information Sciences—Permanence
of Paper for Printed Library Materials, ANSI Z39.48-1984 ∞

Library of Congress Cataloging-in-Publication Data

Rafert, Stewart.
   The Miami Indians of Indiana: a persistent people, 1654–1994 /
Stewart Rafert.
      p. cm.
   Includes bibliographical references and index.
   ISBN 0-87195-132-0 (paper)
   1. Miami Indians—History. 2. Miami Indians—Removal. 3. Miami
Indians—Claims. I. Title.
977.2'01—dc20   95-42296
                                                                      CIP

CONTENTS

■

PREFACE

∎

THIS BOOK IS FOR A GENERAL AUDIENCE AS WELL AS FOR serious students of tribal history interested in the experience of a North American Indian community over three and a half centuries. I could have written a history of the Eastern Miami beginning with removal in 1846, but the previous tribal history and folklife are important in understanding the postremoval tribe. Besides, the 1846 event was far less disruptive to the home Miami community than some observers believed and actually marked the beginning of a revitalization of the community.

Even today most historians devote the majority of their attention to early tribal history, concentrating on the period up to Indian removal or the ending of the frontier, with later history added as an afterthought. This lack of attention to more recent tribal history gives the impression that a group has died out or is so assimilated that there is little history of interest. Change in Indian communities has been constant for centuries, and loss of earlier customs and folkways does not mean the communities have ceased to exist. The surprising fact is the adaptation and persistence of Native American communities into the late twentieth century when many observers felt that the communities would disappear years ago. Such persistence is especially striking east of the Mississippi River where there has been frequent contact with outsiders for three centuries or more.

Overemphasis on tribal history during the frontier period creates a stereotype of Indian life that is a barrier to understanding change in Indian tribes. Without any understanding of change the modern observer of tribal customs and affairs could judge that a people are not Indian because they do not act or appear as they did a hundred or two hundred years ago. Fortunately some historians are reviewing the frontier period with fresh perspectives and are bringing Indian attitudes and viewpoints into Indian history. This kind of research that goes beyond documents is hard work and is comparable to researching modern Native American communities where information is scattered and often hard to analyze. The research must be done, however, if we are to get a more complete understanding of the hundreds of Indian groups that continue to coexist in our larger society.

When I came to the Miami I found them intensely aware of their history and extremely wary of outsiders. They had extensive knowledge of their past, including federal relations following removal in 1846. The very history that they were most engaged in was the history that outsiders had ignored in the mistaken belief that the Indiana Miami were always on the verge of dying out as a distinct population. I soon discovered the Miami had no such beliefs themselves and that they possessed a complex, multifaceted community history and sense of identity that was very powerful and ongoing. In this volume I focus on Miami history in the nineteenth and twentieth centuries and have given a reading of earlier Miami history in light of later tribal experience. Some of my colleagues will disagree with this recasting of the past, but I am concerned with a living community and those elements of the past that have shaped the present.

My research has focused on tribal history after 1846 because the postremoval history of the Indiana Miami is little known to outsiders and because it demonstrates the clear continuity of this important tribe into the present. Indeed, some of the most dramatic Miami history has occurred during the twentieth century. The current struggle for federal status has gained the Indiana Miami national attention on a scale not experienced since the 1830s. The reader who is interested only in modern Miami history may want to skip over the first two chapters and begin with the American period in 1795. I recommend against this because the first two chapters convey many of the folkways and beliefs that have set the tone of the distinct modern Miami community.

My approach throughout the book is ethnohistorical in the sense that I try to incorporate Miami viewpoints and tribal actions in the history. Very often federal officials would attempt to impose new policies on the Miami, only to have them react far differently than expected. Part of the task of the historian is to show these Miami reactions from the standpoint of an ongoing culture that has made many adaptations, but is still distinct. We also tend to think of Indian groups as always moving toward the dominant society as a cultural model, but there are times when they "revitalize" and move toward older beliefs and values. The Miami have been active shapers of their own destiny, and unless we understand Miami actions and processes we will miss a great deal of their history.

The word *tribe* is a fairly modern name for a type of society consisting of several separate communities united by kinship and social units such as clans, religious organizations, and economic and political institutions. There is no general consensus on a precise definition. I use the term in the ordinary sense in which it is applied to Indian groups in the United States which have a sense of separate identity and wish to preserve a cultural heritage. The term *nation* derives from the treaty-making era of United States history. Treaties are kept with diplomatic papers at the National Archives, are ratified by the United States Senate, and are regarded as agreements with independent governments. Chief Justice John Marshall recognized Indian governments as "domestic, dependent nations" in *Cherokee Nation* v. *Georgia* (1831). In the twentieth century the Indiana Miami have again called themselves the "Miami Nation" in their attempts to regain treaty rights.

There is a sharp distinction in American Indian law between recognized and nonrecognized Indian groups. The Indiana Miami at present are not federally recognized, so federal Indian law and protections do not apply to them. Legally they are not a tribe and are called Miami descendants. Under recent federal law Miami Indian artisans cannot sell crafts as American Indians. Other disabilities in the areas of health care, education, and social programs derive from their lack of status under Indian law. The Indiana Miami have challenged their nonrecognized status for nearly a century and always refer to themselves as a tribe or nation. Basing their status on a long history of federal relations and a treaty signed in 1854, their formal organization is called the "Miami Nation of Indians of the State of Indiana."

A few matters of style should be mentioned here. I prefer the singular form when referring to the people of a tribe if the tribal name refers to a collective group as it usually does. Thus, with only a few exceptions, I refer to the Miami, Potawatomi, Delaware, and so on. I also use the modern preferred forms of tribal names such as Ojibwa for the older Chippewa and Lakota for Sioux.

Miami personal names, which are still given, have been spelled many different ways. I use the most common spelling and avoid the garbled spellings of English-speaking clerks and observers as well as the nineteenth-century dashes between syllables. The Miami did not anglicize their names as did the Lakota and many other Plains tribes during the late nineteenth century. The old names live on, though most Miami have forgotten the English translations. Most of the names refer to trees, animals, gestures, sounds, seasons, time of day, and so on. I often give the Miami name alongside the English name and a translation if it is known. A few of the Miami up until the twentieth century did not have English names. Best known were Meshingomesia (Bur Oak) and Pimyotamah (Sound of Something Going By). The current spelling of surnames varies, too. For example, some members of the Bundy family also spell their name "Bondy."

Albert S. Gatschet and Jacob P. Dunn made invaluable lists of Miami words in the late nineteenth and early twentieth centuries. I use the word lists to give a better idea of daily activities and attitudes and to show the persistence of many folkways into the twentieth century. During the 1930s Carl F. Voegelin, a professional linguist, reorganized Dunn's word list and made minor changes in spelling. I make use of Voegelin's work, published as *Shawnee Stems and the Jacob P. Dunn Miami Dictionary*, when quoting Miami words. Rather than undo Dunn and Voegelin's work, I will give the pronunciation for their marked letters. A *č* is pronounced as the "ch" in chair, while an *š* is pronounced as the "sh" in shoe. The Miami word for sandhill crane is written as *čäčakwa*. The *ä* is pronounced like the "e" in "the." The word sounds approximately like "chuhchakwuh." Two syllable Miami words are usually stressed on the first syllable. Three and four syllable words are usually stressed on the second syllable.

I refer to the Miami as Indians because that is what they call themselves when they do not refer to themselves as Miami. They are mainly a rural and small town people, and the term Native American never really caught on with them. When speaking of tribal peoples in general or of government policies I use the term Indian in most cases, though the term Native American fits some urban Indians and the history of the 1960s and 1970s. Non-Indians I call European Americans, whites, or African Americans, or I use their national names. The term white often has racist connotations for Indians, but is generally not perceived that way by the European Americans who make up the dominant society. While I do not like racism, I believe it tends to disappear as groups gain control of their own destinies. In this sense Indian racism toward members of the dominant group in our society reflects a sense of powerlessness.

I came to the Miami as a historian in the late 1970s, interested in how small communities persist and change over time. I quickly realized that an Indian community is very different from the seventeenth-century New England communities I had studied. Here was a community in the late twentieth century with sharp edges and a very long collective memory. My questions sometimes provoked strong responses or were totally ignored. My best tactic was to listen, and in this way the Miami inducted me into ethnohistory far better than any anthropology course could have done.

Many Miami people assisted my work. The Miami memory of the past is pungent, detailed, and often humorous in its details of human foibles. There is also a strong element of anger in memories of injustices, pride in survival, and a warm sense of security within a loving community that tries to take care of its own. Miami recollections often seemed timeless to me because past events are rooted in present reactions. For many Miami history is not something formal and distanced from everyday life, but it is an important part of everyday life and experience. The Miami scorn most formal history as biased and inaccurate. Tribal history is passed down from generation to generation, argued over, defended, and used in the service of the community. This attitude may sound unprofessional until one remembers that professional historians distorted and ignored tribal history for a very long time and wrote Indians out of American history. By and large I found Miami history told by Miami people to be accurate and, most important of all, the Miami steered me to documents that had been long forgotten.

Books about human societies can set forth only roughly the shape of their history and daily life. I will never know the inner experience of being a Miami Indian. My work is meant to suggest as well as describe in the hope that others will join in the study of modern Native American communities. Like canaries in a mine shaft, the fate of such small groups tells us much about the social and legal atmosphere of our larger society and our place in it. In this sense the history of the Indiana Miami is the history of us all.

Newark, Delaware, 25 March 1994

ACKNOWLEDGMENTS

■

THE WRITING OF THIS BOOK WAS PUT OFF FAR TOO LONG, and regrettably, a number of people who helped over the years have died. While one shares the joy of learning from Indian elders, one also experiences lasting grief when they pass on. Swan Hunter (Wapingequah, White Swan) helped me from the beginning of my research with genealogy and later allowed many of her photographs to be copied, several of which appear in this volume. She and her niece, Eva Bossley, told of growing up in Butler Township, Miami County, shared some recipes for cooking milkweed, and gave a good description of the Gabriel Godfroy household in the days when it was a Miami social center. Mrs. Bossley's brother Oliver Godfroy (Swimming Turtle) told me in passionate tones of his efforts to free his treaty land from county taxation, a case that had been in and out of court since the 1870s. Shortly after my interview, he won his case and a few days later died quietly in his sleep.

Carmen Ryan told of the formation of the Miami Nation, the modern tribal government, and of efforts to gain federal recognition in the 1930s. Mrs. Ryan was a constant letter writer, and dozens of her letters written over the past fifty years give a clear idea of Miami governance since the 1920s. Lyman Mongosa, Herman Bundy, Homer "Sid" Mongosa, LaMoine Marks, and others told me of hunting, trapping, and fishing on the rivers and created a vivid picture of everyday life for Miami boys and men. Robert Owens told of life in the Lafontaine house at the forks of the Wabash just west of Huntington, Indiana. Other Miami told of the Maconaquah Pageant in the 1920s and 1930s, of searching for edible and medicinal plants, work in the circuses east of Peru, and episodes of prejudice. The more I learned, the easier it was to ask for more information, a process that has never ceased. This work reflects, so far as possible, the memories of the Miami people coupled with a great deal of research in local and federal records.

The Miami tribe has been documented heavily since the eighteenth century. The documentation continued after Miami removal in 1846, and I have found an astounding array of information on tribal activities scattered in many sources. My task has been to gather many bits of information and to bring them together into a coherent history, not an easy task as anyone who has attempted writing a tribal history must know. The pleasure has far outweighed the pain.

I am indebted to many non-Indians for assistance as well. At the National Archives in Washington, D.C., Richard Crawford, Robert Kvasnicka, Robert Fowler, Renee Jussaud, and many others helped bring Miami items to my attention. In Indiana, Linda Robertson and Ron Woodward, Wabash County historian, were helpful, as were many officials in Wabash, Miami, and Grant Counties.

Among ethnohistorians I must thank James Clifton for searching out my work and providing continuing encouragement to pursue actively and enlarge my research over the years. Historians R. David Edmunds and James H. Madison, both at Indiana University, gave the manuscript a careful reading, as did my colleague in Miami studies, Elizabeth Glenn at Ball State University. Phyllis Miley (Maconaquah) read the work from the Miami perspective and offered many useful comments. Virgil Vogel, expert on American Indian medicine and place names, gave me constant support and was a model of careful scholarship until his death in January 1994.

The Miami Nation hired me to write a petition for federal recognition for them in 1982. I worked closely with the tribal council and many volunteers over an eight-year period. We had a warm and professional relationship, one in which the Miami were clearly in charge. It is a testimony to the strength of Miami governance and self-confidence that I never felt a need to tell tribal officials what to do, though I sometimes made suggestions. Chief Francis Shoemaker, tribal secretary Lora Siders, Robert Owens, Lawrence Godfroy, the tribal council, and the junior council were unfailingly helpful to my work, and I particularly want to thank the tribal leadership and many Miami people for a warm working relationship. I worked especially closely with Chairman Raymond White, Jr., who was a tireless advocate of Indian burial issues and brought national attention to the Indiana Miami tribe, as well as creating a modern tribal center. His foremost goal was to regain federal recognition for the tribe. His life was cut short at the age of fifty-six in March 1994, before he could see that dream of the Miami people come true.

The Indiana Historical Society has supported my Miami research from its beginning. A Clio Grant from the Society funded much of the writing of the book, as did a grant from the Ball Brothers Foundation and from Edmund Ball. The Administration for Native Americans, Department of Health and Human Services, funded extensive research for Miami recognition over an eight-year period, much of which is reflected in the present work.

Family and friends have helped greatly over the years. My wife Nancy has tolerated numerous lengthy stays in Indiana with our growing family. Our three girls, Samara, Kyla, and Jesse, have become adopted midwesterners and have developed a sophisticated knowledge of regional differences. Our friends

Mike and Judi Brown and Rich and Rachael Rogers in North Manchester, Indiana, have hosted many visits and have made continuing low-budget research possible through their generosity. My parents Stewart and Mildred Rafert have wholeheartedly supported my career as an independent scholar and have become surprisingly staunch advocates of Indian rights and self-determination. My late cousin Dr. Allegra Stewart offered unfailing hospitality and a beautiful setting at her home in Indianapolis for talking about the life of native peoples in modern secular society.

I am very grateful to my daughters Samara for writing suggestions and Kyla for help with the computer. Pam Goffinet created the maps.

INTRODUCTION

■

When I try to get a true perspective I so often find my-self despondent because "that world of song and laugh-ter" no longer exists—and the children have tried to adapt to a Puritanical world where God is a severe judge, and they escape in whatever way they find available, sometimes destructive.

Carmen Ryan, 20 August 1983[1]

We've come out from under a rock, and we're going to stay out.

Chief Francis Shoemaker, 6 July 1985[2]

PERIODICALLY OVER THE PAST TWO CENTURIES OUTSIDE observers have predicted the end of the Miami Indians as a rec-ognizable Indian group, either through loss of population or total assimilation into American society. In May 1848 historian John B. Dillon wrote:

At the present day a few small, mixed and miserable bands constitute the remnant of the once powerful Miami nation.

[S]hrouded in darkness, with the lights of civilization and religion beaming around them, the last fragments of one

of the most powerful aboriginal nations of North America
are passing away from the earth forever.[3]

As recently as the 1950s those who knew the Miami and even
some of the Miami themselves expected the disappearance of
the tribe. At the time only a handful of Miami owned a few
acres of the thousands possessed by Miami tribespeople a century earlier. Collections of clothing, beadwork, silver trade
crosses, and peace medals had been sold to collectors long ago,
and tribal craft activity was almost nonexistent. The spoken
language was becoming extinct, most folklore and subsistence
activities connected with the land were gone, and the great majority of Miami were married to non-Indians. It seemed only a
matter of time before there would be nothing left that could be
called Miami.

Remarkably, the Miami Indians continue today not only as a
recognizable community of Indians in Indiana, but also as a
group aggressively seeking restoration of full status as a federal
Indian tribe. Craft activities flourish, and the Twigh Twee
Drum, a group of male singers, perform at various ceremonies
and events in the Midwest. Hundreds of people attend spring
and fall general meetings of the tribe, as well as the Miami reunion held every August since 1903. The tribe is able to hire
legal experts to pursue Miami rights and has funds for a number
of other activities.

Beginning slowly in the 1960s the Miami once again revital-
ized themselves as a tribe. The rebirth of tribalism gathered
strength in the 1970s, fed partly by national trends in Indian
awareness and awards by the Indian Claims Commission, but
much more so by dynamics particular to the Miami, who were
independent of the "Red Power movement" and Indian activism of the time. By the early 1980s the tribe was able to
persuade the Indiana legislature to support full federal recognition and began hiring experts and gathering volunteers to do
the extensive research and administrative work involved in

petitioning the Bureau of Indian Affairs for such status. By the early 1990s the tribe had emerged as a full-fledged tribal organization, able to provide considerable support and services to its people without federal recognition, although that goal remained critically important.

If John Dillon or any of the other doubters of tribal persistence over the years were to come to Peru, seat of Miami County, today they would be surprised at the Miami establishment. There, on Miami Street in the former Peru High School, they would find a tribal headquarters with modern offices, an extensive tribal archive, a cultural center and small museum, day-care center, tribal council chambers, cafeteria, and bingo hall. A few miles east of Peru the tribe has purchased thirty-five acres of land along the Mississinewa River upon which it has built a longhouse for various ceremonies.

How has a small Indian tribe that has lost its land, language, most of its land-based culture, legal status, and even in many cases the stereotypical Indian appearance of its members kept its identity? Further, how has such a group continued in its insistence that it is a North American Indian tribe, despite continuing efforts of the United States government to detribalize the group for nearly a century and a half? This book is an attempt to describe the persistence of a Miami identity up to the present, despite great changes in the tribal culture and community. I describe the Miami as a "hidden community" because when times have been tough, they have gone "under a rock," to use Chief Shoemaker's metaphor. Today, as a sign of strength, they are much less hidden.

The interaction of the Miami people with French, British, and Spanish imperial governments, and with the American federal government, with non-Indians, and with other tribes has been a heavily documented story since the late seventeenth century. The Miami have gone through a number of transformations, sometimes turning up cultural and political blind alleys, but always managing to find themselves again as a people. The

Miami of the late twentieth century are clearly not culturally the same as the Miami first contacted by the French in 1654, nor are they culturally the Miami of the early nineteenth century. If they had persisted in the cultural characteristics of those periods, they would be extinct. Rather the Miami have found continuity and survival as a people through their ability to change.[4] Like the person whose soft tissues and even bones are replaced by new cells over time, the Miami have changed in many ways, while in some ways they have remained recognizably the same over a very long period of time.

Today twenty-five hundred Miami (half the tribe) still live in Indiana. The great majority of the state population is concentrated in Elkhart and St. Joseph Counties and in the old homeland of the tribe in the upper Wabash valley in Miami, Wabash, Grant, Huntington, and Allen Counties. About half the Miami population in Indiana is concentrated in Peru, Wabash, Huntington, Fort Wayne, and South Bend, while the remaining Miami are dispersed among other people and do not see each other as a matter of course. Over three-fourths of the tribe in Indiana live in urban or suburban areas, if one counts small towns. Only one-fourth lives in rural areas, and virtually none of the rural Miami lives on old treaty reserves or village sites.[5]

Half the Indiana Miami live outside Indiana. A quarter of the out-of-state Miami are concentrated in the tristate area centered about Miami, Oklahoma, Baxter Springs, Kansas, and Joplin, Missouri, where they migrated beginning in the 1860s as land was lost in Indiana and the Western Miami reservation in Kansas was allotted and sold. The remainder are scattered over many states. Without federal recognition the Miami receive no direct federal funding as an Indian tribe. Income comes from bingo halls, tribal membership dues, grants available to community groups, and other forms of fund-raising.

In 1846, after about two hundred years of documented history, the federal government split the Miami tribe into two tribes. The Miami who were permitted to remain in Indiana became known as the Eastern or Indiana Miami, while the Miami who were forcibly relocated to Kansas Territory became known as the Western or Oklahoma Miami. A comparison of the two tribes is sometimes helpful. Subsequent movements of tribal population between eastern and western areas has complicated both tribal histories and has at times perplexed federal officials. The federal government has insisted since 1846 that the tribal government resides among the Oklahoma Miami, and has given only the most grudging recognition of the legal rights and needs of the Indiana Miami. The Indiana tribe, three times as large as the Oklahoma tribe, has thus been treated as a stepsister of the Western Miami tribe and as an "orphan" among American tribes.

The return of many Miami to Indiana after removal frustrated the official policy of moving Indians west of the Mississippi River and strengthened the hand of Indian leaders in Indiana. It became an aspect of tribal pride and memory, aiding tribal continuity. Another aid to continuity was extended Miami families or kinship groups. Though the Miami still refer to family lineages as clans, these groups replaced the earlier Miami clans and became social and political entities that jostled against each other and came together only at critical times to resolve issues. When they were unable to achieve unity they existed as competing factions. The combination and separation of these large groups has been a continual theme in Miami history and has greatly strengthened the identity of the Miami as a separate people.

When I came to the Miami in the late 1970s they were recovering from grueling confrontations with each other over tribal leadership and how to handle awards from the Indian Claims Commission. The prospect of receiving some money from the federal government was unsettling, as it forced the Miami to redefine who they were. In the midst of the twenty-year-long claims process, there was a bruising leadership struggle. By the time I arrived leadership was settled and the majority of the claims awards had been paid out to individuals.

My task was to write a history of the Indiana Miami community from removal until the eve of World War II. I began with tribal leaders and elders and went from family to family letting the Miami tell of their community as they saw it. I started as a participant-observer while amassing data on tribal history in local archives and courthouses and at the National Archives in Washington, D.C.

While asking a few key questions and listening to a variety of answers I was unaware that I was being used in a very sophisticated way to transmit messages from one tribal group to another. If a topic or issue was too "hot" for discussion I was misled or steered away. Unknown to myself, I became a means to widen discussion of tribal issues and to help reestablish tribal unity. I gradually learned that the Miami, who were supposed to be almost totally assimilated into modern American culture, had a powerful community of interests and that they were using me to further their agendas while I was studying their community history.

Later I learned I was the latest in a long series of intermediaries, outsiders who were used by the Miami to deal with powerful government officials as well as to smooth the inner dynamics of the community. From the beginning the Miami themselves shaped my community study as much as did documentary sources and the ideas of non-Miami people. After five years of intense apprenticeship with the Miami the tribe hired me as a consultant. In that role, writing grants and working closely with the tribal council and many tribal volunteers, I became very close to the tribal political process. My task was to assemble a petition for federal recognition to qualify the tribe to become a tribe within the definition of federal Indian law.

In field research I developed an intense working relationship with the Miami. I was educated in Miami values and eventually came to "speak" Miami—not the language itself, but the language of the community—its hopes, fears, aspirations, and memories. At the same time the Miami community boundaries were strong enough that I always had a sense of being, ultimately, an outsider. As a scholar this role was important, and I maintained it on my part by scrupulous attention to documentary evidence and other non-Miami sources.

Historians are not trained to work with American Indian communities. Normally such work is left to anthropologists and sociologists. Until recently historians have studied federal relations with tribes, calling these formal relations "Indian history." However, tribal values and beliefs are extremely important in the outcome of Indian history, and until we take them into account, along with documentary evidence, we will push Indian communities into the past, rather than treat them as ongoing societies. Fortunately, a growing body of historians share this outlook. They are joined by anthropologists who are interested in the history of persistence and change in Indian communities. The joining of history and anthropology in the study of societies over time is called ethnohistory. This relatively new field of study makes use of historical documents and the insights of cultural anthropology in an attempt to give a fuller view of Native American communities over a long period of time.

Today the Eastern Miami are in court, attempting to regain their treaty rights and status under federal Indian law. The legal history of the tribe continues, as does the tribal revitalization that began in the 1960s. The Miami people have a strong sense of a common Indian heritage as well as of a Miami heritage. They are in no danger of losing their identity. They are also determined that the United States government has a moral obligation through the Washington Treaty of 1854 to recognize their tribal government. Their pride and determination as Miami Indians remain in place today.

ONE

Miami Refugees
1654–1700

■

> Throw aside your bone bodkins; these French awls will be
> much easier to use. These knives will be more useful to
> you in killing Beavers and in cutting your meat than are
> the pieces of stone that you use.
>
> > *Claude Charles Le Roy, sieur de Bacqueville et*
> > *de La Potherie's account of the first recorded fur*
> > *trade between the Miami and the French explorer*
> > *Nicolas Perrot made in 1665–66.*[1]

THE FIRST EUROPEAN CONTACT WITH THE MIAMI
occurred about 1654 when two French explorers, the famed
Pierre-Esprit Radisson and his businessman brother-in-law, Médard
Chouart, sieur de Groseilliers, found Miami refugees northwest
of Green Bay, Wisconsin, somewhere near the head of the
Fox River. The Miami had fled their territory around the southern
end of Lake Michigan by 1640 or a little earlier, pushed out by
marauding Iroquois war parties armed with guns obtained from the
Dutch in New York.[2] The Iroquois Wars, sometimes called the
Beaver Wars, had begun in 1642, encouraged by the Albany Dutch
who wanted to compete with the French for the fine beaver furs of

the Great Lakes Indians. The wars lasted the rest of the seventeenth century, reshaping every Indian group in the West.[3]

In 1653 a temporary peace was arranged that made possible French contact with the Miami and several other groups the following year. Radisson and Groseilliers referred to the Miami as "Oumamik," from the Ojibwa *omamik,* which is close to the Miami name for themselves in the shortened plural form, *miamiak.* The name "Miami" is of uncertain origin and exists in many forms, including "Maumee." Similar names from other tribes have assumed the same spelling, adding some confusion. Miami, Florida, for example, has nothing to do with the Miami tribe but probably derives its name from a Muskogean term for the river and a Seminole village. The Miami River in Oregon is from Chinook jargon for "downstream," while Miami Mountain in California probably derives from a Yokuts name.[4] The Miami counties of Ohio, Indiana, and Kansas are named for the tribe, as are the Big and Little Miami Rivers, the Maumee River, the seat of Ottawa County, Oklahoma, and many streets, parks, and other sites throughout the Midwest.

British and American colonial authorities consistently referred to the Miami as "Twightwees," with several spellings. In the 1820s the Miami recalled an interesting story connected with the word *twaatwaa,* which was the origin of the English name for the group. In the early days (most likely the 1720s or 1730s) the Miami had "discovered the Cherokee, and were in the habit of making war on them." They had done so three times when the Cherokee decided to counterattack. The Cherokee carefully tracked the Miami until they came to a prairie where they saw two sandhill cranes. Driving the cranes ahead of them, the Cherokee crossed the prairie and ambushed the Miami on the far side. The frightened cranes cried out, and the Miami rushed forward to fight the Cherokee. The cranes called out more loudly and rapidly in the midst of the struggle, then flew off. All the Cherokee but one were killed. When he returned to his village he announced that the war party was defeated not by people but "by the *Twau twau's* who could fly off at will."[5]

European Diseases, Warfare, and Population Decline

To date, archaeological evidence of Miami life in the hundred and twenty-five or so years before meeting the Europeans is very limited. This period, sometimes called protohistory, was important because European diseases brought changes to tribes in the interior well ahead of any actual contact between the two cultures. The principal new diseases brought from Europe were smallpox, measles, and bubonic plague. Indians had virtually no immunity to these killers. Smallpox, along with companion diseases such as pneumonia and streptococcal infections, brought about the most severe but immeasurable population decline. Smallpox epidemics swept the Great Lakes region at least twice, between 1519 and 1524 and in 1639, before the French met the Miami. The 1519–24 epidemic began in the Greater Antilles, spread to Mexico, then south to Chile and all the way through North America to the Atlantic Coast. This first epidemic was probably the most severe and was responsible for a general tribal population collapse in North America, ending prehistory on the continent.[6]

Smallpox mortality is generally about 30 percent in an unvaccinated population, and it can be presumed that at least this many died among the precontact Miami in the first episode in the early sixteenth century. The disruption of food gathering and the pneumonia and streptococcal infections that accompany smallpox could have killed many more. The psychological effects of epidemic diseases would have been enormous as well, especially an unknown disfiguring disease that struck swiftly. Smallpox could transform a healthy person within a few days to a pustuled, oozing horror, barely recognizable to close relatives.[7] Measles was the second greatest killer of Indians. In 1633–34 measles swept through the Great Lakes area, and there may have been earlier epidemics.[8]

Beginning in the early sixteenth century, Europeans brought diseases that spread from eastern Canada, Mexico, and the Caribbean, passing far beyond the limits of face-to-face contacts between Europeans and natives. It is believed that the loss of life was heavy among all groups, though it cannot be quantified. Population decline affected native societies in many ways, striking down leaders, spreading grief and terror, eroding religious beliefs, disrupting planting and harvesting, altering hunting territories, and causing erratic shifts of power among competing groups.[9] Miami population decline probably began in the 1520s and continued, with brief pauses, until the 1880s.

Miami Political Organization and Location in the Early Contact Period

Despite great reductions during the protohistoric period—the century and a quarter before actual contact—the Miami population still numbered many thousands in the early contact period. When Nicolas Perrot, the unflappable French explorer, trader, and expert on day-to-day Indian relations, and his partner Toussaint Baudry visited the Miami village near the head of the Fox River in Wisconsin about 1665, "The great Chief of the Miamis came to meet them, at the head of more than three thousand men, accompanied by the Chiefs of other Nations who formed part of the Village."[10] The huge welcoming party sang the calumet song and presented a ceremonial pipe to the sun and then to the two strangers. The pipe ceremony was followed by feasts, dances, and speeches. Perrot, a great favorite among the Indians, was in frequent contact with the Miami for thirty-five years. In 1671 he spoke of Tetinchoua, head chief of the Miami, who "as if he had been the king, kept in his cabin day and night forty young men as a bodyguard. The village that he governed was one of four to five thousand warriors; he was, in a word, feared and respected by all his neighbors."[11]

Perrot's remarks suggest that the Miami were probably organized as a centralized chiefdom, unlike other tribes of the western Great Lakes. Some writers believe the Miami chiefdom reflected contact with earlier Mississippian cultures. The size and organization of their villages as well as their worship of the sun as a major deity suggests such an influence.[12] The fact that the Miami possessed a soft white corn unlike the flint corn of neighboring tribes also implies distant contacts in the Southwest, but these are speculations without an archaeological basis. The power of Miami chiefs was probably related to the large size of Miami villages, enhanced by refugees from other tribes, the possession of a specialized corn for trade, and by the Miami tendency to locate at key portages. While the Miami liked to cluster together in a few large villages, other tribes of the Midwest generally formed small, scattered villages from which segments would break away from time to time to form new villages.[13]

The Miami-dominated village at the head of the Fox River was the largest ever seen in Wisconsin, with a population of perhaps twenty thousand. Located on an upland near a bluff, there was an abundance of fish, waterfowl, and game, including bison, as well as fertile soil for crops and plentiful supplies of wild fruits and berries. Clay was at hand for pottery, while marshes were thick with reeds for matting. Ever-flowing springs at the foot of the bluff supplied ample fresh water.[14]

Perrot's vivid description of a huge and flourishing Miami-led village aside, life for the Miami in Wisconsin was far from a paradise lost. The area between Lake Michigan and the Mississippi River was not large enough for the refugee Miami, Illinois, Potawatomi, Mascouten, and other groups who found themselves caught between the Iroquois to the east and the Lakota to the west. Warfare and raids between resident tribes were common, as was warfare with intruding Iroquois groups and with the Lakota, who resisted invasions of their hunting territories west of the Mississippi. Accordingly, the Miami shifted locations frequently, sometimes even living west of the Mississippi in Iowa.

French Activities among the Miami

During the 1660s and 1670s the Iroquois threat lessened as the French reorganized the administration of Canada, built a string of forts along the St. Lawrence River, and carried war to the Iroquois home country. It was during this time that the tireless Perrot established good relations with the western tribes. Missions were begun among the Miami on the Fox River (1670–72), and dozens of coureurs de bois (woods runners) fanned out to engage in unregulated trade. French trade items quickly replaced or supplemented stone tools, clay pottery, and many other everyday items used by the Miami. New items were added for everyday use: hatchets, knives, awls, basins, kettles, scissors, silver gorgets, armbands, mirrors, cloth, and, of course, guns. Brandy and tobacco were also trade items. For the imported goods the Miami traded beaver skins and soft white corn.

The opportunity to trade encouraged the Miami to locate at portages between major rivers that they then controlled to their advantage. The Miami continued the practice of locating major villages at portages throughout the eighteenth century. The French administration in turn regulated trade and provided some military protection. During the early trade period most western Great Lakes tribes became allies of the French, some more than others. The Potawatomi became key allies of "Onontio," their name for the governors of New France, and sought to maintain a position of dominance with respect to other tribes. Their unwavering loyalty over the years earned them the title "Keepers of the Fire."[15] The Miami were far fewer in number, relatively concentrated geographically, and therefore less useful French allies. They were sometimes loyal to French interests, sometimes not. While the Miami traded with the French and met some imperial needs, they were more likely to shift loyalty as the occasion demanded.

Officials such as Perrot learned native languages and native ways, as did the coureurs de bois and some of the priests.

Native groups, for their part, supplied furs, aided the French in warfare, and became dependent on French trade. In this way, out of shared needs, the French and Indians created what historian Richard White has called the "middle ground," a Euro-Indian political, economic, and social system based on native and European values that was more or less workable for all. White is careful to note that for all the extensive borrowing and sharing between French and Indians, the French remained French, and the Indians remained Indians. A marriage of convenience, the middle ground lasted as long as neither side dominated the other.[16]

Miami Population

After French contact some shadowy notions of Miami population can be formed. Population estimates are ultimately important because they translate into political authority. Thus, French, British, and American officials of the early republic always estimated warriors as potential allies or enemies in military actions. Later, Indian populations inherently laid claim to some degree of ownership of land and political independence that competed with clear titles by non-Indian populations. Up to the present the political and economic dynamics of Indian population figures have led to inflation or obscuring of Indian population depending on the circumstances and remain a key indicator of Indian influence within American life.

Miami population estimates up to the late eighteenth century are complicated by the existence of six Miami-speaking groups. Three of the groups, namely the Wea, Piankashaw, and Atchatchakangouen, later became tribes. The other three groups, the Kilatika, Pepicokia, and Mengakonkia, gradually joined other Miami groups and disappeared from the historic record by the late eighteenth century.[17] The Atchatchakangouen, or Crane band Miami, derived their lengthy name from the Miami word for the sandhill crane, *čǎčakwa*.[18] The Crane band Miami were the primary ancestors of today's Eastern and

Western Miami tribes. Many of the Kilatika and Mengakonkia may have merged with the Crane band, while the Wea probably absorbed the Pepicokia.[19]

In 1658 when Father Gabriel Dreuillettes reported on Radisson and Groseilliers's visit to the Miami, he stated their population was "eight thousand men, or more than twenty-four thousand souls."[20] Most authorities believe this number is far too high, even if it includes all six Miami groups. At the other extreme is anthropologist James Mooney's estimate, made in 1928, of 4,500 Miami at the time of Columbus's landing in the Americas, a figure that seems far too low considering population declines due to the epidemic diseases discussed earlier.[21]

In 1695 French authorities estimated the total population of two Miami villages to be 1,100 to 1,200 warriors. If one uses the standard multiplier of 3.5 persons per warrior, the villages held perhaps 3,800 to 4,200 Miami.[22] This estimate was made a few years after a massacre of Miami by the Iroquois and an attack by the Lakota in 1687. Without getting into a lengthy technical discussion of population densities and ratios of decline, it can reasonably be asserted that the Miami may have lost two-thirds of their population to disease and warfare during the seventeenth century. Figuring back from the 1695 estimate, which probably does not include all Miami villages, a very rough estimate of 11,000 to 12,000 Miami in 1600 can be made. In 1500, before the great smallpox epidemic of 1519–24, the population was probably larger, but there are no means of making even a general estimate.[23]

The Coming of Peace and the Return of Refugees

Threats from the Iroquois diminished during the 1670s, and the Miami migrated south and east toward their old territory around the southern tip of Lake Michigan. The explorer René-Robert Cavelier, sieur de La Salle, met the Miami there at the mouth of the St. Joseph River in 1679 and built a post called

Fort Miamis at the location.[24] Farther up the St. Joseph, La Salle found a village of Miami and Mascouten at the location of today's South Bend, Indiana. The Indians showed him the portage route to the nearby Kankakee River.[25] By 1681 there were several thousand Miami on the St. Joseph River. The following year La Salle built another post, Fort St. Louis, on the bluffs of the Illinois River near present Utica, Illinois. Many of the Miami moved to this new location from Fort Miamis, only to be struck by renewed raids by the Iroquois in 1684.

The year 1687 was a turning point in western warfare. The carnage visited on the Miami and other tribes by the Iroquois ended as French authorities mustered their Indian allies to carry attacks into the Iroquois homeland.[26] The return of the grizzled old warrior, Louis de Buade, comte de Frontenac, as governor of New France strengthened French morale and defenses in the West and helped to shift the main theater of English-French warfare east to the New England-New York border. Frontenac, called the "Iron Governor," was an expert at manipulating the middle ground to French advantage. On one occasion he gained the loyalty of a party of visiting chiefs by interrupting a conference with a war whoop, seizing a tomahawk, and leading the Indians in a war dance.[27] The Miami, hardened by years of Iroquois attacks on their villages, joined in the raids on the New York frontier.

Late-seventeenth-century warfare was so deeply etched in Miami memory that two chiefs could recall an episode six generations later in 1824. As they told it, a large party of Miami warriors was raiding southern enemies when a band of Seneca warriors destroyed their village and marched the women, children, and the elderly east. An old woman was left for dead, but she recovered to tell the returning warriors the terrible fate of their people. As the Seneca traveled east, they killed and ate a Miami child each night. The following morning they took another small child, drove a stick through his or her head, and sat the child up on the path facing the Miami village to the west.

Miami Locations
circa 1654–1700

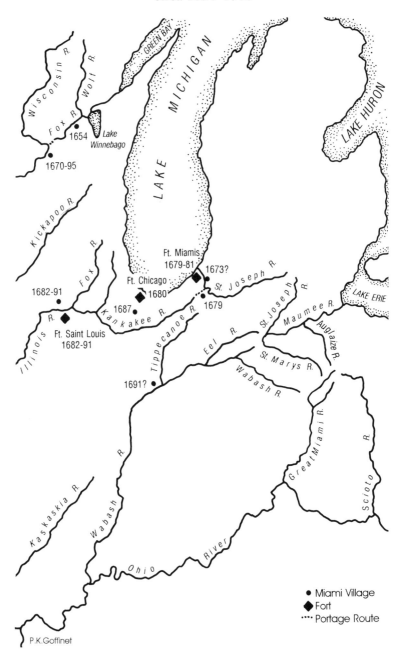

P.K.Goffinet

● Miami Village
◆ Fort
•••• Portage Route

Unknown to the Seneca, the Miami warriors were pursuing their war party. When the Seneca were one day's march from their home village they sent a messenger ahead to tell of their victory over the Miami. The Miami, heartbroken as they recognized the mangled remains of their children, managed to get ahead of the Seneca and ambushed them, recovering the surviving captives and killing all but six of the Seneca men. Two Seneca captives escaped. The Miami killed two of the remaining four, cut off their heads, and perforated their ears. The Miami hung the heads from the necks of the two survivors, whose hands, noses, and lips they cut off, telling them to run home and show their friends the vengeance of the Miami. The two captives who escaped returned to their village to tell of the disaster, but they were ignored in the midst of the victory dance. When the mutilated warriors arrived carrying the heads the dance turned into a scene of horror and confusion.[28]

Peace with the Iroquois was ratified in 1701 when French authorities arranged a great conference in Montreal of all the warring tribes. The Algonkian-French triumph over the Iroquois presented an opportunity for the French to reorganize imperial affairs in the West and to create a new alliance among the tribes, thus ending fifty years of Indian civil war between the Iroquois and the Indians of the western Great Lakes.

Late-Seventeenth-Century Miami Life

Descriptions of life among the Miami during the late seventeenth century are scattered throughout French sources and are only suggestive of the various categories of daily life and beliefs. At times the French sources can be supplemented by later sources. Despite these severe limitations, the earliest accounts of Miami life are important for understanding later adaptations and the persistence of some features of their daily life and beliefs into modern times. Most important, perhaps, are the descriptions of daily activities and beliefs that lend a sense of continuity to Miami life and give a stronger sense of a rooted community actively shaping its destiny.

A French account of 1718 noted that the Miami "are very industrious, and raise a Kind of indian corn which is unlike that of our tribes at Destroit."[29] The Miami were semisedentary, maintaining large, permanent summer villages where they carried on extensive agriculture from April to October. Villages were located near streams or rivers, often at the sites of fords and large springs. Here the mixed river bottom soil types supported the greatest variety of plant life in a small area. Several varieties of corn were the main field crop, as well as melons, squashes, pumpkins, and gourds. Women handled the sowing, cultivation, and harvesting of crops, although men might assist with burning off the stalks of the previous harvest, the clearing of new fields, and harvesting.

Corn was often stored in bark-lined pits that were up to about eight feet in diameter and five or six feet deep. Sometimes corn was left on the ear, the shucks braided, and the long strands of corn hung over poles to dry. Women were vigilant, protecting crops from large flocks of birds.[30] Miami reverence for corn is reflected in a story collected in the early nineteenth century. Once a whole Miami village was punished for failing to respect corn. The villagers had raised a large crop, stored most of it underground, and saved a great deal for immediate use, but the crop was so abundant much of it still remained on the stalks. Some young men broke ears from the stalks and threw them at each other. Soon after, when the hunters left for the fall hunt, they could kill nothing, though wildlife was abundant.

One day a hunter, alone in the woods searching for food for his aged father, came upon a small lodge where he found an old man lying with his back to the fire. The man told the young hunter that the Miami of the young man's village had harmed him, reducing him to his present piteous state. He invited the young man to take some corn from a small kettle and satisfy his appetite. The corn was finer and sweeter than any the hunter had eaten before. After the meal the old man spoke again, saying the Miami had abused him and broken his backbone in many places. He revealed he was Mondamin, the corn spirit, and the contempt shown him was responsible for the failure of the hunt. "Other Indians do not treat me so," he continued, "those tribes who regard me, are well at present. Have you no old men in your town, to have checked their youths in such wanton and malicious sport? You are an eye-witness to my sufferings. This is the result of the cruel sport you have had with my body." With that the old man groaned and covered himself up. The young man returned to the village and reported what he had seen and heard. After that the Miami were careful not to play with corn on the stalk.[31]

The connection of the injured corn with the old man and the fact that the young hunter was looking for food for his elderly father was linked to the Miami practice of feeding ripened corn to the spirits of deceased relatives as a firstfruits rite.[32] The Miami generic term for corn was *minjipi*, a compound word meaning "corn spirit."[33] Thus, corn could keep the elderly alive, and it went to the deceased first.

Through the summer and fall women and children spent their leisure time gathering wild fruits, berries, nuts, and medicinal plants. Wild plants far outnumbered cultivated plants. Since so many foods could be gathered in the wild there was little incentive to domesticate a greater variety of plant species.[34] In August, when plants were fully developed, special attention was given to gathering various barks, roots, fruits, leaves, and berries for medicine.[35]

Hunting supplemented agriculture and was a key component of trade with Europeans. The Miami hunted large animals such as bison, elk, wildcat, deer, and bear. In the seventeenth century bison was the principal game hunted. Large village hunting parties left in the late fall. Circular fires were set in the woods or fields with an opening left where the bison were killed when they tried to escape. La Salle said the Miami sometimes killed as many as two hundred bison in a day. The animals killed were divided according to the number of people or hunters in a family. The meat was sun dried or broiled on gridirons and could be kept for some time.[36] As the large animals became scarcer during the eighteenth century the Miami turned to hunting smaller animals such as porcupine, muskrat, opossum, lynx, woodchuck, and raccoon.[37]

In 1702 one amused Frenchman saw the Miami bringing bears into their village that were tamed in the course of hunting and "driven before them with switches, like sheep to the slaughter house."[38] The Miami seemed to rely little on fishing, perhaps because of the abundance of game. They ate a great variety of ducks as well as passenger pigeons, prairie chickens, quail, wild geese, and turkeys. They also ate soft-shelled and snapping turtles.[39] There is no mention in early French accounts of starvation among the Miami people. In 1688, when the French garrison at Niagara almost perished from a severe epidemic, the Miami kept them well supplied with deer and wild turkeys.[40]

French documents rarely mention Miami shelter. In 1673 Jacques Marquette described lodges covered with mats or bark. These were mainly like the dome-shaped winter lodges built by Woodland Indians from New England to the Mississippi and were used from late fall until well into spring. The Miami called them *wikiami*.[41] The floor was usually oval, and the framework was made of saplings. A fire pit was in the center, storage at the rear, and sleeping platforms along the sides. Women could erect such a shelter in an hour or two.[42]

The Miami also built summer houses at village sites. These were rectangular structures with a high gabled roof—about twelve-by-twenty feet, roughly the same size as a pioneer log cabin—and usually covered with elm bark.[43] In each village there was a longhouse in which councils and ceremonies were held. There were also sweat lodges. People did not spend much time in houses, which were for shelter, sleep, and storage. In good weather most cooking, eating, and working was done outdoors.[44]

Miami men wore utilitarian clothing consisting of a leather shirt or blouse, leggings and moccasins in winter, and breechcloth and moccasins in summer. Moccasins and leggings were often decorated with colored figures or porcupine quillwork. Men were commonly tattooed over their whole bodies, whereas women were tattooed only on cheeks, chests, and arms. Women wore clothing to the knees and added leggings and cloaks when the weather was cold.[45] There is no mention in early records of children's clothing, which probably imitated that of adults.

Perrot, who was with the Miami for long periods from 1665 to 1699, described several aspects of Miami belief. He said their principal deities were the Great Hare, the sun, and various manitous (*manetowaki*) or spirits of animals or natural occurrences to whom one could pray or make supplication. Manitous were divided into those of the sky, the earth, and beneath the earth. Thunder and lightning were manitous of the sky, as were eclipses of the sun or moon, certain phases of the moon, tornadoes, and other unusual winds. Snakes, wildcats, and other animals that competed with the Miami for food or that were considered dangerous or feared were manitous of the earth. Bears and animals that lived in caves or dens were manitous beneath the earth. Some happening or dream would lead to a prayer to a manitou in which food or tobacco was offered in return for mercy or protection.[46]

One of the most feared manitous was the Underwater Panther, called *Lennipinja*, which the Miami believed lived in lakes or deep pools of water. This was the manitou of water and fish, and turbulent water in deep places was believed to be caused by the movement of his tail. The Miami offered gifts of tobacco to this powerful spirit to secure good fishing and to ease their fear of drowning.[47]

One Miami creation story relates to just such a deep pool of water and was not recorded until the early twentieth century. The Miami, according to the story, emerged from a pool of water at *Sakiwayungi*, "Coming Out Place," their name for

South Bend. They called the St. Joseph River *Sakiwasipiwi*, or "Coming Out River." When the Miami emerged from the water they told each other to take hold of tree limbs. This they did and formed a village at the site, which was also the portage between the Kankakee and St. Joseph Rivers. Three common Miami personal names were related to the origin of the tribe: Sakakwatah, "She Takes Hold," Sakakonang, "He Grasps It," and Sakakokwa, "Holding Woman." At the time the brief story was recorded the Miami had not lived at South Bend for two hundred years, but it had remained a general tradition among the older Miami people.[48]

When a woman was about to give birth she was confined to a cabin opposite her husband's. If the delivery was slow or difficult forty or fifty men might rush up to the cabin firing guns and creating a great uproar as though they were enemies. Surprise and fear were thought to hasten delivery.[49] When a woman was ready to return to her husband after giving birth, she bathed and her husband shook all the skins in the cabin, threw out all the ashes of the fire, and, after lighting a new fire, invited her to enter with the child.[50]

Miami children began training for a vision quest when quite young, fasting for periods of increasing length. At puberty boys and girls were expected to undergo more extended fasting. As part of the ritual, boys blackened their faces with paint or charcoal while girls used earth. The full-scale fasting eventually attracted the pity of a spirit, usually in animal form.[51]

The formality of courtship and marriage varied widely, ranging from direct action by the couple to negotiations between families and selection of a marriage partner for a young man by the village chief. Shortly after a couple was married there was an exchange of gifts in which the husband gave his wife a horse, newly saddled and bridled, or some other valuable present, which she in turn offered to her eldest brother. At the conclusion of the hunting season the eldest brother preserved the best meat and gave it to his sister, who presented it to her mother-in-law.

The mother-in-law divided the gift among the family members, who presented a counter gift of vegetables and roots. This final ceremony ended the reciprocal giving of gifts.[52]

Miami men could have as many wives as they could maintain, and plural marriages were a sign of wealth and status. Usually a man did not marry until he proved he was a good hunter. A young man's father announced his son's intentions by having a female relative deliver various gifts—kettles, guns, skins, meat, cloth—to the cabin of the young woman. If the young woman accepted the gifts, she in turn led a group bearing gifts to the young man's family. The mutual acceptance of gifts constituted the marriage.[53]

There was no formality to divorce—a husband or wife could simply walk away from a marriage for any justifiable cause. "Ill conduct" on the part of a wife and cruelty on the part of a husband were perhaps the most common causes of divorce. If a badly abused wife killed her husband his death was unavenged. Adultery was considered criminal for the husband as well as the wife.[54] Because Indian marriages were subject to the high mortality of spouses, an individual commonly had three or more marriage partners during a lifetime. The resulting complex family units depended on strong kin relationships and a kinship system that designated extended family as immediate family.

Miami kinship terminology ignored generations and provided children with a large group of close relatives. Lineage passed in unilateral descent through one's mother's brother. In other words, a mother's brother was an uncle, and his male descendants were also called uncles. The daughters of the uncles were called mothers, and their children were one's sisters and brothers. A child belonged to the clan of the father, and marriage within a clan was prohibited, so all marriages were between people of different clans.[55]

The absence of generations in Miami kinship terms was confusing to European observers. One Frenchman noted that "All call each other relatives—I have seen men of eighty claim that young girls were their mothers."⁵⁶ Plural marriages (more than one wife) confused kinship for outsiders even further. In the case of the death of both parents or of the mother, the children were adopted by relatives. There was no difference in the treatment of legitimate and illegitimate children. The mother was responsible for the immediate care of the children, and the father's duty was to supply food and other items necessary for daily comfort and survival.⁵⁷

Death was followed by a brief wake in which the corpse, bathed and dressed in its finest clothing, was laid out in the lodge. Persons who died in the morning were buried that afternoon or the following morning. Four people unrelated to the deceased were appointed to carry the body to the grave. An elderly person made an address, asking the deceased not to take any of the living with him/her. Food and water were placed in the grave. After the talk the chest of the deceased was uncovered, and the relatives walked around the grave, each one laying on a hand. After this was done the four carriers covered the body with earth. At twilight an elderly person of the same sex as the deceased stayed with the body for four nights. The Miami believed the spirit of the deceased remained about the place where it lived for four days before starting on its journey to the spirit land. The Milky Way, or "spirit path," led to the spirit land. During the journey the spirit of the deceased was tempted by evil spirits, and if it succumbed to temptation it wandered about without reaching its proper destination. Guardian spirits, *paisaki*, accompanied the spirit on its journey.⁵⁸ A person could choose scaffold burial or burial in a seated position, but extended burial in a shallow grave two and a half or three feet deep and lined with bark or planks was most common. A performance of a favorite dance or activity of the deceased was sponsored as soon after the burial as convenient.⁵⁹ A year after the death of a parent the offspring adopted a replacement. The adoption ceremony, which included a dance or a performance of the deceased's favorite activity, marked the end of mourning.⁶⁰

The Miami had a complete round of annual ceremonies. Often called dances by whites, the surviving descriptions are too poor for a reconstruction beyond the names of some of them. There was a calumet ceremony, mentioned earlier, and of course there were ceremonies for the dead. Warriors returning from a battle danced the bison dance.[61] There was a green corn ceremony and undoubtedly other ceremonies concerning the crop cycle. Unfortunately, the Miami ceremonial cycle is one of the most poorly documented features of tribal life.

The Miami ritual activity described in greatest detail over the longest span of time was the Midewiwin (Spirit Doings). The Midewiwin developed among all Great Lakes tribes during French-Indian contact to cope with epidemic illnesses and to meet a need for pantribal institutions that could bring together independent clan groups. The mide men or priests enforced tribal welfare and interests and reinforced traditional standards of conduct through casual and, at times, mysterious death threats.[62] The mide priests conducted rituals for dealing with epidemic illnesses (a new result of European contact) as well as problems of social control within a tribe, managing deviant warriors, and serving to bind clan villages into a tribal society.[63] Henry Rowe Schoolcraft and Gov. Lewis Cass of Michigan Territory observed at least part of a Miami Midewiwin ceremony near Fort Wayne as late as 1821, indicating a degree of cultural conservatism among the Miami ignored by those seeking Miami conversion to Euro-American agriculture and work habits.[64]

While the mide priests assumed the highest rank in the religious hierarchy, they did not replace the older office of the *näpkia*, or healer, who used medicinal plants. Older men or women, the *näpkiaki* or herbalists continued their healing practices among the Miami long after the Midewiwin ceased to exist.[65]

The Miami, like many tribes, had men who dressed as women and took on female occupations—planting, hoeing and harvesting corn, and doing domestic work. The French called such an individual a berdache, and the Miami called him *wapingwatah*, or white face. The berdaches were few in number and took on their female roles during the vision quest. They were generally respected within the tribe, and the fact of their sex was no secret. If a berdache went with a war party, as sometimes happened, he exchanged female clothing for male.[66] French observers were amazed and disapproved of men who acted as women. While observations of berdaches are nonexistent among the Illinois Indians after about 1700, the Miami were able to give a full description as late as 1825, suggesting that the role may have persisted into the eighteenth century.[67] By the early twentieth century the Miami word for berdache was shortened to *wapingwat* and meant simply old bachelor.[68]

The Miami were fond of games, many of them typical of other nearby tribes. Various types of gambling were extremely popular. The plumstone or bowl game, *sänzawitawi*, was popular among women, who sometimes played for days on end. Moccasin or *makesina* was a popular guessing game upon which much was wagered.[69] *Wiwiläkaši* was played with eight or more of the short bones found above the hoof of the deer. The bones were strung on a short string tied to a stick, and the object was to catch as many as possible like a stack of teacups on the stick.[70] Shooting an arrow at a ball of bark thrown high in the air was another wagering game. The snow snake game, in which a hickory or other hardwood bow was slid on ice toward stakes, was a gambling game played between villages. Challenges were sent from one village to another by a messenger who carried a miniature bow ornamented with the articles to be bet upon.[71]

Many games involved contests of strength and skill that were important to hunting, warfare, and craft activities. Among those not mentioned above were swimming games, wrestling, and shooting arrows at various targets. Miami lacrosse, similar to that of other tribes, was played by hundreds at a time and was extremely rough, with many injuries and the occasional death of a player. A single game could take an entire day. Unlike other tribes the Miami used a wooden ball, which they perforated with two holes so it would make a singing noise going through the air.[72] The Miami often dreamed in early life that they would excel in certain games, which they then practiced and worked at, attaining their vision.[73]

The Miami political system appears to have been somewhat more centralized than that of the Sauk, Fox, Potawatomi, and other tribes to the north. It is not certain that a Miami chief controlled villages other than his own, but the size of Miami villages in the late seventeenth century lent power to the office of the chief, and Miami chiefs seem to have had more authority than chiefs in other tribes.[74] Civil chiefs were paired with war chiefs. Civil chiefs were concerned with regulation of the village and negotiations for peace, while the war chiefs sent out war parties, planned strategy, and managed the ritual aspects of warfare. Civil chiefs were prohibited from joining war parties or even to show signs of rage or anger. Their property, including hunting gear and horses, was available to anyone needing it. In exchange, villagers supplied furs and game as a measure of their esteem.[75]

The office of chief was patrilineally inherited from father to eldest son. If a chief had no son the succession went to the eldest son of his eldest daughter. There were female chiefs, the eldest daughters of both civil and war chiefs. They supervised major feasts, reported on the affairs of the village to the chiefs, and helped prepare for war parties. Their power was limited, but important.[76]

Miami chiefs had a steward or *kapia* (crier) responsible for distributing goods or gifts and carrying messages for the chief. A chief who had no descendants might appoint a *kapia* as his successor. The power of appointing a successor was always reserved to the chiefs. The *kapia* often took on the duties of the chief before his death.[77]

The war chiefs, summoned by the *kapia* carrying a wampum belt painted red, met in council to decide on war. Chiefs could demand redress before declaring war on another tribe, and such requests could postpone war for a considerable time.[78] If war was decided upon the war chiefs called a meeting of warriors at the council house to explain their decision. The war party often fasted from time to time in the weeks or months before setting off.[79] The night before departure an all-night war dance was held, and each warrior deposited a token of his personal manitou or guardian spirit on a cloth that was then carried on the expedition by the shaman who led the march. Younger men furnished wood, cooked, and repaired the moccasins, equipment, and clothing of the experienced warriors. Campfires were made along an east-west axis, the established warriors sleeping on the south side of the fires and the young men on the north side.[80]

A woman who lost a close relative and had a dream of leading a war party was sometimes allowed to do so if her vision was accepted by the war chiefs. She also carried the sacred bundle, and her role was ritual rather than military.[81] Miami oral tradition preserved the story of a woman who actually led a war party against the Iroquois. The Iroquois had attacked the Miami and taken many prisoners. The woman dreamed the villagers should pursue the attackers and not only take back the prisoners, but kill all of the enemy. The warriors appointed her head of the war party. Painted black and dressed in a kind of deerskin apron which was also blackened, she led a successful attack on the Iroquois.

A defeated war party returned to the village without ceremony or public announcement. A favorite trick of successful war parties was to send a messenger ahead with news of defeat and the names of dead warriors. The macabre joke was forgiven when mourning villagers discovered that those believed dead were well. Victorious war parties gave notice of their arrival with a yell and entered the village dancing the bison dance. They made their way to the council house, where the sacred bundle or pack, containing objects that symbolized the visions of individual warriors, was hung from a pole in the center. Two elderly women assumed custody of the bundle and sang thanks for the safe return of the group. As each warrior's name occurred in their song he stepped forward with a gift of cloth, beads, or skin for the singers. At nightfall the shaman who carried the bundle in war took the bundle to his lodge. Five or six days later four shamans returned the bundle to the council house where the warriors reassembled. The bundle was later opened and the sacred objects returned to their owners, each of whom gave a small feast for his individual *manitowa* in his own lodge before putting the sacred object away.[82]

The End of the Iroquois Wars and the Return of Peace

The great peace arranged at Montreal in 1701 opened a new century with a greatly strengthened imperial France anxious to exploit tribal loyalties in order to control the hinterland. The Miami had changed in the fifty years since French contact, losing population to warfare and disease while gaining new technology through trade. Such gains were bought at a price of increased dependency on trade goods. The Miami, however, were discovering that they could buy English goods as well and thus could exploit French dependency on the Miami's need for European goods. Although there were Frenchmen in every Miami village, the Miami were far more selective in borrowing from European beliefs than in their borrowings of material items.

By the end of the seventeenth century, after fifty years of contact with Europeans, the Miami were beginning to understand economic needs and resources on their own. They occupied key portages and learned to trade their soft white corn, in effect diversifying their tribal economy away from the undependable fur market where prices could collapse unexpectedly. Small in number and refusing to settle at major French outposts, they could snub French imperial designs and comparison shop among English traders without much danger of punishment.

More important, the Miami were incorporating the French themselves into their society and beginning to create a mixed-blood or métis society of Indianized Frenchmen who could act as intermediaries and further strengthen Miami interests. In effect, they were diversifying their ethnic community as well as creating a more complex society that could respond with greater flexibility to change. They were well prepared for the events of the new century.

TWO

Eighteenth-Century Life in Indiana 1701–1794

■

Kekionga, that "glorious gate which the Miamis had the happiness to own, and through which all the good words of their chiefs had to pass from the north to the south, and from the east to the west."

Miami Chief Little Turtle[1]

The utmost good faith shall always be observed towards the Indians.

Article III, Northwest Ordinance, 1787

MIAMI LIFE BECAME MUCH MORE ROOTED DURING THE eighteenth century as the various groups of Miami-speaking people moved into the upper Wabash valley and settled into locations where they remained until near the end of the century. The Miami people were pushed into interaction with four nations during the eighteenth century—France, England, Spain, and the United States. Their responsiveness to change was severely challenged, but in some ways they were stronger at the end of the century than at its beginning.

The more sedentary condition of the tribe contrasted with the imperial rivalry between Britain and France and long episodes of warfare among other tribes in the western Great Lakes region. The Miami tribe was small and relatively concentrated compared with the Potawatomi, Ojibwa, Kickapoo, and other neighboring tribes. Perhaps for this reason Miami participation as a French ally was uneven. The Wea and Piankashaw groups were larger and more involved, while the Atchatchakangouen Miami, ancestors of today's tribe, were smaller in number and farther from warfare in the Illinois country and in the area of Wisconsin.

During the eighteenth century the political, economic, cultural, and geographic boundaries of the modern Indiana Miami tribe were established. Some of those boundaries were ruptured during the first fifty years of American contact, but in many ways the Miami coalesced as a tribe and gathered a sense of who they were that has persisted to the present. The move into northern Indiana was to become permanent for the main body of the tribe, which remains there today, nearly three hundred years later.

During the eighteenth century the Miami adapted to a number of compelling changes as they confronted French, Spanish, British, and American authorities and entered the nineteenth century with a sense of security. If they had not adapted so capably they might have disappeared as a people, broken into remnants and absorbed by other tribes as were the Illinois Indians.

The French Era in Indiana, 1701–1763

The peace achieved between England and France in 1701 ended fifty years of war between the Iroquois and the tribes of the western Great Lakes. Following the conference, a vastly more powerful France attempted to consolidate trade and defense on the frontier. The very success of the French-sponsored alliance, however, masked changes in the tribal world itself that would bring renewed warfare and the eventual collapse of the French imperial system in North America. Over sixty years of fratricidal warfare had sown tensions among the allied tribes, which were now expanding into territory south and east of the old refugee centers in Wisconsin and coming into closer reach of English traders and the remnants of tribes crossing the Appalachian frontier to establish themselves in the upper Ohio valley.

The Miami had followed the general tribal movement southeastward as peace settled on the western country, abandoning Wisconsin, northern Illinois, and the St. Joseph valley, and finally settling in the upper Wabash valley. Henry Rowe Schoolcraft commented in his great compilation on Indian tribes that the Miami living on the St. Joseph "retired to the Wabash, in so imperceptible a manner, that history hardly takes any notice of the movement."[2] The Miami-speaking groups diverged as they spread out along the Wabash River valley, the Piankashaw settling near today's Vincennes, Indiana, while the Wea (Ouia in French) settled near today's Lafayette. The Atchatchakangouen or Crane band Miami were attracted to the area of today's Fort Wayne. There they established their main village, Kekionga, which was located at the portage between the Maumee and Wabash Rivers. The Wabash-Maumee portage was a key link between Detroit and Vincennes, in the center of the great arc of French settlements that stretched from Montreal in the east to New Orleans in the southwest. The Miami council fire was at Kekionga, making it both an economic and a political center for the tribe.

The Miami location on the upper Wabash was comparatively secure and permitted the small tribe to consolidate relatively free from interference for some ninety years, from the beginning of the eighteenth century to the American military incursions of the early 1790s. The nearly impassable Black Swamp to the east and northeast cut off land transportation, except during extremely dry or cold weather. Communication by water with Detroit was narrowed to the Maumee-Lake Erie route. Although access to the southeast was easier, in the first half of the eighteenth century there were no known Indian villages between the Ohio River and the headwaters of the White River of

Miami Locations
circa 1701–1794

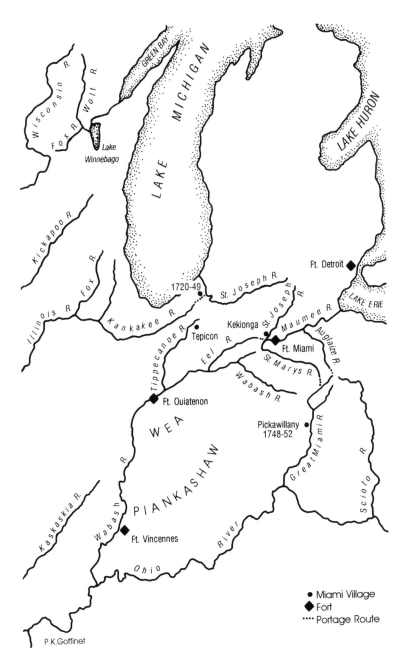

LAKE MICHIGAN

GREEN BAY

LAKE HURON

LAKE ERIE

Wisconsin R.

Wolf R.

Fox R.

Lake Winnebago

Kickapoo R.

Fox R.

Illinois R.

Kankakee R.

St. Joseph R.

St. Joseph R.

Maumee R.

Auglaize R.

St. Marys R.

Ft. Detroit

1720-49

Tepicon

Tippecanoe R.

Eel R.

Kekionga

Ft. Miami

Wabash R.

Ft. Ouiatenon

WEA

Pickawillany
1748-52

GreatMiami R.

Scioto R.

PIANKASHAW

Kaskaskia R.

Wabash R.

Ft. Vincennes

River

Ohio

● Miami Village
◆ Fort
···· Portage Route

P.K.Goffinet

■ 28 ■

Indiana in the area north of today's Richmond, Indiana.[3] Later Shawnee migration was east of the Scioto River in central Ohio, and the Huron (or Wyandot) who left Detroit settled along Sandusky Bay on Lake Erie, some distance from the Miami. The Miami were at a protected but not isolated location, a comfortable distance from both the English and French and on the border between tribes allied to both nations.[4]

Although the Miami by and large stayed out of the Fox Wars, epidemic disease continued to cause a decrease in tribal population and a fragmentation of tribal leadership. In 1715 a measles epidemic killed many, leaving only about 400 warriors (some 1,400 tribespeople using a multiplier of 3.5) according to a French enumeration taken at Kekionga in 1718.[5] In 1733 smallpox struck the Miami, killing at least 150 at Kekionga and disrupting French plans to use Miami warriors against the Fox.[6] Hereditary chiefs among the Miami originally had priestly functions, and it is possible that their inability to ward off epidemics greatly weakened their status. At the time of the epidemics the French noted increasing rivalry and division among Miami leaders.[7] Population loss and increasingly factionalized leadership decreased the usefulness of the Miami as allies and weakened the already shaky Miami-French alliance.

By the late 1720s colonial traders from the Atlantic Coast were again interested in the upper Ohio River region. English goods were of equal or better quality than French goods, and far less costly owing to the rise of the industrial revolution in England. English blankets and strouding, the coarse woolen cloth favored by Indians, was of better quality and lower price than that of the French and became the most important manufactured item in the western trade.[8] The Miami at Kekionga were in a favored location where they could play off British and French trading interests if they chose to. The interplay of Miami leadership and French and British imperial rivalry eventually became a factor in Miami tribal politics. For the time being the Miami remained within the French alliance while engaging in some English trade. French officials encouraged the Miami to raid the Chickasaw, who were England's allies, and they did so in 1734.

Although the French attempted to consolidate their control over the lower Ohio River region through their military posts at Forts Miami (at Kekionga), Ouiatenon, and Vincennes, English colonial traders were entering eastern Ohio, accompanying Delaware, Shawnee, and other tribal refugees from the crowded hunting grounds of western Pennsylvania.[9] Pennsylvania traders dominated the upper Ohio River valley by the late 1730s, and the French-Indian alliance was in a state of perpetual crisis. George Croghan, the rough-natured, wily, and knowledgeable Scots-Irish capitalist who was a prototype of the frontier colonial trader, was sending trading parties from Pine Creek, Logstown, and Beaver Creek on the upper Ohio to Miami villages and as far as Illinois Indian villages in the Mississippi valley by 1744. Complicating the situation further, Virginia speculators and traders, including two of George Washington's older brothers, organized the Ohio Company of Virginia and received a huge land grant on the upper Ohio River. They sent Christopher Gist to explore and survey as far as Pickawillany on the Great Miami River near present-day Piqua, Ohio, only about ninety miles southeast of Kekionga. In 1748 Croghan climaxed his efforts with the construction of a palisaded fort at the village of Pickawillany.[10]

The Miami, never strong allies of the French, were wavering in their support by 1747. In that year La Demoiselle, a minor Piankashaw war leader originally from the mouth of the Embarras River near Vincennes, seized the French post at Kekionga, destroyed some buildings, and took most of the trade goods. La Demoiselle's pro-British stance had surfaced in 1736, soon after the death of François-Marie Bissot, sieur de Vincennes, a strong and popular French leader. La Demoiselle's French name came directly from his Indian name, Memeskia (Dragonfly). The British called him Old Briton. By 1745 he had moved his village near Kekionga, hoping to persuade the Miami to join him in establishing trade with the English. Piedfroid (Wisekaukautshe), the pro-French Miami chief at Kekionga, intervened after the destruction at the French post, and most of the trade goods were returned. Later the fort was rebuilt.[11] La Demoiselle's rebel group, not to be stopped, sent three representatives to Lancaster, Pennsylvania, in 1748 where, in the presence of George Croghan and Conrad Weiser, they signed a treaty with the Pennsylvanians.

By 1749 the pro-British Miami, led by La Demoiselle, had left the area of Kekionga and moved to build a large town near Croghan's fort at Pickawillany. La Demoiselle sought an alliance with the Six Nations Iroquois and opened wide the gates to English trade in the West. He encouraged Piedfroid to move to Pickawillany as well, and within a year most of the Miami did so, but Piedfroid and his extended family remained at Kekionga.[12]

Pickawillany quickly grew to four hundred families, or more than fourteen hundred people from several different tribes. La Demoiselle attracted several minor chiefs of the Wea and Piankashaw, and the Ottawa and Ojibwa of Saginaw promised to join the village. Using the attraction of British trade he had expanded his influence far beyond the Miami-speaking villages of the Wabash to create a large intertribal village that caused the French to fear the loss of the whole Ohio country.

The French attempted to attack Pickawillany in 1751, but were stopped when they lost the support of the tribes living around Detroit. In June 1752 the tide turned when Charles de Langlade, a young métis, or mixed-blood from Michilimackinac, attacked the unprepared village with 250 Ottawa and Ojibwa warriors and a few Potawatomi from Detroit. Only 20 of La Demoiselle's Miami and Shawnee warriors joined the defense, and 14 of these were killed. La Demoiselle was captured, cooked, and ritually eaten. Five British traders and all their trade goods were captured. The influence of English traders in the western portion of the Ohio valley was ended for the time being. The Miami moved back to Kekionga, which gained influence as the Miami political center. Hereafter the French decided to resort to force to hold the Ohio country.[13]

The Pickawillany episode revealed deep changes in Miami leadership, which was influenced by epidemic disease and imperial European competition. Historian Richard White has pointed out that La Demoiselle's rapid rise reflected the death of older leaders and a breaking up of older Miami leadership roles. When La Demoiselle destroyed the French post at Kekionga he was not even a band or clan leader. Piedfroid, on the other hand, was the chief who led the Miami from Kekionga during the devastating smallpox epidemic of 1733. Seventy-five years after his death Piedfroid was still remembered in Miami oral tradition as the most powerful of the Midewiwin priests. It is likely that Piedfroid used his role in the Midewiwin and the power of various manitous to rise to political leadership ahead of hereditary leaders who lacked his curing powers.[14] La Demoiselle, who was not Miami, used the possibility of an Iroquois alliance and the Lancaster Treaty to challenge effectively Piedfroid and the French.[15]

After the destruction of Pickawillany the French constructed Fort Presque Isle on Lake Erie, Fort Le Boeuf on French Creek, Fort Venango on the Allegheny River, and Fort Duquesne at the forks of the Ohio River in the former areas of British influence. The Miami in turn loyally aided the French in the French and Indian War.[16] About 250 Miami warriors helped destroy Maj. Gen. Edward Braddock's forces in western Pennsylvania in July 1755. For two years after the destruction of Braddock's army the Miami joined attacks on English settlements. In June 1756 two hundred Miami warriors accompanied the French commander at Kekionga on a devastating raid to the headwaters of the James River where they killed or captured nearly three hundred Virginians, slaughtered hundreds of cattle, and carried off booty on 120 packhorses.[17]

In the fall of 1757 a dynamic new English government led by William Pitt was able to rise above poor military leadership and bickering colonies to borrow huge sums of money and to send much larger armies into the fight against France. French defeat in the West was assured in 1758 with the capture of Fort Frontenac near the eastern end of Lake Ontario. The surrender of that outpost meant that Canada was cut in two and the way was open for British conquest of the interior. By the fall of 1758 a force of six thousand men, led by Brig. Gen. John Forbes, was slowly cutting across Pennsylvania to Fort Duquesne, which surrendered on 24 November. The following year Fort Niagara, at the western end of Lake Ontario, surrendered, and French control of the West was over.[18] The Treaty of Paris in 1763 gave England all the French territory east of the Mississippi and Spain the Louisiana Territory west of the Mississippi.

Miami Persistence and Change during the French Era in Indiana, 1701–1763

Miami cultural change during the first half of the eighteenth century was conditioned by location and interaction of elements of Miami culture with that of other tribes and that of the French and British. From the very beginning of contact trade goods quickly replaced many native items, particularly stone and ceramic tools, implements, and wares. Table 2:1 gives an itemized listing of French and British trade goods commonly available from 1680 to 1760. Although the Miami settlement at Kekionga was influenced by trade, the Miami maintained a degree of independence by living on the boundary between French and English trade and political and military influence. The Miami strengthened their independence by trading their specialized soft white corn and by levying tolls at the Wabash-Maumee portage. Though the Miami had become somewhat dependent on European trade, they retained a high degree of autonomy. While they adopted a narrow range of trade goods and some Frenchmen lived at Kekionga, changes came only to the periphery of Miami life, leaving the center intact. What the Miami accepted from the French was converted to fit Miami beliefs and values.

Table 2:1. French and British Trade Goods, 1680–1760[19]

Tools/ Weapons	Domestic/ Apparel	Personal	Food, Liquor, Tobacco
guns	kettles	earrings	brandy
powder	basins	rings	rum
lead	tin pots	Morris bells	whiskey
swanshot	scissors	bells	tobacco
wad extractors	needles	beads	tobacco tongs
flints	thimbles	mirrors	corn
arrowheads	leggings	vermilion	wheat
knives	cloaks	combs	barley
butcher knives	capes	Jew's harps	oats
hatchets	plain shirts	pipes	pork
large axes	ruffled shirts		beef
hoes	jerseys		bacon
awls	shoes		bread
gimlets	stockings		flour
net cords	gartering		salt
	shoe buckles		tea
	hats		
	doublets		
	sleeves		
	blankets		
	handkerchiefs		
	stroud		
	woolen cloth		
	duffel		
	bed lace		

Miami relations with the French were reasonably harmonious until the 1750s because the French had little need to dominate the tribe. As Richard White has shown in his book of the same title, a "middle ground" developed where Miami and French could meet mutual needs without conflict. In the overlapping world of the middle ground, shared systems of meaning and accommodation were worked out in a multitude of compromises that did not require great changes for the French or the Indians. The Miami developed a dependency on French trade goods, while the French could at times depend on Miami military support. Change for the Miami was selective and permissive rather than coercive.

The end of French political authority in the western Great Lakes eventually doomed the middle ground of shared understandings and permissive acculturation that had grown out of a century or more of French-Indian relations. Tribes entered a new era of contested sovereignty in which extensive Indian-white warfare replaced the older era of European contact. The middle ground persisted in some ways until 1815, but never again would the interests of tribes and outsiders be balanced in any sort of meaningful equilibrium.

Though the middle ground of French-Indian relations eventually perished, the French element persisted in the Miami and other western tribes into the distant future, which influenced the dynamics of tribal government in subtle ways up to the present. While new sovereignties—British, Spanish, and American—challenged Indian communities, nearly all had a métis, or mixed-blood, population formed by the offspring of French-Indian marriages and sexual alliances. Often called "Canadians" in local communities, the métis grew in numbers with later marriages among French traders and by intermarriage with other tribes. In some tribes the mixed-blood people, who tended to be more acculturated, achieved wealth and higher social standing through their dealings with white officials. In other tribes they pursued leadership within the confines of more traditional tribal leadership roles and did not differentiate themselves as a separate social class. In either case the métis frequently acted as intermediaries between tribespeople and white officials, and white officials, whether British or American, tried to exploit and manipulate tribes through the métis.

French-Indian liaisons were not, of course, the only source of mixed-blood Indians. Captives were another source, and almost from the beginning of Indian-European relations there were mixed marriages and children produced by casual encounters. Intertribal marriages also became much more common during the eighteenth century as villages clustered for the purposes of trade or war alliances. Tribes like the Miami, which had suffered a severe population decline and were situated on the ethnic frontier, were more likely to take in outsiders from all of these sources and to assimilate them.

The social culture of the Miami and other western Great Lakes tribes changed slower than the material culture, though it too became somewhat more similar. The Midewiwin religion spread its influence through all the tribes, helping to unite villages and promote the rise of nonhereditary leaders. French and British officials seized upon this development to favor certain chiefs whom they expected to act as their agents. La Demoiselle was the first notable example of this phenomenon among the Miami-speaking groups. The Miami themselves preferred quiet, inward-looking, generous, and mild-mannered leaders who thought first of kin-based villagers. Leadership struggles in the coming years revolved about tribal and extratribal sources of influence, often resulting in the rejection of a leader who became too dependent on outside influence.

The British Era and the Miami, 1763–1783

Conditions for the Miami were changed very little by the defeat of France. Access to British trading goods became easier, but everyday life continued much as it had before. The Europeans who lived among the Miami were French, not English, and the Miami continued to acculturate in the direction of French manners. Occasional intermarriage between French traders and village residents continued, and some Miami spoke French.

While the Miami quietly occupied Kekionga, three European empires—Great Britain, France, and Spain—and the emergent United States engaged in increasingly intense economic, military, and diplomatic competition for the rich land of the trans-Appalachian West. Most documentation concerns the rapidly shifting expedients of European powers, with the Miami appearing from time to time as shadowy figures in the background.

Pacanne, a prominent chief of the Miami from the 1750s until his death about 1815. This likeness is the earliest known of a Miami Indian, sketched by Henry Hamilton, commander at Detroit, 1778.

By permission of the Houghton Library, Harvard University

The Miami continued undisturbed at the Wabash-Maumee portage during the British era. In 1778 the Miami occupied two villages in the area, Kekionga and a smaller village whose name, if it had one, has not survived. Pacanne (Pacani, Nut) led the larger village, while Le Gris (Nakakwanga, Crippled Ankles) led the smaller village. There were also two smaller villages, a Miami-Potawatomi village on the Elkhart River and another called Kenapacomaqua at the mouth of the Eel River near present-day Logansport.[20] The British estimated there were two hundred fifty warriors, suggesting an approximate population of one thousand.[21]

The Miami leadership that came to power during the British interregnum bears mention because the same leaders remained in place until the War of 1812 and contended with American leaders as well. Pacanne was probably a nephew of Piedfroid, who died of smallpox in 1752, and Le Gris was likely the nephew of La Grue, who also died of smallpox the same year. Thus, both were hereditary leaders. Henry Hamilton, the lieutenant governor at Detroit, mentioned two additional Miami chiefs in 1778, Le Gros Loup (Big Wolf) and Hibou (Owl). Le Gros Loup is not mentioned again, but Hibou, whose Miami name was Meshingomesia, Le Gris, and Pacanne were prominent Miami chiefs well into the early nineteenth century. Owl in later years became a speaker for Pacanne and his nephew Jean Baptiste Richardville.[22]

It was in 1780 that Little Turtle (Mishikinakwa), the most famous Miami leader, first became known through his destruction of a small French military force led by Augustin Mottin de La Balme, who was acting on American interests. Little Turtle's ancestry is not clear. Roy Harvey Carter, the Turtle's most recent biographer, believes Little Turtle's father, Ciquenackqua, signed the Lancaster Treaty with the Pennsylvania authorities in 1748. If so, he was loyal to the British-leaning Piankashaw-Miami group led by La Demoiselle. Ciquenackqua's wife was a refugee Mahican woman, giving Little Turtle mixed tribal lineage. His status came through war exploits and was not hereditary.

As the American population increased in Ohio in the 1780s refugee Indian groups joined the Miami at the Wabash-Maumee portage. In 1785 the Delaware established their first town on the east bank of the St. Joseph River. In 1787 two more Delaware towns located nearby on the St. Mary's River. In 1788 and 1790 Shawnee from Chillicothe and Piqua set up villages nearby on the Maumee.[23]

The material culture of the Miami—the items used in everyday life—grew more complex during the British era. As southern Ohio became more settled, a larger volume of trade came up the Great Miami, Whitewater, and other rivers, and more trade was carried on pack animals.[24] Trade items became much more diverse as sources and outlets for trade goods became more numerous and as the British attempted to maintain their alliances through goods. Because of technical advances in the British textile industry, a wide variety of types and colors of cloth and clothing became available. Various types of horse tack (saddles and bridles) became common, indicating a more general use of horses. Farm tools, house construction materials, and a wider variety of common domestic items indicated increasing acculturation of the Miami and neighboring tribes. Other goods were manufactured exclusively for the Indian trade: leggings, Indian coats, tomahawks, pipe tomahawks, scalping knives, silver jewelry, gorgets, crosses, and arm and wrist bands.

Miami wampum belt, 1775–1800. The belt is green, representing the Wabash River, and was purchased from Camillus Bundy, Peoria, Indiana, 1925.

The Detroit Institute of Arts, Courtesy Cranbrook Institute of Science, Robert Hensleigh, Photographer

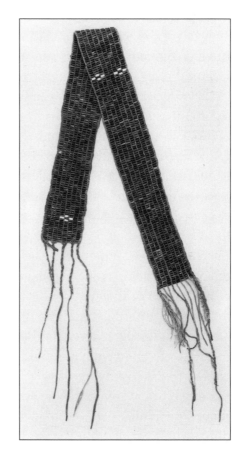

Some of the Miami folkways and beliefs of the British period are preserved in interviews with Chiefs Jean Baptiste Richardville and Le Gros in 1824.[25] Both men had grown to manhood during the 1780s. A comparison of their recollections of ceremonies and customs having to do with birth, puberty, marriage, warfare, death, and the Midewiwin religion shows little change from the descriptions given by French observers recorded in the seventeenth and early eighteenth centuries, as described in the last chapter. Establishing a chronology for changes in customs is risky because information is scarce and Chiefs Richardville and Le Gros were able to recall events such as the 1752 smallpox epidemic and the Seneca raid on the Miami that took place long before they were born. Without more comparative information, it is safest to say that there was slow change in tribal social culture, and Miami social culture of the late eighteenth century was recognizably similar to that of a hundred years earlier.

Miami material culture, in contrast to social culture, came to resemble that of the Europeans in many regards by the late eighteenth century. Middle ground villages like Kekionga displayed high levels of acculturation to European-American material goods, while behaviors and beliefs stemmed from Indian culture. Such communities could be confusing to outside observers who expected a sharp contrast between "primitive" Indians and civilized European Americans. The addition of several Delaware and Shawnee villages at the Wabash-Maumee portage was the final element in a middle ground community, which was often a collection of mixed tribal groups.

British authorities spent the time between the fall of France and the outbreak of the American Revolution attempting to create a workable Indian policy. At first many tribes had welcomed the British, expecting a flood of trade goods after the scarcity of the war years. The British, though, were facing economic difficulties of their own, after spending lavishly to defeat the French, and were in the mood to economize. Lord

Jeffrey Amherst, the military commander of North America, was a first-class Indian hater who genuinely believed the only good Indian was a dead one. In 1762 he eliminated the ritual of gift giving and slashed the budget of the Indian department 40 percent, making the middle ground of French-Indian relations a thing of the past. Tribes, unaware of British fiscal problems and sensing the harsh tone of the new government, quickly turned sullen and resentful. Their attitude was not helped by a flood of plundering and cheating traders and land speculators who talked openly of thousands of whites ready to come across the mountains.[26]

The Miami, true to their cautious stance, remained to one side for a time and declined to join an anti-British uprising in the winter of 1762–63. In the spring of 1763, however, they joined Pontiac's Rebellion (really a series of rather disconnected episodes), captured the entire British garrison at Kekionga, and killed the two ranking officers.[27] The following year the Miami took Capt. Thomas Morris, who was en route to the Illinois country from Detroit, prisoner at Kekionga. Pacanne, the young civil chief, intervened, freeing Morris who was forced to return to Detroit.[28] In 1765 the Miami finally acquiesced to British authority, permitting George Croghan to travel from Vincennes to Detroit without interference. Croghan, who had always promoted trade with the "Twightwees," was now promoted to deputy commissioner of Indian affairs. He stopped at Kekionga in August, leaving this description:

> within a Mile of the Twightwee Village I was met by the Chiefs of that Nation who received us very kindly. the most Part of these Indians Knew me and conducted us to their Village where they immediately hoisted an English Flag which I had formerly given them at Fort Pitt.
>
> The Twightwee Village is situated on both Sides of a River called St. Josephs.... The Indian Village Consists of about 40 or 50 Cabins besides nine or ten French Houses.[29]

The Proclamation of 1763, forbidding settlement west of the Appalachians, was part of a new British attempt to stem Indian fears of a white invasion of the Ohio country. However, any positive effect of the decree was destroyed by the swarms of surveyors and aggressive traders who entered the Indian country hoping to exploit development all the way to the Mississippi River. George Washington and Patrick Henry were busily sending surveyors into Kentucky and lobbying for land grants in areas supposedly off-limits to whites. At the Treaty of Fort Stanwix (1768), the Six Nations Iroquois ceded land south of the Ohio River used as hunting grounds and occupied by the Shawnee and other allied tribes. The treaty unleashed a tidal wave of land speculation in the Ohio country.[30] The Shawnee were joined by the Delaware, Wyandot, and some Seneca in the brief but bloody Lord Dunmore's War in 1774, instigated when Michael Cresap and a party of land jobbers murdered a peaceful hunting party. The war soured the temper of Indians west of the Ohio and was a sure sign of the breakdown of authority in colonial culture.[31]

The Miami sent some war parties to fight in Lord Dunmore's War and occasionally raided into Kentucky in the mid-1770s. In June 1777 the Miami were drawn toward taking sides in the Revolutionary War when they attended a council at Detroit sponsored by Lt. Gov. Henry Hamilton. The "year of the three sevens" saw a number of devastating Indian raids on the frontier. Also in this year George Rogers Clark of Virginia began to plan military action in the Illinois country to pressure the neutral tribes to take sides. He was encouraged by Gov. Patrick Henry, who believed "Savages must be managed by working on their fears."[32] Clark himself was a surveyor, large-scale speculator in Kentucky and Tennessee land, and an Indian hater who later told Hamilton that he expected to see the whole Indian race exterminated, and "for his part he would never spare Man woman or child of them on whom he could lay his hands."[33]

Using the news of an American-French alliance to great effect and aware of tribal anger over British mismanagement of Indian affairs, Clark set out from Fort Pitt in May 1778. Within a few months he had captured Kaskaskia, Cahokia, and Vincennes and neutralized tribes over most of the western Great Lakes region. Hamilton, Clark's British counterpart, left Detroit in October to recapture the lower Wabash villages that had fallen to Clark. En route he raised a war party from the two Miami villages at Kekionga. Hamilton peacefully reoccupied Vincennes during Clark's absence, but Clark returned and recaptured the post in February 1779, taking Hamilton and his men prisoners. Clark's victories, however, were not lasting, as he could not leave a large enough military garrison to sustain an American presence, and the Continental Congress could not afford the gifts necessary to uphold its new Indian alliances.[34]

Though far from Kekionga and the Miami, a family tragedy of the late 1770s eventually became embedded in Miami tribal history. The family tragedy was rather simple and commonplace. The scene was set when a Quaker named Jonathan Slocum led his wife Ruth Tripp, her father, and their nine children from Warwick, Rhode Island, to the Wyoming valley of Pennsylvania to establish a farm. The Slocum family was among the few who remained in the valley after Sir John Johnson and "Butler's Rangers" along with Seneca warriors destroyed Forty Fort near Wilkes-Barre in July 1778 with the loss of 360 American lives. After the surrender of the fort all the settlements of the valley were looted and burned, and most of the civilians fled to the mountains.

At Wyoming, both sides were arranged in a regular skirmish line. Although there was neither a massacre nor torture of prisoners, survivors spread stories of atrocities that became exaggerated in the telling, and Wyoming became a symbol of Indian "savagery." Thinking their Quaker beliefs and friendly relations with natives would protect them, the Slocum family remained in the valley. On 2 November, while the father and grandfather were away, three Delaware Indians attacked the homestead, killed a neighbor boy who was visiting, and captured his brother and five-year-old Frances Slocum. A little over a month later Indians again caught the grieving family by surprise, killing the father and grandfather and injuring one of the sons.[35] The Slocum family searched for the "Lost Sister" for many years. She was finally discovered by accident near Peru, Indiana, in 1835, where she had lived for many years among the Miami. By then she was completely Indian in culture.[36]

The Miami were nominally pro-British during the Revolutionary War, but were willing to trade with the French and Spanish on the Mississippi as well as with the British. Spain had acquired Louisiana at the end of the French and Indian War, and the Miami had traded with the Spanish at St. Louis as early as 1769.[37] The war came briefly to the Miami in October 1780 when Augustin Mottin de La Balme attacked and destroyed Kekionga. La Balme's intentions remain obscure, but he had arrived at Vincennes in July of that year, claiming to be under instructions from Congress. While at Vincennes and Kaskaskia he raised a force of some eighty French and Indians and set out, ostensibly to attack Detroit. He arrived at Kekionga, which the Miami had evacuated, and destroyed the villages of Pacanne and Le Gris. After plundering Kekionga for twelve days La Balme withdrew his force a few miles west. On 5 November 1780, Little Turtle attacked the force, killing La Balme and thirty of his men and ending the threat. Little Turtle's victory gave him the status of a leading war chief. He was to be a major force in Miami affairs for the next thirty years.[38]

The surrender of Maj. Gen. Charles Cornwallis in October 1781 and the signing of the Treaty of Paris in 1783 ended twenty years of British rule over the tribes of the Old Northwest. At the same time Canada was only a hundred miles from Kekionga. The conflicting interests of the new American government, British traders, and various tribes within the Ohio country soon brought renewed warfare that lasted until the defeat of the Miami confederacy at Fallen Timbers in 1794. For a time the Miami were at the center of resistance to American intentions in the Old Northwest.

The Search for an American Indian Policy, 1783–1789

American Indian policy from the Treaty of Paris in 1783 to the conclusion of peace with Indian tribes at the Treaty of Greenville in 1795 was badly muddled. The American government attempted to pay war debts by encouraging land sales in the West, a policy sure to bring renewed Indian conflict. From 1783 to 1787 Congress, under the Articles of Confederation, followed a course of action that repeated some of the mistakes of Lord Jeffrey Amherst at the conclusion of the French and Indian War twenty years earlier. The new American government did not want an Indian war; it wanted Indian land. The rapid acquisition and sale of public land would ease government war debt and stabilize the currency. The simplest expedient was to conduct Indian policy on the premise that the Indians were conquered peoples and the British had ceded the land of the Old Northwest to the American government under the articles of peace that ended the Revolutionary War. The Confederation government proceeded to dictate four treaties highly disadvantageous to the tribes: the second Treaty of Fort Stanwix (1784), Fort McIntosh (1785), Fort Finney (1786), and Fort Harmar (1789). The Fort Stanwix treaty set the tone: negotiations were held at gunpoint, hostages were unexpectedly demanded, and the American commissioners were rude and insulting. The Fort McIntosh and Fort Finney treaties were negotiated under similar circumstances. All three were soon repudiated by the tribes.[39]

The humiliating Fort Stanwix Treaty inflicted on the Six Nations stimulated the tribes west of the Ohio to attempt to form a new confederation to replace the defunct Iroquois Confederation. The new western confederacy held its first meeting at Detroit in the fall of 1785, demanding that the United States government deal with the confederacy rather than individual tribes. The following fall the tribes rejected the treaties dictated by the United States and declared that the Ohio River was the boundary between the United States and Indian country.[40]

The United States chose to press the political advantage it believed it possessed through the three dubious treaties of 1784, 1785, and 1786 and ignored the western confederacy. Goaded by large-scale land speculators and the need to pay war debts, Congress enacted the Ordinance of 1785, which specified the survey of public lands into townships and the sale of land at one dollar per acre. By limiting purchases to a minimum of 640 acres (a square mile), the way was opened for wealthy speculators to purchase large blocks of land that then could be retailed to pioneer farmers. The long-term effect of the law was to encourage speculators and local politicians to press for the cession of vast tracts of Indian land at dubious treaty negotiations far ahead of any actual need. In 1787 Congress enacted the Northwest Ordinance, by which most of Ohio was opened for settlement and the apparatus for making states of the rest of the Old Northwest was put in place.[41]

The result of dictated treaties and the invasion of the Ohio country by squatters and surveyors was the outbreak of ugly border warfare, with atrocities committed on both sides. The western Indian confederacy had high morale and was encouraged to stand its ground by the British. The Indians also were encouraged by past successes, for they had defeated George Rogers Clark and had virtually paralyzed American actions north of the Ohio River during the American Revolution.[42] The expense of further Indian war would cancel any advantages of land sales, if any sales could be made.

With border warfare in full swing, American officials became aware that a more liberal policy toward the Indians of the Old Northwest was necessary. Article III of the Northwest Ordinance reversed the conquest theory and recognized Indian ownership of the soil:

The utmost good faith shall always be observed towards the Indians; their lands and property shall never be taken from them without their consent; and in their property, rights and liberty, they never shall be invaded or disturbed, unless in just and lawful wars authorized by Congress; but laws founded in justice and humanity shall from time to time be made, for preventing wrongs being done to them, and for preserving peace and friendship with them.[43]

Article III was made part of the constitutional law of all the states later formed from the Northwest Territory.

The Miami at Kekionga remained aloof from American policies during the 1780s and did not attend any of the American treaty sessions. As American attention turned toward the upper Wabash valley the Miami tribe found itself split between pro-British and pro-American inclinations. While some Miami journeyed to Detroit in the fall of 1785 and endorsed the positions of the western confederacy, Pacanne, the civil chief of one of the Miami villages at Kekionga, was friendly toward the Americans, even though American settlers had attacked some of his group and some friendly Piankashaw, killing six of them in the spring of 1786.[44] In the summer of 1788 there was another unprovoked attack on some members of Pacanne's band and some Piankashaw on the upper part of the Embarras River in present-day southeastern Illinois in which nine Indians were killed. Pacanne was on a mission for Maj. John Francis Hamtramck, the American commander of Vincennes at the time.[45] Later that year Pacanne traveled on to Spanish Louisiana, where in January 1790 the commander of Fort Don Carlos III on the Arkansas River noted his arrival with thirty-three people. Pacanne received permission to live in Spanish territory and informed his host that he intended to travel to Ouachita (near Arkadelphia, Arkansas) to visit another Miami chief, Owl or Hibou.[46]

Henry Hay, an intelligent observer, visited Kekionga in the winter of 1789–90 and kept a journal. His comments offer a view into this important middle ground community and Miami life on the eve of four years of destructive warfare that ended nearly a century of Miami residence in the area. Hay was himself an interesting example of the middle ground. His father Jehu Hay was deputy Indian agent at Detroit. During the American Revolution George Rogers Clark captured Jehu Hay and sent him to prison at Williamsburg, Virginia. Henry Hay's mother was French, and his given name was Pierre. As a child he had been a close friend of Le Gris's children.[47]

At the time of Henry Hay's visit Pacanne was in Spanish Louisiana, and his nephew Jean Baptiste Richardville was acting chief of Kekionga. Richardville (Peshewa, Wildcat) was a métis or mixed-blood, son of Tacumwah, Pacanne's sister, and Antoine Joseph Drouet de Richardville, a trader at Kekionga who moved to Canada about 1770. J. B. Richardville was equally comfortable in the world of French traders and Miami Indians. He was a trader as was his mother, who was married a second time to Charles Beaubien, another influential trader at Kekionga.[48] Tacumwah also had a business transporting goods over the portage, employing a number of Indians and their horses for that purpose and making a large profit.[49]

At Kekionga the ways of the Miami and the French community frequently overlapped, although the two groups were culturally distinct. Shortly after Hay's arrival Little Turtle arrived with a war party and two captives, an African American and a white. Le Gris, the civil chief, commandeered a pirogue and ordered some French boys standing by the riverbank to unload it so as to take the warriors across the river. Le Gris then billeted the warriors among the French residents, taking care to trouble the families as little as possible and ordering the arrangements "in a very polite manner, but quite like a general or a commandant."[50] Little Turtle and Le Gris soon left for their winter hunting camps as did four to five hundred of the Miami, but they broke their hunt on 1 January to celebrate the New Year with the French inhabitants. Shortly after, the bulk of the Miami returned to their camps.[51]

The Kekionga Hay visited was swollen with refugee villagers moving from the Ohio frontier, and signs of frontier conflict were common. Prisoners were brought in, including a captive from Kentucky who expected to die but was instead adopted into an Indian family. Just before Hay returned to Detroit the Miami returned their war bundles to the council house and danced to them from seven in the evening until the following daybreak.[52] Just eight months later an American army under Gen. Josiah Harmar completely destroyed the local villages, and a year after that the mild-mannered Little Turtle orchestrated the destruction of almost the entire standing American army.

The War for the Northwest Territory and the Greenville Treaty, 1789–1795

While Gov. Arthur St. Clair inflated the achievements of the worthless Fort Harmar Treaty, the tribes of the Old Northwest were rapidly forming a united front against American pretensions. The Shawnee dismissed the treaty, saying "the lands belong to us all [the confederacy] equally, and it is not in the power of one or two nations to dispose of it."[53] War broke out soon after in the form of raids, skirmishes, and outright battles that disrupted life on the frontier for five years.

In October 1789 President George Washington instructed Governor St. Clair to determine the attitude of the lower Wabash and Miami Indians toward the United States. At Kekionga civil chief Le Gris said the Miami could not give a positive response without consulting neighboring tribes and emphasized that nothing could be done without unanimous consent among the tribes.[54] Blue Jacket, the spokesman for the Shawnee, was more blunt: "From all quarters we receive speeches from the Americans, and not one is alike. We suppose that they intend to deceive us."[55] The tribes were uniformly put off by the demanding tone of the peace proposal, and let it drop.

While waiting for a reply from St. Clair, President Washington was receiving a flood of complaints from Kentucky over Indian attacks. For months backwoods merchants, citizens, and civil and military officials had been demanding federal action against Indian depredations on the frontier. In June 1790 Washington, fearful of losing the loyalty of Kentuckians who were desirous to form a new state, decided to punish the Miami and Shawnee at Kekionga, who led what Americans had come to term the "Miami Confederacy." Secretary of War Henry Knox, who had worked to maintain peace on the frontier by sponsoring liberal policies toward Indians, suddenly reversed direction and with Washington's permission instructed General Harmar, his senior military commander, "to extirpate, utterly, if possible, the said [Indian] banditti."[56]

Ironically, measures to conciliate tribes and to calm the frontier moved forward in tandem with war preparations. Congress passed a series of laws "to regulate trade and intercourse with the Indians." The first of these measures became law on 22 July 1790; it declared the purchase of lands from the Indians invalid unless made by a public treaty with the United States. To help settle Indian complaints, provision was made for the punishment of murder and other crimes committed by whites against Indians in Indian country.[57] As if to compound the irony of the new warlike American stance, a delegation of Potawatomi and Miami arrived at Vincennes to discuss peace at almost the same time that St. Clair and Harmar were finishing their plans for an autumn offensive. An annoyed Major Hamtramck brushed off the delegation.[58] The die was cast.

Secretary of War Knox's instructions to General Harmar, issued on 14 September 1790, were to punish the Miami, Shawnee, and Delaware villages at Kekionga "by a sudden stroke, by which their towns and crops may be destroyed."[59] Harmar led his army north from Cincinnati along the route of the old Miami war trail to present Xenia, then up Loramie's Creek northwest to the St. Marys River and along its north bank to its junction with the St. Joseph River.[60] The seven villages at Kekionga were deserted when Harmar arrived on 17 October, and Harmar ordered dwellings and crops destroyed on 20 October. Many Indians lived in log houses, 185 of which were burned. The corn crop was not harvested, and an estimated twenty thousand bushels of corn on the ear were destroyed, testimony to the quality of Indian agriculture.[61] Harmar started for Cincinnati in late October, pausing while a large detachment of militia went back to Kekionga in hope of surprising the returning villagers. Instead, they marched into an ambush prepared by Little Turtle, perhaps the best Indian tactician in the Old Northwest. The Americans lost 183 lives in the attack.[62]

It is not known how many Indians lost their lives fighting Harmar's army, but the destruction of the villages at Kekionga was nearly complete. Worse yet, the Miami accidentally burned two boxes containing belts and pipes recording different events in their history. Years afterward the Miami pled ignorance of the early history of the tribe due to the loss of these important memory devices.[63]

General Harmar's embarrassing defeat made another expedition against the Kekionga villages necessary in the fall of 1791, this one under the direct command of St. Clair, newly appointed major general of the United States army. Congress added a full regiment to the regular army and authorized the recruitment of two thousand volunteers for the attack.[64] Washington had been present at the destruction of Braddock's army as a young major in 1755 and cautioned St. Clair personally to "beware of surprise," a phrase he repeated. Hampered by various supply delays and deficiencies, St. Clair finally marched forth from Cincinnati in early September, building Fort Hamilton and Fort Jefferson in a fairly direct line of march to Kekionga. Plagued by supply problems, the army moved slowly forward, being kept under constant surveillance by small Indian scouting parties.

Led by Little Turtle, the Miami and their allied tribes, the Shawnee, Delaware, Wyandot from Sandusky, ten Six Nations warriors, and some Ottawa, Ojibwa, and Potawatomi, kept constant watch on the American army. In all, the Indian defenders numbered over a thousand warriors.[65] Little Turtle's forces attacked the American camp southeast of Kekionga at about 6:00 A.M. on the morning of 4 November 1791. The American army, totally surprised and in disarray, found itself completely surrounded. The disoriented army put up a half-hearted defense for three hours before St. Clair ordered a retreat. The retreat turned into a rout, and the seven-acre campsite was left littered with personal goods, equipment, wagons, tents, cannons, and howitzers.[66]

The loss and suffering of that early November day was profound. Official sources listed the 630 officers and enlisted men killed but left out the perhaps 100 women and children camp followers who also lost their lives. When informed of the disaster by his private secretary, Washington exploded in a towering rage, cursing St. Clair. It was a virtual replay of Braddock's disastrous defeat of 1755 and was by far the largest defeat ever suffered by an American army at the hands of Indians—or anyone else—with a 32 percent overall loss of manpower.[67] Indian forces had destroyed nearly the entire standing American army. The Miami and their allies probably lost no more than 150 men killed in the grisly victory. The defeat was so total that it was nearly three years before another army was sent to the Old Northwest.

After much debate Maj. Gen. Anthony Wayne was chosen to lead the third and largest expedition against Kekionga. He was a controversial choice. A man of strong contrasts, he loved military life and was a man of action, not a deep thinker. He was an emotional, ambitious person who left a trail of broken friendships behind him. Wayne had been involved in unethical business practices and was near bankruptcy at the time of his appointment. Like many Americans of his time, Wayne was a heavy drinker, afflicted with gout. His nickname "Mad Anthony" went back to an episode with a deserter in 1781. Its connotation at the time was of mental imbalance, not anger, as in "Mad Hatter." At the same time his Revolutionary War record suggested that he was a conservative strategist and a strong disciplinarian. Above all else he was an ardent competitor who, given a goal, would persevere by finesse or brute force. He was, in short, a far more capable and formidable soldier than Washington or the public realized.[68]

Wayne began training and equipping a new army. During the preparations the army was put in a strictly defensive posture while various peace overtures to the tribes were attempted. Wayne was a harsh disciplinarian—within five weeks in the fall of 1792 he had seven deserters executed, and lashings were common. He also conducted realistic war games, with riflemen in the role of Indians, "highly painted" and yelling ferociously.[69]

At the end of June 1794 Little Turtle probed Wayne's defenses at Fort Recovery, which had been constructed in December 1793 at the site of St. Clair's defeat, with over a thousand warriors and was repulsed. Afterward many of the Ottawa and Ojibwa returned to their homes.[70] In July Wayne marched his army north toward the Maumee villages and Kekionga. He had a group of Choctaw and Cherokee scouts, old enemies of the Miami. More puzzling was the help of William Wells, a white captive who was raised among the Miami and was married to Little Turtle's daughter. Now, at about age twenty-four, he left his Miami wife and children to work for the Americans.[71]

In early August Wayne decided to build Fort Defiance near Blue Jacket's deserted Shawnee villages on the Maumee River at the site of present-day Defiance, Ohio. Wayne, raised among the rich cornfields of Chester County, Pennsylvania, paid the ultimate tribute to Indian agriculture, commenting that he had never before "beheld such immense fields of corn, in any part of America, from Canada to Florida."[72]

Shortly after Wayne built Fort Defiance, the allied tribes held a council at which Little Turtle spoke for a negotiated peace, believing he could not develop tactics to counter

Wayne's well-disciplined and well-supplied army. Unable to convince his allies and representing the smallest of the tribes, Little Turtle gave up overall command to the bellicose Blue Jacket of the Shawnee and led only his own Miami warriors.[73]

Wayne pressed battle on the confederated tribes in the area of an old windfall called Fallen Timbers left by a tornado near present Toledo, Ohio, on the morning of 20 August 1794. His well-trained troops moved forward in two columns, one for a frontal attack and the other to fire into the left flank of about eight hundred warriors crouching behind fallen tree trunks. For a time the Indians held their ground, but then broke and ran. The battle of Fallen Timbers was over in less than two hours and less than a hundred lives were lost by both sides—thirty-three Americans and about twice as many Indians. The fleeing natives withdrew a few miles to Fort Miami, where to their intense frustration they found themselves locked out by the British garrison.[74]

Unknown to the Indians, the radicalization of the French Revolution had pushed the United States and Great Britain into each other's arms by 1794 and had caused the withdrawal of British support for Indian defense of the Old Northwest. At the very time Wayne was moving his army north, John Jay was negotiating the withdrawal of British military posts from the Old Northwest. The signing of Jay's Treaty with Great Britain in November 1794 called for the removal of the British posts and the end of British support for an Indian barrier state in the Ohio country.[75]

Shortly after the victory at Fallen Timbers Wayne cut a road along the north side of the Maumee River to its source at Kekionga, where he arrived for the first time on 17 September. Entering the Miami heartland he found over five hundred acres of cleared cropland. The Miami, along with the Shawnee, were among the best horticulturists in North America, a fact that was totally lost on later reformers who wished to make farmers of Indians. At the time of Wayne's arrival most of the Miami lived in log houses and used most of the same manufactured items as pioneer settlers. Such similarities in material culture masked profound differences in cultural and spiritual values, despite 150 years of contact with Europeans.

After the defeat at Fallen Timbers the Miami abandoned their old political and trade center at Kekionga for other village sites along the Wabash, Eel, and Mississinewa Rivers. The building of Fort Wayne ended Miami use of Kekionga after nearly a century of occupation. As the Miami faced the new century, they could no longer play off French and British interests or hope to defeat an American army. Not all was lost, however. The Miami had emerged as a tribe with well-seasoned civil and war leaders who felt they were equal to the American challenge. The Miami soon discovered how severe that challenge was to be.

THREE

Treaties, Trade, and Attrition
1795–1815

■

I have ... always believed it an act of friendship to our red brethren whenever they wished to sell a portion of their lands, to be ready to buy whether we wanted them or not, because the price enables them to improve the lands they retain, and turning their industry from hunting to agriculture, the same exertions will support them more plentifully.

Thomas Jefferson to Little Turtle[1]

Young Mayjr Dark Rec[eive]d a wound
Just By his fathers Side
those feeble hands shall bee Revengd
for my Sons Death he Cryd
and like a man Destractd out
of the lines he flew and
Like a bold verginion a
Savag there he Slew.

Inscribed on the cover of a journal kept by John Tipton during the campaigns of 1811[2]

THE DECISIVE AMERICAN DEFEAT OF THE TRIBES OF THE Old Northwest at Fallen Timbers brought radical changes in Indian-white relations over the next twenty years. Restless American officials were more interested in exploiting tribal land than in trading with natives and sought to incorporate Indians into the dominant society as small-scale farmers. Native resistance to forced assimilation and land cessions was met with various social experiments, disguised by humanitarian rhetoric but backed by military force when failure threatened. Eventually, Indian resistance to American experimentation and aggression led to renewed warfare. In the meantime the middle ground of the French and British era disappeared for the Miami as American officials and settlers manipulated treaty cessions, invented their own idea of the "Indian," and attempted to force Native Americans to live as European Americans.[3]

The middle ground where whites and Indians peacefully blended European-American culture with native ways of life and belief was abhorrent to American reformers and officials. White men who assimilated Indian ways and married Indian women were referred to as squaw men, while Indians who were of mixed race were referred to as half-breeds. Middle ground communities were neither Indian nor white according to American ideology, and were therefore repellent. Equally disturbing was the fact that the acculturation that had taken place in the Old Northwest was frequently toward French ways rather than Anglo-American.[4] In the early nineteenth century middle ground or creole communities were frequently portrayed as dirty, drunken, slothful, and without religion.

Attitudes toward Indians varied greatly between officials in the East and the frontiersmen on the edge of Indian country. American political leaders were generally well educated and often believed in the "noble savage" who could be remade into family farmers. Frontiersmen, frequently of Scotch-Irish descent, commonly had two or more generations of violent contact with Indians, which led them to view the Indians as part of the fauna, deeply feared and to be rid of like wolves or bears. The Miami were faced with a two-pronged attack on their Indian identity, facing pressure to take up European-style farming and civilization on the one hand and murderous assaults on their persons on the other.[5]

The Miami, though fewer in number and less powerful than the invaders of their territory, maintained their own perspective on how to live and survive in their homeland. They were not going to take up new ways and be displaced from their land easily. The very smallness of their number was in some ways a protection, enabling them to live in a few closely located villages, making for easy communication and comparatively unified leadership. Miami leadership itself was stable, and well-experienced. The same leaders who had faced British authorities now confronted American officials. They would not easily be bent.

The Treaty of Greenville, 1795

The lengthy negotiations for the Treaty of Greenville, which began 15 July, were the first major contact between the Miami and American officials. The Miami were relatively unknown to American authorities since they had not appeared at any previous treaty council. Eleven tribal groups were represented at Greenville, and over eleven hundred Indians assembled on the treaty grounds in western Ohio, twenty miles west of Pickawillany and the same distance south of Fort Recovery. Maj. Gen. Anthony Wayne quickly established a friendly but firm tone, setting a slow pace for deliberations and encouraging open communications.

Wayne began the negotiations with warm praise for the hollow Fort Harmar Treaty of 1789. Little Turtle immediately challenged Wayne's position, saying "there are men of sense and understanding among my people, as well as among theirs, and [they say] that these lands were disposed of without our knowledge or consent."[6] Wayne was on the defensive and adjourned the council without an answer. He reopened the next council with Blue Jacket, now a secretly paid ally, who led a chorus of praise for the Fort Harmar Treaty. Wayne explained the treaty and said the United States was willing to pay again for the ceded land.

Little Turtle was not satisfied with Wayne's response and defined Miami lands as extending from Detroit due south to the Ohio, west to the mouth of the Wabash, north to Chicago, and east to Detroit, an area including the western third of Ohio, all of Indiana, and parts of eastern Illinois and southern Michigan. Little Turtle's claim included lands of the Potawatomi and other tribes, but it was a counter to Wayne's claim of joint ownership of much of the Miami domain. Wayne disputed Miami ownership of such a large region, saying that at least six other tribes claimed some of the same area. He then produced a copy of the 1783 peace treaty ending the Revolutionary War and asserted that the British turned over the Old Northwest to the new American government, saying the United States might have claimed all of the land but, being benevolent, chose not to take advantage of the situation.[7] Little Turtle was outraged, but received no support from the other chiefs. Each tribe was called forth to sign the treaty on 3 August. Of the 107 Indian signatories over one-fourth were Potawatomi, reflecting the strength and size of that tribe compared to others. Only three Miami initially signed the treaty: Le Gris, Jean Baptiste Richardville (Peshewa), and Wapamungwah (White Loon). Metocina (Indian), who had a village on the Mississinewa, did not sign, nor did Pacanne and Owl, an indication of future trouble.[8]

Greenville set the pattern for the 361 treaties that were to follow between the American government and various tribes from 1795 to 1871.[9] It specifically repudiated the conquest treaties of the 1780s and recognized Indian rights to the land they occupied. It established a boundary for Indian country while setting aside sixteen reservations of land for forts and trading posts. The treaty specified that only the United States could purchase land from Indians, and the government was bound to protect Indians from squatters and was to provide them licensed traders. Finally, Indians were allowed peaceful hunting privileges in the land

According to Miami tradition, this pipe tomahawk was presented upon the signing of the Treaty of Greenville in 1795 and was purchased from Camillus Bundy, Peoria, Indiana, 1925.

The Detroit Institute of Arts, Founders Society Purchase with funds from Flint Ink Corporation

they had ceded. To help bind the various tribes to the agreement, $9,500 in trade goods were promised in perpetuity. The Miami share was $1,000. As an encouragement to "civilization," tribes could, if they wished, take a portion of their annuities in the form of domestic animals, farm implements, or as pay for "skilled artificers" to live among them.[10]

Jay's Treaty, signed between England and the United States in November 1794 and ratified in June 1795, was nearly as relevant to Indian affairs in the Old Northwest as the Greenville Treaty. A major issue of Jay's Treaty was the presence of British military and trading posts on American soil, particularly at Michilimackinac and Detroit. Negotiations for the treaty in the summer of 1794 had caused the British to withdraw support from Indians of the region, assuring Wayne's military victory at Fallen Timbers. The treaty called for the evacuation of British troops by the summer of 1796, but British traders were free to cross the American boundary to continue trade as before. Indians with trade goods also were allowed free passage of the border.[11] As a result, a close connection continued for many years between the Miami and "British" traders, nearly all of whom were French Canadians or métis who often resided in Miami villages. The Miami continued to enter Canadian territory for trade and sometimes for refuge until the end of the War of 1812.

The wording and tone of the Greenville negotiations were such that most Indians believed they could occupy most of the Old Northwest for as long as they wished. Article V stated:

> The Indian tribes who have a right to those lands, are quietly to enjoy them, hunting, planting, and dwelling thereon so long as they please, without any molestation from the United States; but when those tribes, or any of them, shall be disposed to sell their lands, or any part of them, they are to be sold only to the United States.[12]

The article appeared innocent and straightforward, but the second part—the exclusive right to preemptive purchase by the United States at later treaties—provided a powerful opening for further land cessions in the Old Northwest. When the desire to buy land became strong enough, the disposition to sell could be manufactured.

In 1797 Little Turtle journeyed east to Philadelphia with his interpreter William Wells. Little Turtle, who had crushed St. Clair's army in 1791, was treated as a celebrity. President Washington presented him with a ceremonial sword, and he had his portrait painted by Gilbert Stuart. Taking advantage of modern medicine, he allowed himself to be vaccinated against smallpox. C. F. Volney, a world traveler and friend of Thomas Jefferson, thought Little Turtle resembled Chinese Tartars he had once seen, despite the blue suit and black hat he wore. Volney was intensely interested in languages and in a few interviews gathered the first extensive word list of the Miami language.[13]

Establishing a New Tribal Home

The Miami, who had taken in so many refugees during their last years at Kekionga, were themselves refugees after the Americans occupied their old village sites and the Wabash-Maumee portage. Fort Wayne was an American administrative and military center, not a place for the Miami to stay. At Greenville the Miami had ceded the portage and its large revenues, one of the key advantages of the location. Although Little Turtle promised to remain near Fort Wayne to maintain peace with the Americans, the main body of the Miami tribe abandoned the new American center and resettled down the Wabash in a series of villages concentrated at the Forks of the Wabash west of today's Huntington and along the lower Mississinewa near today's Peru. Though a council house was built at Fort Wayne in 1802 and annuities were paid there, the seat of the Miami council was with the new villages and was referred to as the Mississinewa council.

Accounts of tribes on the edge of settlement in the Old Northwest in the first decade of the nineteenth century stress rapidly growing dependency with the overhunting of game animals, social breakdown with the arrival of floods of alcohol, and even periods of starvation. This situation was truer of tribes such as the Shawnee who lived south and east of the Miami and closer to white settlements. After leaving Kekionga the Miami found a new refuge that was comparatively isolated from the worst features of the frontier. At their smaller village sites located along the Wabash, Mississinewa, and Eel Rivers the Miami were more dispersed and could make better use of subsistence sources than they could in the large, closely located villages at Kekionga. Indeed, the dispersal of the Miami into much smaller villages indicates a need to make greater use of subsistence activities to replace the market activities lost when the Miami abandoned Kekionga. Some Miami had lived along the Mississinewa since about 1790, and the tribe had nearly a generation to adapt to the new location before warfare returned.

The village sites of the Miami along the Wabash, Eel, and Mississinewa Rivers became the permanent home of the Miami, and the Miami remain in the general area today. The character of the modern Miami tribe was shaped along the rivers two centuries ago, and everyday life on the land—the tribal economy and folkways—requires a brief comment to balance the sketchy and often biased comments of white observers at the time.

Along the Wabash, Eel, and Mississinewa, the Miami continued the many activities of the annual subsistence cycle, growing fields of corn, beans, squash, some European garden vegetables, and wheat, making use of the rich riverine ecosystem with its many soil types and plant and animal environments ranging from wet and marshy on the floodplains to dry on the limestone bluffs and the uplands. Many medicinal plants grew in the mixed soils and microenvironments along the rivers and uplands: goldenseal (yellow root), dog fennel, boneset, yarrow, pennyroyal, bloodroot (puccoon), and sweet flag (calamus) were a few that were commonly used.[14] A great variety of edible foods grew in abundance as well. There were wild plums, strawberries, grapes, papaws, persimmons, crabapples, and many varieties of berries. The acorn of the bur oak, Indian potatoes, and tubers of the water chinkapin, arrowleaf, and Jerusalem artichoke supplied starch. Common milkweed, flowers of the mulberry, early shoots of skunk cabbage, sour dock, wild onion, and a number of other plants were prized as greens. Teas were made from spikenard, spicebush, sassafras, and several other plants. Maple sugar and honey were used as sweeteners, as were dried fruits and berries.[15]

The spread of European and Asian weed plants added to the Miami diet in the late eighteenth and early nineteenth centuries. Weeds were spread by domestic livestock, birds, and human activities years ahead of any pioneer settlement. In this way dandelion greens, mustard greens, and lamb's-quarters entered the Miami diet, as did honey from bees introduced from Europe.

The disappearance of bison and the overhunting of large mammals such as deer, bear, and elk in the early nineteenth century did not automatically cause starvation among a tribe, as some writers have implied.[16] As the larger meat animals disappeared, the Miami turned increasingly to the rivers as a protein source. Semiaquatic mammals such as mink, river otter, beaver, and muskrat still populated the region, as did other small mammals—porcupine, fox squirrel, rabbit, woodchuck, and opossum. All were eaten. There were many kinds of fish, which were caught by netting, spearing, hooking, gill grabbing, shooting with bow and arrow, and basket seining at weir dams.[17]

Fowling was another common and important food gathering activity, often omitted in accounts of the time. The Miami trapped quail, prairie chickens, and passenger pigeons and hunted turkeys. Waterfowl were plentiful, and every variety of duck was eaten, as were geese.[18]

The Miami along the upper Wabash still kept some cattle, pigs, and chickens as they had at Kekionga. Officers John Payne, William Russell, and others who led attacks on Miami villages in 1812 and 1813 commented on the quantities of corn that they destroyed. One militiaman recalled seeing "very good log-cabins" and said that ox teams, brought from Canada, were in use.[19] There is no evidence of starvation or general hunger among the Miami in the period up to the War of 1812. When four Miami villages were destroyed in the fall of 1812 three of them were "remarkably flourishing," and troops destroyed a large quantity of corn.[20]

Although the Miami began moving toward dependency and subordination to the American system after 1795, dependency was not a critical issue until after the War of 1812. The lack of interest in male-dominated agriculture using horses to plow is a sign that female agriculture remained viable. During the interwar years the Miami apparently were able to reestablish themselves successfully as a community. The tribal population, which perhaps had numbered a thousand in the 1770s, had risen to fourteen hundred by 1817, despite the warfare of 1791–94.[21] An increasing population is the best indicator of successful adaptation to change. Marriages with the local French traders increased, and the tribe became more racially and ethnically diverse. During the interwar years the Miami were slowly evolving into a more complex community, assimilating outsiders who could in turn help the tribe accommodate to later American demands.[22] In short, the Miami were successfully adapting to change at their own pace.

A Flurry of Treaties

William Henry Harrison, who was Maj. Gen. Anthony Wayne's aide-de-camp at Fallen Timbers in 1794, quickly became a powerful advocate of easy land sales in the Old Northwest. Selected by the legislature of the Ohio Territory in 1799 as the delegate from the Northwest Territory to the United States Congress, Harrison chaired the Committee on Public Lands that introduced the public land act passed in 1800 allowing the purchase of 320 acres at two dollars an acre, with one-fourth paid down and four years to pay the remainder. The Northwest Territory was split into the Indiana and Ohio Territories in the same session of Congress, and Harrison was appointed governor of Indiana Territory at the young age of twenty-seven. The creation of the Ohio Territory and the more liberal land laws led to a flood of western settlement and statehood for Ohio in 1803.[23]

The boundaries of the Greenville Treaty sessions had not yet been surveyed when Harrison arrived in the Indiana Territory to take up residence at Vincennes. There was constant friction between Indians and whites, and Little Turtle journeyed to the new capital of Washington, D.C., to ask, among other things, that firm boundary lines be drawn between white settlements and Indian lands.[24] Harrison used Little Turtle's request to survey the Vincennes tract as an opening to press for land cessions, going far beyond the cessions of the Greenville Treaty. Harrison began with old claims of the Wabash and

Treaty Cessions
1795–1809

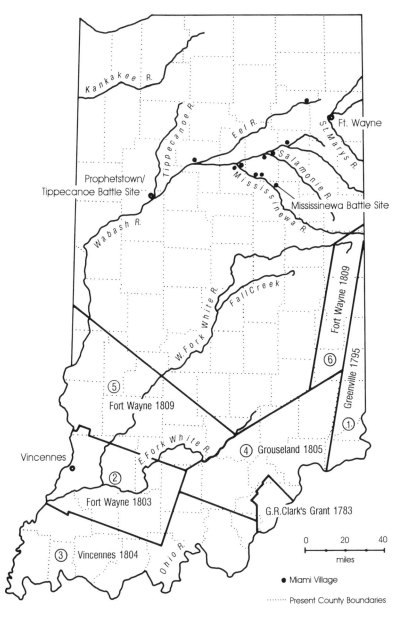

Kankakee R.

Tippecanoe R.

Eel R.

St. Marys R.

Ft. Wayne

Salamonie R.

Prophetstown/
Tippecanoe Battle Site

Mississinewa R.

Mississinewa Battle Site

Wabash R.

W. Fork White R.

Fall Creek

Fort Wayne 1809

⑥

Greenville 1795

⑤

Fort Wayne 1809

①

E. Fork White R.

Vincennes

④ Grouseland 1805

②

Fort Wayne 1803

G.R.Clark's Grant 1783

③ Vincennes 1804

Ohio R.

0	20	40

miles

● Miami Village

········· Present County Boundaries

P.K.Goffinet

Illinois land companies, which Congress had invalidated twice.[25] Although the tribes concerned strongly rejected these empty claims, Harrison managed in the fall of 1802 to get four chiefs to sign an unusual "preliminary treaty" accepting the claims. The chiefs were the now strongly pro-American Little Turtle and Richardville of the Miami and Topnebi and Winamek of the Potawatomi. Harrison granted Little Turtle a personal annuity (i.e., a bribe) of $150 at the time of the signing.[26] Topnebi and Winamek, from the St. Joseph River area in southwestern Michigan, had long been identified as pro-American chiefs who were taking advantage of the Miami and trying to expand their influence far into Indiana.[27]

Not long after concluding the highly questionable preliminary treaty, Harrison received an urgent and confidential letter from President Thomas Jefferson in February 1803. Jefferson, who strongly favored the settlement of the Old Northwest, suddenly felt the task was urgent because Spain had secretly ceded the Louisiana Territory back to France. French influence so close to its former native allies, Jefferson said, "is already felt like a light breeze by the Indians . . . under the hope of their protection, they will immediately stiffen against cessions of land to us. we had better therefore do at once what can now be done."[28]

Jefferson's private letter to Harrison went beyond urging land cessions. Jefferson did not want self-sufficient Indian societies living in American territory. Chiefs should be encouraged to run up large debts among traders, he said, to create massive dependency among Indians so they would have to sell land whether they wanted to or not:

> we shall push our trading houses, and be glad to see the good & influential individuals among them run in debt, because we observe that when these debts get beyond what the individuals can pay, they become willing to lop th[em off] by a cession of lands.[29]

Anticipating Indian removal, Jefferson suggested that Indians would either incorporate into the American system or move beyond the Mississippi. By incorporation he meant the disappearance of Indian culture and the eventual intermarriage of Indians with whites. "Your blood will mix with ours," he told Indians more than once.[30] If a tribe resisted forcible acculturation, he concluded, "the siezing [*sic*] the whole country of that tribe & driving them across the Missisipi, as the only condition of peace, would be an example to others, and a furtherance of our final consolidation."[31] In 1805, when Congress passed legislation for the government of the Louisiana Territory, Section 15 of the act authorized the president to give the land west of the Mississippi to the Indians in exchange for land they were occupying east of the river. The mechanism for Indian removal was in place, although it would be some years before it was used.[32]

Encouraged by Jefferson's diatribe, Harrison pressed on to reduce native resistance to a new treaty, announcing that goods and annuities set forth in the Greenville Treaty would go only to those tribes that attended a treaty conference. Given the choice between attendance or widespread suffering among their people, most of the chiefs came.[33] The Fort Wayne Treaty of 7 June 1803 was the first of four treaties negotiated with the Miami from 1803 to 1809, all but the last signed by just two or three chiefs. In 1803 only Little Turtle and Richardville signed for a large land cession in southwestern Indiana that continued into Illinois.

In August 1804 Harrison negotiated two treaties with the Delaware and Piankashaw, who relinquished more land in southern Indiana along the Ohio River. Little Turtle and Richardville recognized Delaware title to this land in the 1803 treaty, despite strong opposition among the Miami tribe at large. In August 1805 Harrison called a new treaty session at Grouseland, his Vincennes home, to settle the difficulties with the 1804 treaty. Harrison conceded that the land the Delaware ceded rightfully belonged to the Miami and he used Topnebi and Winamek to pressure the Miami. Through the bribery of Little Turtle and the payment of additional annuities, Harrison managed to get Miami agreement to the flawed 1804 treaty and the additional cession of land in southeastern Indiana. For the first time Owl signed an American treaty, as did two other unidentified Miami headmen.[34] (See map on p. 67.)

The civilization policy went forward in tandem with the treaties. President Jefferson and other federal officials believed that Indian men who took up plow farming would not need land for hunting, which they then would be more willing to sell. The Baltimore Yearly Meeting of Friends (Quakers) dispatched tools and equipment to a training farm a few miles west of present Huntington, Indiana, in 1804. Philip Dennis demonstrated plowing with horses and other European-American farming techniques, but the Miami were not interested in what was considered female work or in using their prized ponies to pull plows. Dennis quit after a season, to be replaced two years later by William Kirk, who failed in his mission as well. Kirk went to Black Hoof's Shawnee village at Wapakoneta in western Ohio and was successful among that more acculturated group.[35] Harrison accused William Wells, the Indian agent and interpreter at Fort Wayne, of interfering in the work of civilization, even though it is clear that the Miami had no need for a radical change in their culture, especially in a time of turmoil over land cessions.[36]

Harrison's land hunger and hard bargaining at treaty sessions produced great anxiety and anger among the tribes of the Old Northwest. Surveyors were busily marking off a number of new boundaries between Indian and white lands in many parts of Indiana and Illinois Territories. By 1805 the Greenville Treaty, signed only ten years before, was for all practical purposes dead. In just four years Harrison had persuaded the natives of the Northwest to cede more than twenty-nine million acres or forty-six thousand square miles to the United States for a few cents an acre.[37] President Jefferson, oblivious to worsening conditions in Indian country, continued to speak as though the Greenville settlement was being carefully observed and that the tribes were happily ceding lands they no longer needed or wanted.[38]

By 1805 evidence of widespread discontent, sense of loss, and social confusion and breakdown was reflected in frequent charges of witchcraft within some tribes and the rise of Tenskwatawa, the Shawnee Prophet, and his brother Tecumseh, an experienced military leader and masterful political organizer. Tenskwatawa's teachings of rejecting European-American influences and Tecumseh's message of common Indian ownership of the land and of a pan-Indian confederacy to rid Indian country of whites were not equally appealing to all tribes. The Miami resisted Tecumseh, based on their firm belief that they owned the lands of Indiana and that other tribes were there at Miami invitation. The Miami had no intention of acknowledging pan-Indian ownership of the upper Wabash.[39] The Miami were further displeased when Tenskwatawa established a settlement called Prophetstown near the juncture of the Tippecanoe and the Wabash Rivers, just north of present-day Lafayette, Indiana. Although some young warriors joined Tenskwatawa, most Miami resisted his doctrines because the authority of the chiefs, some of whom were Midewiwin priests as well, remained strong and they and their followers resisted the new doctrines. The Miami were also farther from the liquor trade and had suffered less from it.[40]

The breaking point in Little Turtle's leadership came at negotiations for a new treaty at Fort Wayne in 1809, when he again acknowledged the Potawatomi grant to the Delaware along the White River, although these lands were clearly recognized as Miami by the Greenville Treaty in 1795. What was worse, Little Turtle cooperated with Harrison in admitting a large number of Potawatomi warriors from the St. Joseph River area to the treaty grounds. Led by Winamek and the son of Five Medals, the Potawatomi went so far as to threaten war with the Miami if they did not cede the lands in southern Indiana. This was no idle threat as about half the Indians present at the treaty grounds were Potawatomi who expected to get the largest share of the treaty goods for their support of Harrison during the negotiations.[41]

Expecting a repeat of earlier negotiations, Harrison ran into a stone wall of resistance. The Mississinewa Miami, led by Pacanne, Richardville, Owl, and Metocina, expressed open hostility to Little Turtle and the Potawatomi and for days refused any sale of lands. Harrison finally got agreement only by openly acknowledging that the Mississinewa chiefs, not Little Turtle, were the real representatives of the Miami nation and that he would always recognize them as such.[42] By cooperating too closely with Harrison and by admitting the Potawatomi to the treaty grounds, Little Turtle had cut himself off from the Miami leadership, who forced Harrison to admit that Little Turtle was not even Miami. Future chiefs who strayed too far from the consensus of the tribal council met the same fate. Little Turtle was forcibly retired from Miami affairs, and the foundation was laid for the Mississinewa council to lead Miami affairs at critical moments in tribal history up to the present. (See map on p. 67.)

A broader spectrum of Miami chiefs signed the 1809 treaty, reflecting the revolution in tribal affairs: Pacanne, Owl, White Loon, and Shapenemah signed in addition to Little Turtle. White Loon had a village on the Mississinewa and had signed the Greenville Treaty. Silver Heels (Ambahwita, He Flies), a young Delaware chief with a Shawnee wife and who had a village on the Mississinewa, signed as well.[43] Le Gris and Richardville, who may have been away, did not sign.

Early in 1809 the Illinois Territory was split from the Indiana Territory in preparation for Indiana statehood. The land cessions from 1803 to 1809 left the northern half of the proposed new state in Indian hands. The rising influence of Tenskwatawa and his brother Tecumseh grew from Indian resistance to further land cessions, as well as the social breakdown caused by alcohol, a fall-off in game, and a collapse in fur prices. The 1809 treaty was the last straw for Tecumseh, and thereafter tensions heightened throughout the Old Northwest.

War on the Wabash

The two years between the Fort Wayne treaty and the Battle of Tippecanoe in November 1811 were filled with alarms on the frontier. Frequent raids on the American settlements around St. Louis and into Missouri were launched from Prophetstown.[44] During the summer of 1810 the Miami tribe held a council to decide whether or not to support Tecumseh at Prophetstown. A year later, in July 1811, Harrison demanded that the Miami dis-avow any alliance with Tenskwatawa. Lapousier, a Wea chief speaking with the support of Pacanne and Le Gris, replied:

> We have told you we would not get angry for light causes. We have our eyes on our lands on the Wabash with a strong determination to defend our rights.... You have now offered the war club to us, you have laid it at our feet, and told us we might pick it up if we chose. We have re-fused to do so, and we hope this circumstance will prove to you that we are people of good hearts.[45]

The chiefs declined warfare knowing the destruction it could bring to Miami villages located on the route from Vincennes to Detroit.

In the fall of 1811 Harrison attacked Prophetstown, dealing a fatal blow to Tecumseh's hopes of a solid confederacy of tribes to oppose American authority in the region. After the Battle of Tippecanoe, the influence of the pro-American chiefs Pacanne, Le Gris, Owl, and Metocina was strengthened. At the same time Harrison distrusted the Miami and was concerned be-cause Miami villages on the upper Wabash were at the center of the Wabash-Maumee route from Vincennes to Detroit, the seat of British influence.

The slow simmer of causes leading to the War of 1812 finally came to a boil on 18 June when Congress declared war against Great Britain. Little Turtle died a month later. Fort Michilimackinac surrendered on 17 July, leaving the northern frontier exposed. On 15 August Brig. Gen. William Hull surrendered Detroit, and Fort Dearborn at today's Chicago was evacuated the same day. Fifty-two of the evacuees were killed as they left, including William Wells, Little Turtle's son-in-law. Harrison, now appointed a general of the United States army and no longer governor of Indiana Territory, left his post at Cincinnati early in September, moving with twenty-two hundred troops to Piqua, then on to Fort Wayne, which was under siege. The garrison at Fort Wayne was safe, but the factory (government trading post) and public buildings had been burned. The Miami took no part in the attack on Fort Wayne, although some warriors did go down the Wabash to attack Fort Harrison.[46]

After the attack on Fort Wayne Harrison wanted to prevent any grouping of Indians on the Wabash-Maumee route that could interfere with his plans to retake Detroit, and so he decided to treat the Miami as a hostile tribe. In fact, the Miami were made the primary target of Harrison's Indiana Indian campaigns, although the Potawatomi were unequivocally pro-British and posed a far greater threat as a military force. Miami hostilities toward Americans were minor compared to those of other tribes in the region with the exception of the Delaware. The Miami, who were the primary proprietors of central Indiana, had become obstinate about making further land sales after the Treaty of 1809. The destruction of Miami villages could have the effect of softening Miami resistance to further cessions of their land. Though not mentioned in Harrison's plans, this more nearly explains the destruction visited on the tribe. Following his plans, stated or unstated, Harrison then ordered the destruction of all Indian villages within a two-day march of Fort Wayne. Thus perished Little Turtle's village near present-day Columbia City, Indiana, and three flourishing Miami villages at the Forks of the Wabash near today's Huntington. All Miami property and crops were destroyed.[47]

After ordering the destruction of the Miami villages around Fort Wayne, Harrison decided to attack the Mississinewa villages, home of the main body of the Miami tribe, to eliminate any potential threat when he moved against Detroit the following year. His orders to Lt. Col. John B. Campbell were to avoid harm to Pacanne, Richardville, White Loon, and the Delaware chief Silver Heels if possible.[48] Campbell attacked Silver Heels's village near today's Marion in bitterly cold weather on 17 December, taking forty-two Delaware Indians prisoners. He then moved down the Mississinewa where he attacked and destroyed at least two Miami villages. The Miami, who were not expecting an attack, had not evacuated their villages, and a number of Miami, including women and children, were killed.[49] On 18 December Campbell returned to the site of Silver Heels's village where he was attacked by the Miami before daybreak. Ten men were killed and forty-eight were wounded. He then retreated to Greenville. The following July Harrison ordered another demoralizing attack on the Mississinewa villages. Crops and houses were destroyed, but this time the Miami had evacuated the area.[50]

On 5 October 1813 Harrison defeated the British at the Battle of the Thames at Moraviantown in Ontario. Tecumseh's death in the battle brought about the end of Indian resistance and made the military frontier in the Old Northwest secure. A few days later the Miami chiefs and the chiefs from six other tribes came to nearby Detroit to offer token help to Harrison in return for an armistice. The following July (1814) Harrison called a peace council at Greenville to enlist the support of all the northwestern tribes in the cause of the United States. Over four thousand Indians attended. In Article I of the treaty Harrison and Gov. Lewis Cass of Michigan, on behalf of the United States and its Indian allies, the Wyandot, Delaware, Shawnee, and Seneca, extended peace to the Miami Nation of Indians and to certain bands of the Potawatomi.[51]

In 1815 Harrison held a final treaty session, this time at Spring Wells near Detroit to end formally the War of 1812. This treaty pardoned chiefs and warriors who may have committed hostilities against the United States. The second Greenville Treaty marked the end of Miami military power and influence on the frontier twenty years after Wayne's defeat of the tribe at Fallen Timbers. British influence in the Old Northwest was finished, and the finality of American power at last ended the middle ground of accommodation and power sharing between native and white cultures. The Miami suddenly faced political subordination, social inferiority, and cultural discrimination. As if to signal this profound change, Le Gris, Pacanne, and Owl died between 1813 and 1815. Under new leadership after 1815 the Miami faced a world behind the American frontier where blending new ways with old would be far more difficult.

FOUR

Behind the Frontier
1816–1846

■

You have made a request of us for our land, which we have already refused. I told you our situation. We have a right to trade or exchange our property, . . . if we cannot agree and trade, we can seperate [*sic*] in peace. But it is not so here, for you ask us after we have refused. When I was at Washington last winter you told me to take care of our lands, and to think a very great deal of them. You now ask us for our very beds, for the means of our subsistence.

Chief Le Gros to Gov. Lewis Cass, 12 October 1826[1]

Dr Sir, after the repeted requsts of my neighbours and our Settlement I do adress these fewe lines to you . . . disiring you to call the indians out of our vicinity which you have premited to hunt on Wildcat . . . we are ceerously injured by them for the[y] are Pilligon our corn fields and Cribs Burning our Range Destroying our pastures killing our hogs . . . not only this but keeping our famelys continuely in feare and unhappy for the name of an Indian is a terrer to weomen and children.

W. W. Douglass to John Tipton, 10 November 1828[2]

BY 1816, A SHORT TWENTY YEARS AFTER THE SIGNING OF the Greenville Treaty, the Miami found themselves a conquered people on their own land. They were now behind the American frontier, and their only claim against American authorities was their ownership of most of the remaining land in Indiana. Other tribes—the Delaware, Piankashaw, Wea, Kickapoo, and some Potawatomi—had already moved beyond the frontier to the Louisiana Territory or into Michigan, Wisconsin, and Ontario. Although Miami groups had often spent much time west of the Mississippi during the eighteenth century, the main body of the tribe had always remained in the area of Kekionga. While many of the Indian tribes in Indiana left ahead of white settlement, the Miami and Potawatomi elected to stay in their homeland. Eventually the Potawatomi were forced to leave as well, and only the Miami remained as an organized tribe within the boundaries of the state.

The Miami decision to stay in Indiana was courageous in the face of heavy odds against survival as a tribe. The next thirty years were to be the most difficult and dangerous for the Miami since the Iroquois invasion of their lands nearly two hundred years earlier. This time the invaders were Americans, arriving in bewildering numbers and bearing the accumulated prejudices of two centuries of warfare with Indians. The loss of tribal land and the cutting up of hunting territories as well as competition for game greatly reduced Miami subsistence activities. Just as dangerous to tribal welfare were traders and white officials who brought quantities of alcohol and large sums of money in their efforts to pry the Miami from their land. As older ways of life were disrupted, the Miami became strangers in their own country and died off in alarming numbers. They were not wanted, but eventually they frustrated federal removal policy and remain in their homeland today. How they did so is a remarkable story.

The Miami rebuilt their villages along the Wabash and Mississinewa Rivers after their destruction in 1813. They returned to the annual subsistence cycle, raising and harvesting various crops from spring to fall, going on long winter hunts beginning in November, and maple sugaring early in March. Though they were more dispersed than they had been at Kekionga in the eighteenth century, they remained closely grouped in eleven villages along the upper Wabash valley, within easy walking or riding distance of each other.

Benjamin F. Stickney, Indian agent at Fort Wayne, reported on the situation of the Miami in 1817 to Thomas L. McKenney, superintendent of Indian Affairs in Washington, D.C. Stickney was anxious to see the Miami take up American culture and emphasized the lack of acculturation among the tribespeople:

> They have places that are commonly called villages, but, perhaps not correctly, as they have no uniform place of residence. During the fall, winter, and part of the spring, they are scattered in the woods, hunting. The respective bands assemble in the spring at their several ordinary places of resort, where some have rude cabins, made of small logs, covered with bark; but more commonly, some poles stuck in the ground and tied together with pliant slips of bark, and covered with large sheets of bark, or a kind of mats, made of flags.[3]

According to Stickney alcohol was a severe problem among the Miami and Potawatomi under his charge. He reported that both tribes were highly suspicious of whites, feeling that whites were motivated more by trade and speculation than anything else.[4]

Stickney's letter tells a great deal about the Miami situation in the new state of Indiana. They were apparently poorer than they had been at Kekionga, where they enjoyed the revenues of the portage and two-way trade, but their population had increased from the estimates made forty years earlier of roughly one thousand to about fourteen hundred. While alcohol was undoubtedly a problem it had not yet caused the tribal population to plummet. The Miami expressed confidence in their way of life, feeling it was superior to that of whites, who they believed were deceitful and enslaved by their work. According to Stickney, they listened to the religious opinions of others and felt the same respect was due their beliefs. In fact, he said, "There is no people who appear to be more firmly fixed in their theological faith."[5]

The Miami remained less "missionized" than the Potawatomi and other neighboring tribes such as the Shawnee at Wapakoneta, Ohio. Isaac McCoy, the itinerant Baptist missionary to Indians, worked among the Miami in Fort Wayne for two and a half years, but had little success with them. He moved on in 1822 to the St. Joseph River in southern Michigan where he set up Carey Mission and had some success in converting the Potawatomi. The Catholic Church maintained missions among the Potawatomi at St. Joseph in Michigan and at other locations, but the Miami had had no missionaries among them since the French Jesuits left sixty years earlier. The Midewiwin religion remained a powerful influence in their lives. In 1821 Governor Cass of Michigan Territory and Henry Rowe Schoolcraft, both amateur anthropologists, witnessed a Miami Midewiwin ceremony near Fort Wayne.[6]

The New Dependency Economy

The Treaty of St. Marys, Ohio, of 6 October 1818 reflected the outcome of the War of 1812 and redirected the Miami economy away from the fur trade toward direct purchase of goods on credit, rising debt, and further land sales. At St. Marys the Miami ceded most of central Indiana, allowing the survey and platting of the new state capital, Indianapolis. For 4,291,500 acres (called the New Purchase), the tribe eventually received 6.4 cents an acre. Their permanent annuity under the treaty was increased to $18,400, a large sum in those days. The Miami kept their principal winter hunting grounds east of present-day Kokomo as part of the Miami National Reserve, an area thirty-seven miles square containing some 875,000 acres.[7]

The remaining Miami landholdings were fragmented into six village reserves of a few square miles each and twenty-four individual reserves. The individual reserves were a new feature in

American treaties after the War of 1812; however, private grants to Indians were first made in Massachusetts Bay Colony in the 1600s. Thomas Jefferson revived the concept in order to emphasize the benefits of property—civilization, he believed, required individual ownership of land.[8] Protected from sale without the approval of the president, the individual treaty grants were the beginnings of the allotment system and the eventual breakup of Indian lands held in common across the United States. The treaty grants were also a means of bribing influential tribal leaders. Conveniently, sections of land (640 acres) could be exchanged for debts to traders. Traders could easily obtain valuable Indian land grants at choice locations for a nominal price with a recommendation from the Indian agent to the president that he approve the sale, usually a formality.[9]

Private grants were awards to Miami leaders and others who had close business dealings with the tribe. Officially, such grants were given to more "civilized" Indians to promote private ownership, but in reality they were used to reward those who helped secure treaties—mostly mixed-bloods and traders. Twenty of the twenty-four individual treaty grants went to mixed-bloods and their children in the 1818 treaty; the names read like a roll call of French traders and their Miami descendants: Josetta Beaubien, Antoine Bondie, Peter Labadie, François Lafontaine, Peter Langlois, Joseph Richardville, and Antoine Rivarre. The largest grants went to chiefs: J. B. Richardville, designated "principal chief," received 5,760 acres and François (or Francis) and Louis Godfroy each received 3,840 acres.[10]

The treaty of 1818 and subsequent treaties quickly involved traders in large-scale speculation in Miami land. As large annual cash payments increased the purchase of goods and consumption of alcohol among the Miami, the fur trade declined in relative importance and the subsistence economy was subverted. Tribespeople quickly found themselves becoming dependent on their annuities and credit with traders, in effect trading land instead of furs. With land thrown into the equation, the traders became the

Treaty Cessions
1817–1840

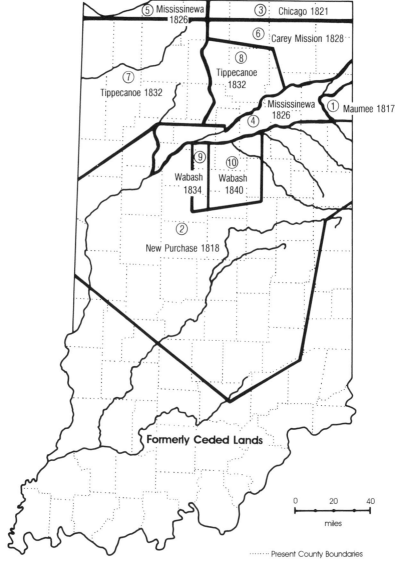

P.K.Goffinet

mechanism for divesting Indians of land and income, pauperizing the Indian community and enriching themselves and the public officials who issued them trading licenses.[11]

Annuity payments replaced the fur trade as the primary source of income for the Miami after the War of 1812, although the fur trade remained important. Once a year Fort Wayne became a day and night center of horse racing, drinking, gambling, debauchery, extravagance, and waste when the boxes of silver coins arrived. A bustling fair was created where traders set up log trading posts and the finest imported goods were sold at high prices. The result was a great deal of drunkenness and violence among the Indians and the immediate exchange of money from government agent to Indian chiefs to traders. With British trading firms finally excluded from the market, American firms took over the trade, beginning with John Jacob Astor's American Fur Company in 1818. Astor's firm was followed by Alexis Coquillard, who was one of the founders of South Bend, Indiana, Coquillard's partner and brother-in-law François Comparet, Samuel Hanna, and the Ewing brothers, George Washington and William G., who were soon joined in Fort Wayne by Cyrus Taber and Allen Hamilton. All were young products of the frontier and aggressive capitalists looking for the main chance.[12]

The European-American traders were faced by a new class of Miami leaders and intermediaries following the deaths of Little Turtle, Pacanne, and Owl. These new leaders were dominated by chiefs from the métis French-Miami trading group. Foremost was Jean Baptiste Richardville (Peshewa, Wildcat), who had learned Indian politics in the old world of the Midewiwin and the middle ground of British-Indian relations under his uncle Pacanne. Richardville had become an astute trader under the tutelage of his father, a Canadian trader, and in particular under his mother Tacumwah, Pacanne's sister. Born in Kekionga about 1760, Richardville was of the right age, fifty-five, to become a seasoned leader when Pacanne died in 1815. Having cast aside some of the frivolity

Chief Jean Baptiste Richardville
(Peshewa) as he appeared in 1826.
Painting by J. O. Lewis.

IHS C2581

Francis Godfroy (Palonswah) as he
appeared in 1839. Painting by
George Winter.

*Tippecanoe County Historical Association, Lafayette,
Indiana. Gift of Mrs. Cable G. Ball*

of his youth, he was fully prepared to deal with the demands
of his American counterparts.

Joining Richardville was another métis leader, François
Godfroy (Palonswah, the Miami pronunciation of François),
born about 1788. Godfroy was also a trader who had reached
his maturity at about the time of the War of 1812 and was a junior partner of Richardville in trading activities. Godfroy, like
Richardville, was the son of a French trader who married a
Miami woman.[13] They were followed by a growing population
of métis within the tribe, fathered by French traders living in
Miami villages. Richardville and Godfroy were fully aware of
the value of land and of the profits to be made in trade as well
as in brokering treaties with white officials. At the same time
they identified culturally as Miami and worked as intermediaries to protect tribal interests along with their own in the
dynamic capitalistic world of American society.[14]

The distribution of private Miami treaty grants to the French-Indian métis signaled a shift in the trading system. The young American traders taking root in Fort Wayne were mainly of Scots-Irish and Anglo-Saxon background. As this aggressive group moved onto the ground floor of development in the region, the older French traders of the middle ground lost status and in effect took refuge with their Indian brethren. The older French traders continued their traditional role as middlemen between Americans and the Miami, and if they were of Indian blood, as many of the second and third generations were, they shared the fate of the tribe as well as much of the profit of land redistribution from tribal to private ownership. The métis also exploited a special relationship with the federal government as interpreters, treaty-signing chiefs, and brokers of tribal affairs with federal officials.[15]

An Endangered Society

The granting of village and individual reserves opened the remaining Miami land to white settlement and made islands of the Indian settlements. The fragmentation of Indian lands and the "Europeanization" of the countryside into small private landholdings separated the Miami from their hunting territories, fishing weirs, and maple sugar camps, and made other subsistence activities more difficult. The Miami continued to hunt, fish, gather, and forage, but at increasing risk to their safety as they crossed pioneer settlements. As the Miami commons was reduced and converted to private landholdings, they were forced into greater competition with whites for the means of survival.

Small hunting parties working far from home villages for months at a time were particularly vulnerable to violence from Indian-hating frontiersmen. In one incident a mixed group of nine Shawnee and Miami were assaulted by five whites near today's Pendleton in 1824. All nine Indians were murdered, including three women and four children. The event became famous because the whites were brought to trial, and three of them were executed for the crime.[16]

The Miami were not always helpless victims of violence in the great majority of cases where the white judicial system failed to punish whites. One example, perhaps one of several in the early nineteenth century, occurred near Fort Wayne. There an Indian-hating white shot and killed a Miami man who was quietly fishing. The man's wife observed the murder from a hiding place and informed the people of her village. Following a lengthy discussion the villagers arrived at a consensus that the murderer should die. After nearly two years of planning and observation the Miami carried out the sentence of death by burning him in his cabin.[17]

The Miami were sometimes killed or injured by whites, but murder and violence within the tribe were much more common. The breakup of Miami lands and their invasion by frontiersmen who viewed Indians as a nuisance increased the sense of vulnerability among the Miami. Alcohol abuse became far more common than before the War of 1812, and the effects of violence and disease showed up in a rapid population decrease. From 1,400 enumerated in 1817, the Miami and Eel River Miami population dropped to 1,073 in July 1825, a decrease of 23 percent.[18]

In 1824 Governor Cass of the Michigan Territory sent Christopher Charles Trowbridge to question the Miami concerning their customs and traditions. Cass also circulated the same lengthy list of questions to the Delaware, Shawnee, Kickapoo, and Wyandot tribes.[19] Trowbridge began his interviews in mid-January 1825 and finished a month later. His two informants were Chiefs Le Gros and J. B. Richardville. As Le Gros and Richardville recounted earlier Miami history and customs, they occasionally commented on the changed condition of the tribe in the 1820s. The chiefs noted that the age of marriage dropped from twenty-three or twenty-five in former years to sixteen or seventeen in some recent cases,[20] and it was common for unmarried young women to have children. Quarreling and wife beating had become much more frequent with heavy drinking. It was clear that the Miami community was smaller, more violent, and less playful than in the past. Little Turtle, the war chief, had been so ruined by American manipulation that even this hero was debunked. Le Gros and Richardville recounted his mixed ancestry and repeating the language of the Miami chiefs at the Fort Wayne Treaty of 1809 offered the opinion that Little Turtle was not even a Miami.[21]

Although Thomas Jefferson and other officials talked much of civilizing Indians after 1800, little was done, except two brief attempts to teach the Miami European agricultural methods in 1804 and 1806. In 1819 Thomas McKenney, superintendent of Indian Affairs, persuaded Congress to appropriate ten thousand dollars annually for the "purpose of providing against the further decline and final extinction of the Indian tribes . . . and for introducing among them the habits and arts of civilization."[22] The appropriation was far too small, and most of it went to small missionary schools for Indians. The Indian agent at Fort Wayne received only $183 in 1823, and this money was sent to Isaac McCoy for his Carey Mission school.[23] The Miami, with a large annuity income and plentiful land, found it far easier to contract out farm labor. Federal documents in the 1820s are sprinkled with agreements for clearing and plowing land, fencing, harvesting, and storing crops—the money to be paid when annuities arrived.[24]

No Miami chiefs would send students to Carey Mission, and only a few children went to the Choctaw Academy in Kentucky.[25] As a result, the Miami were not exposed to the long-term efforts of local missionaries who might have introduced reading, writing, and simple arithmetic, useful skills for dealing with white authorities at a critical time in tribal relations. As it was, the Miami had to rely on outsiders for all of their written communications.[26]

By the 1820s the civilization policy had run its course. Governor Cass, a careful and unsentimental observer of Indians, wrote that, "There seems to be some insurmountable obstacle in the habits or temperament of the Indians, which has heretofore prevented, and yet prevents, the success of these labors."[27] Indians were clearly not assimilating into white society, and state officials did not want Indian societies behind the frontier. As settlement accelerated, reformers turned toward the expedient of removing Indians from the East and taking them west of the Mississippi River. There the goal would still be civilization, but over a longer time and in a different location.[28]

Final Treaties and a Brief Revival of the Middle Ground System

During the 1820s the administration of Indian affairs evolved rapidly along with the development of the American economy and the onrush of settlement in new western regions. After the War of 1812 the cotton gin, the steamboat, and enormous new public works such as the Erie Canal, the National Road, and a large system of canals, followed shortly by the first railroads, began to transform the American economy and speed settlement of the Mississippi valley frontier. In harmony with the new spirit of entrepreneurial capitalism, the government dismantled its factory system in 1822 and left the Indian trade wholly to free enterprise. In 1824 the Bureau of Indian Affairs was created, and in 1832 its head was designated as commissioner of Indian Affairs in order to relieve the secretary of war of some of the burden of Indian administration.

With the approaching development of northern Indiana, the Miami tribe occupied some of the most valuable potential commercial sites in the state, astride proposed canal and highway routes and at the locations of future towns and cities. The Miami National Reserve occupied 875,000 acres only thirty miles north of Indianapolis. Potawatomi land to the north and west of the Wabash River, characterized by extensive wetlands, was not as desirable for agriculture and was farther from the development spreading from the south. The more valuable Miami land gave the tribe greater leverage in treaty negotiations, as did the smaller size of the tribe itself under the seasoned leadership of Jean Baptiste Richardville, himself an experienced trader. The combination of astute leadership, valuable assets, and the move of pioneers toward northern Indiana enabled the Miami tribe to play off officials desiring Miami removal against a group of traders and land speculators who benefited by keeping the tribe in the state.

In March 1823 John Tipton was appointed Indian agent at Fort Wayne, a highly desirable federal position with its control of traders' licenses, negotiation of treaties, and distribution of annuities. Tipton was of the same social and cultural background as many of the traders establishing themselves in Fort Wayne at the time. Born on the Tennessee frontier in 1786, his father was killed by the Cherokee when Tipton was seven. As a young man he fought in the War of 1812, including the Battle of Tippecanoe, and rose rapidly through the militia ranks to brigadier general by 1817.[29]

When General Tipton was appointed Indian agent, northern Indiana was still an unsettled frontier with only a few hundred white inhabitants, many of them of French ancestry, and about five or six thousand Indians. Tipton's primary task was to regulate trade with the Indians as well as he could, to distribute annuities with as little violence and fraud as possible, and to seek further land cessions. His secondary purpose, closely related to his federal appointment, was to build a personal political base by dispensing federal patronage in northern Indiana. His control of several jobs and licensing of traders meant that local office seekers and merchants had to court his friendship and promote his political aspirations to advance their own fortunes.[30] When Tipton moved to Fort Wayne in 1823 it had fewer than five hundred inhabitants. The principal traders in the village were François Comparet (partner of Alexis Coquillard), Samuel Hanna, and the Ewing brothers George W. and William G.[31]

The history of the Ewing family in the Indian trade bears some comment because of the host-parasite relation that developed over the years between the Ewings and the Miami and because of the Ewings' ability to influence General Tipton and federal Indian policy to their advantage. The Ewing brothers had moved to Fort Wayne in 1822. Their father, Alexander Ewing, Jr., had been active in the Indian trade for many years, beginning with the Iroquois fur trade near Buffalo, New York, in 1787, then moving to Detroit around 1800 and to western Ohio in 1807. By the time the Ewings, father and two sons, arrived in Fort Wayne, they had thirty-five years experience in the Indian trade, which meant intimate knowledge of, but not necessarily respect for, the ways of the Indians.[32]

At the time Tipton arrived in Fort Wayne the nature of Indian trade was quickly changing over from purchasing furs from the Indians to supplying goods for annuities and credit, a far better source of steady income for the traders. Whereas the fur market suffered frequent and violent price fluctuations, annuities were steady and paid in silver coins, not in highly discounted local bank notes. The promise of future treaties and a further rise in annuities brightened the prospects of traders and land speculators and enhanced Tipton's power as he controlled trading licenses and conducted treaty negotiations.

From the time of his arrival in Fort Wayne until his remarriage two years later, Tipton made his home at Washington House, Alexander Ewing's combination boardinghouse, store, and tavern. Within a short time the Ewings were making contracts for plowing, clearing, and fencing land near Miami villages along the Mississinewa. As agent, Tipton drew up contracts authorized by the Miami chiefs to pay whatever price he thought proper out of the tribal annuity.[33] Tipton played a key role in transactions between influential whites and Indians, backed by the authority—and cash—of the federal government.

The New Purchase area ceded by the Miami in 1818 was soon carved into twenty-two counties as a flood of settlers rushed into central Indiana. By 1829 it was estimated that a hundred thousand people lived in the area.[34] The completion of the Erie Canal in 1825 and the westward extension of the National Road from Columbus, Ohio, unleashed a further flood tide of settlement, much of it aimed toward the northern third of Indiana. The state also formed plans to build the Michigan Road from Indianapolis to South Bend to open travel directly to the north.

Anxious to open northern Indiana to settlement and development in which he was personally involved, Tipton opened negotiations for treaties with the Potawatomi and Miami in October 1826. Tipton's task was complicated by conflicting purposes. On the one hand, the federal government and state officials were anxious to remove the Potawatomi and Miami, the last remaining tribal groups, from the state entirely in an American version of ethnic cleansing so development could go forward. On the other hand, the tribes, particularly the Miami, brought large quantities of money into the state with the attendant patronage and political influence. If the tribes were removed immediately, this source of income and influence would disappear. The tug-of-war between state officials who wished to see the Miami removed and traders and land speculators who benefited as long as the Miami stayed enabled the Miami to play off one side against the other for a lengthy delay in removal. It was an old game the Miami had mastered in the eighteenth century, and its revival in the 1830s worked to the long-term advantage of the tribe.

The commissioners for the 1826 treaties were Tipton, Lewis Cass, governor of Michigan Territory, and James Brown Ray, governor of Indiana. None of the commissioners saw a permanent place for Indians in white settlements. Tipton was already speculating in Indian lands, Ray was an intimate friend who favored rapid development of the state, and Cass was a slavish supporter of the big trading companies. The speeches made at the Potawatomi treaty crystallized the position of white officials and Indian chiefs concerning land cessions. Governor Cass set the tone with what was by now a ritual speech evolved from two centuries of British-American Indian dealings:

> Your Great Father, whose eyes survey the whole country, sees that you have a large tract of land here, which is of no service to you. You do not cultivate it, and there is but little game upon it.... There are a great many of the white children of your Father, who would be glad to live upon this land. They would build houses, and raise corn, and cattle and hogs.... Your Great Father is not only anxious to purchase the country of you, but he is desirous, that you should remove far from his white children. You must all see, that you cannot live in the neighborhood of the white people.[35]

Chief Le Gros responded for the Miami, who were partners in the cession, his answer shaped by two centuries of Indian relations with white authorities:

> Father, when you collected us here, you pointed to us a country, which you said would be better for us, where we could live.—you said we could not stay here, we would perish.—but what will destroy us.—It is yourselves destroying us, for you make the spirituous liquor. You speak to us with deceitful lips, and not from your hearts.... You point to a country for us in the west, where there is game. We own there is game there, but the Great Spirit has made and put men there, who have a right to that game, and it is not ours.... The land we have we wish to keep to live on—it was given to us by the Great Spirit for the means of our subsistence.... It was told us by our forefathers, that we should stay on the land which the Great Spirit gave us, from generation to generation, and not leave it.[36]

Tipton, Ray, and Cass negotiated a Miami treaty the week after the Potawatomi treaty, but at a price that bordered on the grotesque. Over $31,000 in cloth, blankets, and ornaments were distributed immediately (over $600,000 in current dollars), and another $41,259 in goods was to be distributed over the next two years. Tipton sanctioned the liberal distribution of alcohol to Indians, though prohibition was the official policy on treaty grounds. The tribe was to receive two hundred cows and two hundred hogs. In addition, nine Miami chiefs were to be given a wagon, a yoke of oxen, and a house worth $600. Also the Miami annuity was increased to $25,000. In the face of mounds of finery, offers of houses and private land for chiefs, and the flow of mind-dissolving hard liquor, the Miami relented and signed the treaty. The main importance of the Potawatomi treaty and its Miami companion was the opening of land for the construction of the Michigan Road and the Wabash and Erie Canal.[37] (See map on p. 82.) The Miami treaty was not popular in Indiana or Washington, D.C., because little land was ceded and the cost was far higher than other treaties. Tipton frankly admitted that without the extravagant giveaway of goods and the building of houses for nine chiefs, there would have been no treaty at all.[38]

The influence of the traders was evident in the large number of individual land grants in both the Potawatomi and Miami treaties, 106 in all (20 in the Miami treaty). Land exchange from Indians to traders had become a formality. Influential land speculators selected many individual grants for métis at prime locations. Soon after a treaty the traders would receive the land as payment for some small debt. The Indian agent, who was obligated to traders for support in treaty negotiations, then reported favorably to the president on the transaction and got approval for the "sale."[39] Although less acculturated village chiefs usually kept the land where their villages were located, the tendency was to concentrate tribal populations on smaller and more separated areas of land. The fragmenting of the Miami land base was reflected in the large number of "chiefs" who signed the treaty, thirty-seven in all.[40]

The Miami paid a heavy price for the 1826 treaty despite the quantity of goods and the increased annuity they received.

Land north of the Wabash River was fragmented into village reserves, which increased Miami dependency by making hunting and other subsistence activities more difficult. The influence of traders over tribal affairs was greatly increased, with the danger that all tribal assets would eventually pass into their hands. Finally, the term "perpetual annuity" was dropped, to be replaced by an annuity payable "as long as they exist together as a tribe," a clear hint of future efforts to terminate tribal government and the existence of the tribe itself.[41]

Tipton was personally interested in some of the Indian reserves. Four days after signing the treaty, the elderly Le Gros willed him the four sections of land set aside in his name as well as all of his personal property. Two months later Le Gros died. When his heirs learned of the will, they protested. Years later Tipton paid them $4,000, but the Miami never forgot the incident. Tipton also bought two reserves at the future site of Logansport, then got the Miami agency moved there in 1828. He argued reasonably enough that moving the agency nearer to Indian lands was best for Indian welfare, but he also profited handsomely from the development of the town. The Fort Wayne traders soon moved to Logansport, as did the liquor traffic, and no improvement in Indian sobriety was noted.[42]

In 1828 Tipton secured a minor treaty that bears mention because of the difficulties it caused some Miami. He persuaded the Eel River Miami, of whom there were perhaps no more than a hundred remaining in Indiana, to give up their hundred-square-mile reserve at Thorntown near today's Lebanon and to move back to the lower Eel River near Logansport. The Eel River Miami "tribe" consisted of a single village whose inhabitants had left the Logansport area sometime after the Kentucky militia destroyed their village in 1791. With the help of Little Turtle this small Miami subgroup gained an annuity at Greenville in 1795 and official recognition as a tribe, settling by 1818 at Thorntown.[43] Unfortunately, Tipton did not bother to consult with the Mississinewa council when he negotiated the

Eel River treaty, and after a few years the Miami chiefs refused to allow distribution of annuities to the Eel River people.[44] Later remnants of the group joined the Miami near Peru where they were given refuge.

The Path to Removal

Northern Indiana developed rapidly between 1830 and 1840 as roads and canals were built, land was cleared, and extensive swamps and marshes were drained. The white population north of the Wabash River rose nearly twentyfold in the decade, from 3,380 to 65,897. The Miami and Potawatomi Indian population, which was not included in the census, dropped from five or six thousand in 1830 to about 800 Miami in 1840. Indian landholdings totaled about 3,900,000 acres in 1831 (the Miami owned about 900,000 acres; the Potawatomi about 3,000,000 acres) and perhaps 30,000 acres—less than 1 percent of the 1831 holdings—in 1840.[45] Conversely, in 1830 there were only four organized counties north of the Wabash— by 1840 there were twenty-one. After construction of the Wabash and Erie Canal began in 1832, land sales at the Fort Wayne Land Office increased to third highest in the nation in 1836, reflecting the transition.[46]

The rush of settlement toward northern Indiana coincided with the enactment of Indian removal legislation in 1830. The bill that narrowly passed Congress called for the exchange of land west of the Mississippi for Indian lands east of the river and the deportation of tribes to their new lands. Indiana officials were anxious to clear the state of Indians, and from 1829 to 1831 the state legislature petitioned Congress six times for the extinction of Potawatomi and Miami land titles in the state.[47] Hysteria over the Black Hawk War in 1832 added to the demands for removal of both tribes.

In 1834 the Miami signed a new treaty, which fell far short of extinguishing the still extensive Miami landholdings in the state, and removal was not mentioned. The treaty ceded

208,000 acres of the Miami National Reserve (often called the "Big Reserve") at a dollar an acre, with fifty thousand dollars of this sum to be allotted to traders for Indian debts. Most of this money went to the Ewing brothers. For the first time fee simple patents were issued for 14,720 acres that could be sold without approval of the president. Because the treaty did not call for Miami removal, President Andrew Jackson refused to accept it, and it was not ratified until 22 December 1837.[48] (See map on p. 82.)

In trying to extinguish the Miami land title and remove the Miami from Indiana, state and federal officials were facing two formidable forces, Chief Richardville and the Ewing brothers. The Ewing firm could not survive without Miami annuities, and the Miami could not have resisted demands for removal as long as they did without the influence of the Ewings. Richardville was a trader who was keenly aware of the value of tribal land and retained the respect of the other village chiefs so long as he resisted removal, even though he enriched himself in the process. Tipton summed up Richardville's influence over the Miami tribe in a letter to Secretary of War John Eaton in 1831: "The Miamies are reduced to a small number,–but well organized in their kind of government, and with one of the most shrewd men in North America at their head."[49]

Removal of the Potawatomi from Indiana came in 1838, a calamity that highlighted the heavy-handed manipulation and carelessness of many such episodes. The deportation was based on a series of treaties rammed through by Indian agent Abel Pepper in 1836. One leader, Menominee, refused to go along with the charade. Tipton finally took charge in August 1838, capturing Menominee by a trick and having 850 people sent west under a military guard. The Potawatomi were in poor physical condition, and most had to walk. Typhoid fever struck them as did dysentery, diarrhea, and the effects of malnutrition. Forty-two people, mostly children, died along the way, while more than fifty escaped.[50]

The Miami were now the only tribe remaining in Indiana to interfere with settlement. In the fall of 1838 they agreed to negotiate another treaty. Agent Pepper appointed Allen Hamilton a fellow commissioner. By the late 1830s Hamilton, with his partner Cyrus Taber, controlled one of the most powerful trading houses on the Wabash.[51] Despite the pressure on the Miami, the 1838 treaty was another compromise affair, with some advantages gained by both the Miami and federal and state officials. The outcome, however, was important to the location and legal status of the postremoval Indiana Miami tribe. In many ways the treaty created the foundations for the future Indiana tribe and represented a subtle undermining of federal removal policy. Forty-three individual land grants were made, an unusually large number, but this time the Miami shut the door on nontribespeople who had shared at times in both land and annuities. In the past the tribe had expanded through the acceptance of outsiders, mainly the métis traders with whom the tribe had formed a longtime working relationship. Those times were now gone. Looking to the future, the tribal council declared in article six of the treaty that no one other than Miami Indians should have a right to land or annuities unless those persons were adopted into the tribe by the council itself.[52] Control of tribal membership was an essential aspect of tribal government. Control also was critical if the tribe were going to prevent outsiders from undermining tribal affairs and draining off tribal resources. The era of open membership and free land for those who married into the tribe was ending.

While the tribe did not agree to removal in 1838, an offer was accepted to send six chiefs west of the Mississippi River into Kansas Territory to examine a possible new reservation that the United States would "guarranty to them forever" when they might be *"disposed to emigrate from their present country."* Richardville, nearly eighty years old, along with his family, was exempted from removal. This single exemption, plus the clause granting the tribal council control of membership, became the foundation of the future presence of the Miami in Indiana as an organized Indian tribe.[53]

The cost of the 1838 treaty was enormous, far larger than for treaties with other tribes less well situated than the Miami. The tribe was paid $335,680 (over $7 million currently). A debt commissioner was to be appointed to certify all traders' claims against the tribe, and $150,000 of the settlement was to pay such claims. Tipton and Hamilton each received one-third of the $7,000 profit from the excessively high priced goods sold by the Ewing brothers.[54] Richardville was allotted a further seven and a half sections of land (4,800 acres) and Chief Godfroy six sections (3,840 acres).

Ten square miles along the Mississinewa River were reserved for the heirs of Metocina, to be held in common. Metocina had died in 1832, and this group of Miami was led by his eldest son Meshingomesia. Other one-square-mile reserves went to Miami living between Godfroy's lands and Metocina's lands between Peru and the future village of Marion. The family reserves set aside for Ozahshinquah, Maconzequah (the wife of Benjamin), Osandiah, Tahconong [Tahconah], and Wapapincha were important because along with the Godfroy and Meshingomesia reserves they became a refuge for a majority of the entire Miami tribe after removal. (See map on p. 120.)

Two years after the 1838 treaty the Miami unexpectedly notified Agent Samuel Milroy that they were ready for a new treaty and for removal from Indiana. Milroy was surprised since the Miami village chiefs had resisted any talk of removal for twenty years. According to tradition, Richardville drew up the treaty and informed Milroy the tribe was ready to sign. In fact, Hamilton wrote the terms of the treaty, which were greatly favorable to traders and Richardville. Milroy immediately accepted the treaty proposal on his own responsibility, without any instructions from the Indian Office. Only Hamilton assisted in the negotiations. In addition to owning a major trading firm, Hamilton by this time was the business adviser of the elderly Richardville and for years had been involved in the purchase and sale of Miami land.[55]

The Ewing firm had neared bankruptcy in 1839 in competition with the American Fur Company, thus the new Miami treaty was a means of salvaging its business. In the summer of 1840 the Ewings purchased sixty to eighty-five thousand dollars in goods for the Miami store at Peru. Four company clerks, led by James Miller and George Hunt, all speaking the Miami language, sold goods at a marked price, usually about 100 percent over New York prices. The Miami bought cloth, blankets, shawls, silk handkerchiefs, and ribbons. By November 1840 the Ewings held bills of credit on the tribe for $113,230.30. This indebtedness was the key to getting a new treaty. As William G. Ewing bragged later, "The only means to succeed was by a *large profuse* and general indebtedness of the tribe, made by the knowledge and concurrence of many officers of the Indian Department."[56]

The 28 November 1840 treaty was the twelfth signed by the Miami in the forty-five years since the Greenville Treaty of 1795. The last of the Miami National Reserve or Big Reserve was ceded, "being all their remaining lands in Indiana."[57] This clause was misleading as there were many reserves restricted to sale by approval of the president and the one commonly held reserve in the name of Meshingomesia. The treaty jargon simply meant that the tribal government was to be moved west with a portion of the Miami people, and any lands remaining in Indiana, even if held in common, were supposedly no longer "tribal." In exchange for the five hundred thousand acres of the Big Reserve, the Miami were offered a new reservation of five hundred thousand acres west of the Missouri state line in Kansas Territory and were to be removed within five years.

While the Miami at last accepted removal, the treaty allowed two more exemptions. Francis (as it was now written) Godfroy died in May 1840, and his many minor children by his two wives were permitted to remain on their land in Indiana. The same privilege was extended to Meshingomesia, his sister, six brothers, and their families. The United States would pay the cost of removal for the remainder of the tribe. Only two grants of land were made—seven sections (4,480 acres) to Richardville and one section, or 640 acres, to his son-in-law Francis Lafontaine. Richardville was also granted $25,000 and the estate of Francis Godfroy and $15,000 for money owed their trading houses by tribespeople.[58]

In return for ceding their land and accepting removal, the Miami were paid $550,000, or $1.10 an acre (about $11 million today). Two hundred and fifty thousand dollars was to be paid in annual installments, and $300,000 was reserved for claims against the tribe. Fifty thousand dollars of the $300,000 was reserved for debts contracted from the signing of the treaty and its ratification by the United States Senate. Traders and citizens were delighted with the treaty. The Ewing brothers sold an additional $139,821.99 to the Miami in a sales orgy lasting a mere three months from 28 November 1840 to ratification on 25 February 1841. Because it was the last Miami treaty, the Ewings began switching their business from Indiana to trading posts among the western tribes in Kansas and Iowa, even though they planned to continue with the Miami in Indiana, who still drew $25,000 in annual annuities plus an additional $12,500 annual debt settlement for twenty years.[59]

Richardville died on 13 August 1841 at his home on the St. Marys River a few miles southeast of Fort Wayne. An often retold legend called him the "richest Indian, so far as known, in this country."[60] During his lifetime he was granted 28,320 acres of land in various Miami treaties and $31,800 in settlement of claims, but there is no evidence he left great wealth. Much of his land went almost directly to Hamilton and others closely associated with him. The same was true of Godfroy, who received 10,880 acres and $17,612. The only lands the chiefs kept were

Francis Lafontaine (Topeah), last principal chief of the Miami before removal in 1846. Portrait by R. B. Crafft.

IHS LP3

the several hundred acres where they lived, which became places of refuge for their families and landless Miami.[61] Hereditary chiefs among the Miami were expected to be generous to their people, and Richardville fulfilled this role. Aiding the distressed in the tribe was the key to his leadership status. While he added to his personal wealth to an unknown extent, he also managed to delay removal for the Miami.

After Richardville's death his son-in-law Francis Lafontaine (Topeah, Frost on Leaves) was elected chief by the tribal council. Born about 1810, Lafontaine was married to Richardville's daughter Catherine (Pocongoquah) and maintained a store at the Forks of the Wabash, west of today's Huntington. Lafontaine was young and pliable, and the traders sensed he would be far more accepting of their demands than Richardville. They were not mistaken for he turned over the entire $12,500 annual payment from the 1840 treaty to various creditors without any written agreement.[62]

Persistence and Change in the Miami Community, 1816–1846

Easy access to whiskey, large annuities, and credit had a predictable effect on the Miami after the War of 1812. Easy money and quantities of alcohol, along with a breakup of land and subsistence activities, severely disrupted Miami society. The tribal population, which had been stable or perhaps rising from the 1770s to 1817, began a precipitous decline from 1,400 in 1817 to 1,025 in 1825 and to about 800 in 1840. By 1846, the year of removal, the population was probably less than 500, a loss of two-thirds in little over one generation.

Conditions worsened for the Miami as a pioneer population swept into northern Indiana in the 1830s. The close proximity of whites interfered with Miami hunting and fishing, and virtually unlimited credit and cheap, easily obtainable alcohol encouraged violence. Nathaniel West, who was appointed commissioner to verify trading debts, was shocked by conditions among the Miami in 1839. During his interviews there were six cases of bloodshed, one of them fatal, near his cabin. He observed that all the Miami, male and female, carried a knife (often a Bowie knife) and a loaded pistol to their interviews with him. He declined to ask them to put aside their weapons, "as they are tenacious of the privilege of going armed." Chiefs informed him that between 1838 and 1839 over sixty Miami had died, mostly by violence.[63] Violence varied greatly by sex, however, and men were far more likely to die than women. Agent Samuel Milroy reported in 1840 that there were nearly three Miami females to one male, with half of the deaths of adult males by assassination.[64]

The loss of so many males tended to raise the status of females. European-American observers stereotyped Miami women as drudges who did the farming and most of the heavy work while the men stood idly by. Sources on Miami women's lives are extremely limited, but it is known that they did much of their farming and other work together, while the children played nearby. Miami women's roles were more diverse than those of the pioneer women, and their activities often shocked white observers. They delighted in gambling with the plum stone game, raced horses, and quickly divorced bad husbands. Throughout the eighteenth century Miami women such as Tacumwah were regents who directed the affairs of young chiefs until they were ready to take on the role. More generally, Miami women carried forward tribal culture as the male population declined. Women were at their cabins and fields, going out little, and more often were monolingual, speaking only the Miami language.

The discovery of the "Lost Sister of Wyoming" attracted attention to the Miami and inspired some interviews and journals that shed a great deal of light on Miami women and Miami life in general in the 1830s. In 1778 Delaware Indians captured five-year-old Frances Slocum near Wilkes-Barre in the Wyoming valley of eastern Pennsylvania. George W. Ewing happened to discover her origin by accident while visiting her log house along the Mississinewa River in 1835. He wrote a letter to a general post office address in Lancaster, Pennsylvania, but the letter was not found and published until 1837. At that time two elderly brothers and a sister of the captive journeyed to Indiana to visit their sister. They met a completely Indianized woman known as Maconaquah (Little Bear Woman), who had to speak to them through an interpreter. Once the shock of time and change had worn off, they commented on her situation. She was a widow, lived in a double log cabin, and appeared to have most of the amenities of any farm woman of the time. She was perfectly content where she was and refused an invitation to return to her birthplace, saying she would be "like a fish out of water."[65]

In 1839 a brother and two nieces visited Slocum. Hannah Bennett, a niece, kept a diary in which she recorded a number of details of Miami life. Her aunt's house had a kitchen with a table and split-bottom chairs and the common cooking utensils of the time. A cloth was put on the table and the visitors were offered fried venison, tea, and shortcake. There were six beds made of folded blankets. A number of necklaces hung about the house. Maconaquah and her two grown daughters Kekenakushwa (Cut Finger) and Ozahshinquah (Yellow Leaf) were dressed in typical clothing of the fur-trade era. The mother wore a short blue calico gown with a fold of blue broadcloth lapped around her, red leggings, and buckskin moccasins. She wore seven pairs of earrings, while her daughters wore perhaps a dozen pairs.[66]

Artist George Winter visited Maconaquah's "village" immediately after the Slocum family, commissioned by them to paint a picture of the "Lost Sister." Years later Winter recalled walking nine miles on the Indian trails of the Miami reservation to the captive's home on a lovely autumn day, drinking from springs, and admiring the huge trees. From time to time he passed an Indian cabin, with small fields of ripening corn, and where he was greeted by barking dogs and the stares of the residents. Arriving at Maconaquah's tiny settlement in the late afternoon, he observed that her double log cabin had two or three smaller cabins attached to it. A tall corncrib was some distance behind the main cabin, while nearer on the right was a good-sized stable.[67] Wealth was counted in horses, of which the settlement counted between fifty and sixty. There were also a hundred hogs, seventeen head of cattle, and geese and chickens.[68]

Winter's many paintings and sketches of the Miami offer insights into Miami acculturation in the 1830s. They dressed in a mixture of European and Indian clothing, often elaborately decorated to show wealth. Men usually wore frock coats and ruffled shirts similar to those of prosperous white settlers on the Indiana frontier. At the same time the shirts were worn over the traditional breechcloth and leggings, and the men wore moccasins rather than shoes. They also liked to wear scarves wrapped around their heads in the form of turbans.[69] Women wore dark, full, broadcloth skirts that came almost to their ankles, with loose fitting, brightly colored blouses. They carried

White captive Frances Slocum and her two daughters in 1839. Kekenakushwa (Cut Finger) faces the artist, while Ozahshinquah (Yellow Leaf) faces away. Painting by George Winter.

Tippecanoe County Historical Association, Lafayette, Indiana. Gift of Mrs. Cable G. Ball

Deaf Man's Village as it appeared in 1839. Deaf Man, a Miami chief, was Frances Slocum's husband. The site was occupied by descendants until the 1920s. Painting by George Winter.

Tippecanoe County Historical Association, Lafayette, Indiana. Gift of Mrs. Cable G. Ball

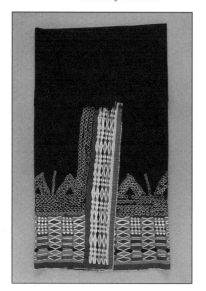

Miami skirt made of wool fabric, with German silver ornaments and silk ribbon appliqué with glass bead fringe, 1820–1840. Collected at Peoria, Indiana, in the 1920s.

The Detroit Institute of Arts, Courtesy Cranbrook Institute of Science, Robert Hensleigh, Photographer

Miami dress mocassins with silk ribbon appliqué and glass bead decoration, 1820–1840. Collected in Wabash County, Indiana, in the 1920s.

The Detroit Institute of Arts, Courtesy Cranbrook Institute of Science. Robert Hensleigh, Photographer

elaborately decorated shawls that could also serve as a head covering. The women wore leggings bordered with ribbon work. Many women carried broadcloth blankets decorated along the borders with silk appliqué and dozens of silver ornaments. The women also wore several pairs of silver earrings.[70]

Acculturation was uneven by the late 1830s as not all tribespeople had equal access to land or credit. While many Miami lived in log houses similar to those of pioneer whites, a large proportion still made use of the bark- or mat-covered *wikiami* common in the eighteenth century and earlier. Almost unlimited credit at the end of the 1830s allowed most Miami to purchase expensive items of European clothing. Such clothing usually was worn for special occasions or given as grave goods or as wedding dowries and obviously was not worn while working. On those occasions plainer, more durable items of apparel were worn, and the Miami were beginning to use what would be called "citizens dress," the same everyday clothing that non-Indians wore.

The Miami still practiced plural marriages that were nearly all "by Indian custom" and not recorded by civil or religious authorities. Burial practices were similar to those of a century earlier in general outline. Although evidence for social practices is sketchy for this period, it is safe to say that Miami beliefs and values were changing quickly. High death rates, common violence from within and without the Miami community, and the constant insecurity of rapid change were bound to erode confidence in older patterns of life and beliefs. Even so simple a matter as speaking the Miami language was becoming tenuous as more women married outside the tribe and as the Miami-speaking community shrank in size and became split apart.

Maconaquah's household was an extended family. Her oldest daughter and husband lived with her, as did three grandchildren by her younger daughter. The son-in-law was a métis, Jean Baptiste Brouillette (Tahquakeah), who occupied himself hunting. The youngest daughter, about twenty-nine years old, had been married four times. Her third husband had died in April 1839. She married her fourth husband in June; he was killed by another Indian in August.[71] An African-American laborer lived in one of the attached cabins. He had assimilated into Miami culture, married a Miami woman, and spoke the language fluently. When Winter arrived he was busy replastering a chimney. Maconaquah's village was typical of the Miami community by 1840.

Frances Slocum and her family were scheduled for removal with the rest of the Miami. In 1845 Alphonso Cole, a Peru attorney, petitioned Congress to allow Maconaquah to remain in Indiana since she was elderly and her daughters owned a treaty reserve. On 3 March 1845 Congress passed a joint resolution allowing her family, by then consisting of twenty-one people, exemption from removal.

Removal

Four groups of Miami were exempt from removal in 1845, and the rest of the tribe were not inclined to leave the state. The small size of the Miami tribe, the botched Potawatomi removal of 1838, and the value of the land and size of Miami debt settlements all conspired to delay and frustrate their removal years after other tribes had been taken from the Midwest. The contract for the Miami removal took on a perverse life of its own. Thomas Dowling of Terre Haute originally received a contract for nearly sixty thousand dollars to remove six hundred Miami to Kansas Territory. Later, Dowling sold the contract to Robert Peebles of Pittsburgh. Peebles in turn sold the contract to three groups of investors, the Ewing brothers, Samuel Edsall, brother-in-law of Indian agent Joseph Sinclair, and Alexis Coquillard. Coquillard had carried out the brutal removal of the Potawatomi in 1838. As an experienced "conductor" he was put in actual charge of the Miami removal.[72]

Coquillard had gone west many times, making a profession of moving the Potawatomi from one location to another.[73] He was dreaded by the Miami who called him "Cutiah," their way of saying his last name. Miami dread was based on some terrifying episodes. On one occasion in the 1830s Coquillard dunned a Miami chief at an annuity payment. Taking the chief's reply as an insult, he lunged at the man and tore off his ornaments and clothing and took them to his cabin. When the chief returned later, Coquillard stepped behind the door as he admitted him and knocked him senseless from behind.[74]

In August 1845 a delegation of five Miami leaders traveled to Kansas Territory to inspect the new reservation. Several older leaders had died in the 1830s, so the inspection group included a new generation of leaders who represented all the Miami groups.

George Washington Ewing
(1804–1866). Ewing was a
tireless manipulator of Miami
affairs in Washington, D.C.,
and his letters offer the best
insight into conditions among
the Miami in the twenty years
before removal in 1846.

Louise Hay

Included were Tahquakeah (J. B. Brouillette), Pimyotamah, Chapendoceah, Louis Lafontaine, and George Hunt. Francis Lafontaine, the ostensible "principal chief," sent his sixteen-year-old-son Louis. George Hunt was a half-blood Miami who worked for the Ewings in their Peru store.[75]

Miami acceptance of removal was not improved by what the visitors saw. The heat was suffocating during their visit, the land scorched, and most of the creeks dry. George Ewing encountered the Indians in St. Louis on their return trip and reported they did not like the land, that it was a miserable place, and that they would so report to the rest of the tribe.[76] Even though Ewing opposed Miami removal at the time because he had no financial interest in the outcome, his impression of Miami feelings was probably not exaggerated. Chief Lafontaine was also dragging his feet on removal, pleading for an extension of the 1845 deadline in order to get the land and debt concerns of the tribe settled.[77]

Miami delaying tactics were successful, and removal did not take place in 1845. George Ewing, who was still angling to make money on the deportation, commented acidly on the humanitarian arguments of Hamilton and others that the Miami would be better off west of the Missouri. Ewing often traveled through the region of the new reservation and noted that it bordered the Missouri state line, where there would be many sellers of whiskey. In fact, he said, "many of those despicable rascals are already stationed along there in advance, anxiously awaiting the arrival of their victims."[78] Two months later, when the Ewing brothers purchased a third of the removal contract, such concerns disappeared from his correspondence, to be replaced with a firm commitment to deport the Miami from Indiana.[79]

During the summer of 1846 Lafontaine apparently lost his effectiveness with the other Miami leaders who were opposed to removal. Attempting to mend matters, he took Pimyotamah and other village chiefs on an unauthorized trip to Washington, D.C., to confer with President James K. Polk. Although the tribal leadership was exempt from removal, their resistance was making the removal of those who were not exempt impossible to orchestrate. Lafontaine was caught in the middle between federal officials demanding removal and virtually the entire tribe that was against it.

Hamilton, always the humanitarian, argued against the use of troops to coerce the unwilling Miami. Withholding annuities would get the proper results. "Let them," he wrote the commissioner of Indian Affairs in August, "be without their usual resources for one winter only, and their state of starvation will teach them in a forcible manner the absolute necessity of complying with their solemn stipulations." Hamilton had not seen the proliferation of grogshops along the border of the sweltering Miami reservation and assured the commissioner in Washington that "feeling for the welfare of the Indians, as we do, we wish sincerely to see them removed far from the corrupting influence of white people and placed under the immediate protection of the government."[80]

Without the support of the traders the Miami could no longer delay migration. In March the Ewing brothers reached a settlement of their outstanding Miami claims and with the permission of Chief Lafontaine and the Indian Office had gained control of the entire $12,500 annual debt installment. The Ewings now warmly supported Miami removal. On 7 September 1846 Commissioner of Indian Affairs William Medill ordered Joseph Sinclair, the Miami subagent, to demand a council with the Miami and to inform the Miami and the traders that there would be no more annuities or debt awards paid until removal was complete. Sinclair called for a small military force, and on 22 September Capt. W. R. Jouett arrived in Peru with sixty-four privates from Newport Barracks near Cincinnati.[81] By 1 October not a single Miami had come to the collection point, and Sinclair announced that troops would begin to search for fugitives in two days. After that threat the Miami gathered. The removal began on 6 October when three canal boats loaded with Miami and their effects departed on the Wabash and Erie Canal. Two more boatloads of Miami were collected at Fort Wayne.[82]

Several whites accompanied the group, including William G. Ewing. They proceeded northeast to Toledo, where they turned down the Miami and Erie Canal, passing through Dayton to Cincinnati, roughly retracing the route of the 1790s military expeditions sent against them. At Cincinnati they were transferred to the steamboat *Colorado*, on which they traveled down the Ohio River to the Mississippi, then up the Mississippi to St. Louis, where they arrived 20 October. At St. Louis they transferred to the *Clermont II* and steamed up the Missouri River to Kansas Landing (now Kansas City). Here they unloaded and traveled fifty miles overland to the reservation, where they finally arrived on 9 November. The local Indian agent certified the arrival of 323 Miami, with the death of six and the birth of two.[83]

George Ewing came from the Sac and Fox agency in Iowa to meet the migrating Miami on 3 November and accompanied them on the last leg of their trip. His assessment of the removal gives a grimmer picture than the brief report filed by the Kansas agent:

> They have suffered considerable from sickness on the way and some have died. They have lost, in all, since they left Peru, Indiana and up to this time [November 24th] 16 persons—all but 5 of these were children and infants. I am informed that much sickness prevailed amongst them previous to their departure.[84]

Removal had finally taken place. Ewing summed up the years of delay and resistance and in his matter-of-fact way went to the heart of the matter: "The *real* cause of their unwillingness was this—they dreaded the very idea of leaving that splendid Indian country where they had lived all their lives."[85]

The division of the historic Miami tribe, itself a fragment of a larger Miami-speaking group, into two tribes, the Eastern, or Indiana Miami tribe, and the Western, or Oklahoma Miami tribe, occurred on 9 November 1846. The Miami had come through fifty years of rapid change, unlike any they had known before. In the last thirty years they had endured rapid population loss at the same time their ownership of prime real estate, good leadership, and an alliance with powerful traders had enabled them to play off powerful groups in American society.

Both tribes now faced an uncertain future, one on the western edge of the eastern woodlands in a country far harsher than the one they had left. The other tribe remained in its homeland, but with an uncertain legal status, a tiny land base, and in the midst of a rapidly populating, dynamic European-American culture. The remainder of this work concerns both change and persistence of older ways in the eastern branch of the Miami tribe in their Indiana homeland. Some of those Miami found a new future in the West, of their own choice, and many of the Miami taken west returned to their homeland, further frustrating federal intentions and complicating the work of the historian. The Miami people were doing as they always had, seeking opportunity and adapting to change, but remaining Indian.

FIVE

Years of Consolidation
1847–1872

■

I was drinking a good deal then—I was drunk all the time.... I was like a horse in fly time—I would go one place and another. Meshingomesia told me I might make improvements here and make what I could off it and quit going in debt to anyone.... I want to live here so when I die I will have a place.... I don't care how poor I am here—I want to be poor in heart so when I die I will have a place [of] peace for me.

Sasaquasyah, testimony before commission to allot the Meshingomesia reservation, May 1873[1]

REMOVAL ENDED AN ERA FOR THE MIAMI. THEY HAD come through a half century of war, social disruption, drastic decline in their numbers, cession of most of their land, and now a division of their rapidly dwindling population. They found themselves a tiny minority behind the frontier in a rapidly populating midwestern state. National attention shifted to the tribes that had been moved west, and the Miami remaining in Indiana quickly became a hidden community, little noticed outside the areas in which they lived. Only 148

Miami were legally allowed to remain in Indiana, and they lived in tiny groups scattered along the upper Wabash valley from Lafayette to Fort Wayne. These small clusters of Miami were separated by more than distance. Uneven acculturation sharply marked off the comparatively affluent Richardville, Godfroy, and Lafontaine families near Peru, Huntington, and Fort Wayne from the far poorer and less acculturated families living up the Mississinewa River.

The remnants of the Miami in Indiana were expected to melt into the general population within a generation. The Miami agency in Fort Wayne was closed soon after removal. As far as the federal government was concerned the Miami tribal government was now in Kansas Territory. Any business the Miami Indians of Indiana had was expected to be conducted through the tribal government in Kansas. In 1847 the dreaded Alexis Coquillard was authorized to collect the Miami who were missed or who escaped removal in 1846. Coquillard combed every Indian community, spreading fear and confusion among the Miami who were not sure of their status in Indiana. The tribe was charged $4,215.40 for the search.[2]

Abandonment of the Indiana Miami by the Bureau of Indian Affairs and the traders soon proved to be an advantage due to changes in federal Indian policy and the oncoming settlement of the trans-Mississippi West. Not long after the deportation of the Miami in 1846 it was realized that the Kansas reservation was in the immediate path of railroad development and waves of incoming pioneers. The rapid settling of Kansas forced changes in federal Indian policy. In 1849 the Bureau of Indian Affairs was taken from the Department of War and placed in the newly created Interior Department. Indian affairs, except in cases of war, were now under the control of a civilian agency. In the same year Commissioner of Indian Affairs William Medill proposed the establishment of a new reservation system in which local Indian agents would have almost total control and supervision over the lives of the Indians in order to force male horse-plow farming and the breakup of reservations into individual farms.[3] This was to be the final effort of the civilization policy that had failed east of the Mississippi. The changes signaled the end of "permanent" reservations for Indian tribes and the beginning of the final efforts to dispossess Indians of their land totally and to end their tribal governments.

The Western Miami found themselves in the heart of "Bleeding Kansas," their reservation invaded by hundreds of squatters. Within a few years of removal John Brown settled at Osawatomie on the border of the reservation and began murderous raids against proslavery whites in the area. Worse yet, a "Miami Claim Association" was formed with the sole purpose of undermining federal protection of the newly relocated Indians. Popular sovereignty quickly replaced tribal sovereignty, and the hapless Western Miami nearly drowned in a sea of alcohol just as George Ewing had predicted.[4]

The Indiana Miami, free of federal supervision and the heavy handed control of a local Indian agent, went about rebuilding their lives behind the frontier. The "government chiefs" were now in the West, while the Mississinewa council, representing all of the Miami groups and tracing its roots back to late-eighteenth-century leaders, remained in Indiana. Without the need for a principal chief, the Eastern Miami could revert to their old system in which village chiefs made decisions as a group. The Indiana leaders were sober and well experienced in tribal affairs. They knew that the preservation of tribal existence relied heavily on good governance and the ongoing legal status of the tribe. They also realized that removal had created a dilemma in Miami governance. The federal government insisted that the small group of chiefs in the West, representing only two or three families, were the sole Miami government. The much larger group of chiefs in Indiana, representing all the village groups, insisted that they were the Eastern Miami tribal government. Defending the legal status and prerogatives of the

Indiana Miami government soon became a critical task that has continued to the present day.

Though federal officials insisted that the Indian title was extinguished in Indiana, the claim was again a legal fiction because the Eastern Miami retained core holdings of land on which they resided. Just east of Peru, Francis Godfroy had left 2,500 acres of treaty land to his family, stipulating that it was not to be sold until his minor children reached adulthood. Two miles up the Mississinewa, Ozahshinquah owned a square-mile reserve plus land she inherited from Tahconah [Tahconong], one of her husbands, a total of 805 acres. Five or so miles farther up the Mississinewa, Meshingomesia held a ten-square-mile reserve in common for all of his father's descendants. Francis Lafontaine had a square-mile reserve west of Huntington, and J. B. Richardville had left over 2,400 acres to his family southeast of Fort Wayne in Allen County and in Huntington County. Finally, the Miami family of Pierre Langlois, the trader with the Eel River Miami at Thorntown, held a square mile near Lafayette. The Eel River Miami were landless.

By 1846 the remaining Miami landholdings in Indiana amounted to perhaps 15,000 acres. The population of outlying Miami settlements near Lafayette, Huntington, and Fort Wayne was quite small, sometimes consisting of only one or two families. The great majority of the Miami population took refuge on about 10,000 acres between the Wabash and Mississinewa Rivers in a rough triangle bounded by Peru, Wabash, and Marion.[5] (See map on p. 120.)

The Miami reserves in the Peru-Wabash-Marion area were within easy walking distance of each other along old paths, trails, and traces. The land was located on the rivers, with easy access to hunting, trapping, fishing, gathering, and small-scale horticulture. It was a prime subsistence-cycle habitat. The larger Wabash River fell slowly through a broad, flat valley and was characterized by alternating deep stretches and boulder-strewn shallows. The Mississinewa was entirely different,

falling more rapidly over limestone shelves, with high limestone bluffs rising sharply from the river and occasional deep
pools. The area between the two rivers contained a number of
soil types, as well as marshes, small ponds, and prairies. Large
springs and occasional flooding moistened the lowlands, while
the limestone slopes and uplands had dry open places. Slopes
faced south and north, and valleys harbored a diverse mixture of
plant species, some left from cooler glacial times from the far
north and others on warm slopes from regions far to the south.
The Wabash valley was a minor tributary of the Mississippi fly-
way, with large numbers of migrating birds. The area was warm
enough that some geese and other species wintered over.

The Wabash and Mississinewa were as yet untainted by industrial pollution and were heavily populated with fish, turtles,
and shellfish. Complementing the waterfowl and fish were a
number of small mammals that could be exploited for furs and
food. The heavy, old-growth forests were largely intact on Indian land, moderating the heat of summer and sheltering the
landscape from powerful winter winds. The Miami had occupied the area for fifty years or more and had made extensive use
of subsistence resources. The relative calm that settled on tribal
affairs after removal allowed tribespeople to return to ancient
patterns of hunting, fishing, and horticulture. The ending of virtually open credit with traders meant that tribespeople once
again had to depend on their own efforts for economic survival.

Although the population of northern Indiana more than doubled between 1840 and 1850 to 165,286, settlement was spread
thinly over a large area. The largest cities along the upper
Wabash were Lafayette with 6,128 population and Fort Wayne
with 4,282. Both were over forty miles from the main Miami
settlement. The county seat towns were still villages in 1850,
Wabash counting 964 citizens, Marion 703, and Peru 1,266.[6]
Usable roads were almost nonexistent. As late as 1857 one resident of Wabash complained that "the mud is from two to seven
feet deep on every Road leading to Wabash" and that it recently

Major Miami Sites
circa 1847–1872

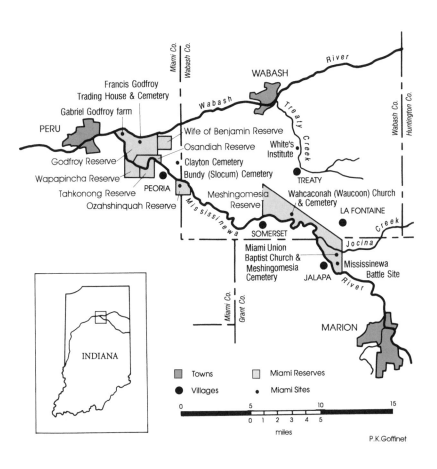

took three to five hours to go nine miles to the village of Somer-set.[7] Although canals opened in the 1840s and the first railroad was operating in the late 1850s, it was to be some time before decent market roads connected outlying towns to transportation centers. The Miami were still comparatively isolated from the pressures of settlement and a commercial economy. In terms of involvement with traders, they were less a part of the market economy than in the 1830s and 1840s.

The Political Consolidation of the Tribe: New Leadership

The most important task of Miami leaders after removal was to gain legal status for the tribe under federal Indian law. Officially the Indiana Miami were not a tribe but a collection of Indian descendants. Miami leaders, however, had long fought removal itself and were not ready to accept detribalization. While the federal government had enhanced the status of Chiefs Richardville and Lafontaine in the 1830s and 1840s, the village leaders had maintained a close watch on the American chiefs ever since the corruption of Little Turtle by William Henry Harrison. With the death of Francis Godfroy in 1840 and J. B. Richardville in 1841, the older generation of leaders reaching back to the early 1800s was gone. Younger leaders, nearly all born in the early 1800s, came to power: Meshingomesia (Bur Oak), son of Metocina; Tahquakeah (known as Jean Baptiste or Capt. Brouillette), son-in-law of Deaf Man (Shepaconah); Peter Bondy (Wapapetah); Pimyotamah (The Sound of Something Passing By), brother-in-law of Francis Godfroy; Mezequah; and Francis Lafontaine (Topeah), son-in-law of J. B. Richardville. These village leaders constituted the new tribal leadership after removal.

The deaths of Richardville and Godfroy increased the power of the village chiefs who sat as the Mississinewa council. Chief Lafontaine, favored by the Miami agent, struggled to maintain his authority in the six years after Richardville died. Lafontaine went west with the removal group and died suddenly in the spring of 1847 at Lafayette on his journey home from Kansas.

Lafontaine's death freed the village chiefs from further interference from the federal government and traders in Indiana. The Miami were able at last to maintain a tribal council form of government without a compromised chief. Meshingomesia, as the leader of the largest Miami group with the largest landholdings, assumed the role of lead chief. The majority of Miami leaders were of mixed blood, but they were of equal standing on the council and did not try to dominate the tribe.

Meshingomesia remained lead village chief of the Indiana Miami for the next thirty-two years, until his death in 1879. Born about 1800 he was the oldest of the ten sons of Metocina, who had signed the Greenville Treaty in 1795 and was descended from the Miami who had traded with the English at Pickawillany. Sometime after 1752 those Miami had been the first to settle along the Mississinewa. During the 1830s and 1840s the group avoided running up debt and were little acculturated to individual property. They were the only group granted communal lands in the 1838 treaty. As power moved to more culturally conservative leadership after removal, members of the Richardville family began to move west, where they could have greater impact on Miami affairs. Louis Lafontaine, son of Chief Lafontaine, moved to Kansas and joined the Western Miami tribal council. He was followed by Thomas Richardville, a grandson of Chief Richardville, in 1860. Other members of the Richardville family continued to move west during the remainder of the nineteenth century. As American influence over the tribe waned, so did the role of the more acculturated mixed-blood leaders associated with preremoval affairs.

Consolidation of the Tribal Population

The nucleus of the Indiana Miami tribe began with the Richardville family who were exempted from removal in 1838. In 1840 the Francis Godfroy family and Metocina's family were likewise exempted. In 1845 Congress exempted the family of Frances Slocum. These four groups totaled 148 people. The

Meshingomesia (ca. 1800–1879)
encouraged formal education
and American-style horse
agriculture among
his followers. Photo by
L.F. Craven, Marion, Indiana.

IHS C6389

consolidation and growth of the Indiana Miami population began on the very day of removal. A small group of Miami in Coquillard's camp in Peru stoutly refused to go aboard the canal boats, claiming they were Eel River Miami. They were left behind. In 1847 Coquillard scoured Miami villages and collected 78 more people for removal—"everything in the shape of an Indian," as he put it—including the hapless Eel River group. James Aveline, a trader with the Eel River group, successfully sought a writ of habeas corpus from Judge Albert Cole and got the release of the 17 Indians, all girls and women, who were allowed to remain in Miami County.[8]

As it happened, Judge Cole's son Alphonso A. Cole was the attorney for the Eel River Miami. Learning from George W. Ewing that this group was owed several thousand dollars in back annuities, Cole was soon working with the wily Ewing to obtain the funds for himself, James T. Miller, and James Aveline.[9] As Ewing walked Cole through the minefields of official Washington, he cautioned secrecy and proper timing and emphasized, "don't *fool yourself* with Indians, They are the *goddamdest ingrates* in the world."[10] By 1851 Ewing was able to assure Cole from Washington that the entire Eel River annuity—$16,000—was being sent to Indiana, "so set your traps & make all safe at pay[men]t." Ewing could speak with assurance because the paymaster in Fort Wayne was his brother-in-law Smallwood Noel.[11]

The population of Miami in Indiana was swelled mainly by returnees from Kansas, numbering about 60 people. Most were from the family of Chief Mezequah, who became involved in a blood feud on the Western Miami reservation. These Miami, also with the help of Alphonso Cole, petitioned Congress to receive their annuities in Indiana in 1850. On 1 May Congress passed a joint resolution extending exemption from removal to 12 additional Miami who held treaty reserves in Indiana and their descendants. Included in the exemption were Mezequah's two wives and children, Osandiah, and the families of nearly every other Miami village chief, including those of Seek, Black Raccoon, Black Loon, and the wife of Benjamin. The Miami families of Pierre Langlois and Anthony Rivarre were also allowed to stay, although they had never left the state. In all, 101 more Miami were legally permitted to remain.[12]

With the addition of the Kansas refugees and the other families, the Miami population in Indiana rose to over 250 by 1850. The Miami population in Kansas declined to about 100, with only 12 adult males in 1868.[13] Divided into seven distinct groups, the Indiana Miami tribe had achieved a large enough population to maintain itself as a separate cultural, political, and social group from the dominant society. Marriage taboos prohibited marriage within one's extended family, and the addition of three groups to the original four who were exempted from removal facilitated a high rate of intermarriage within the small tribe for another generation, greatly enhancing tribal cohesion. The returnees altered the political balance of the tribe as well. Invited to settle among the Godfroy family near Peru, the Mezequah family provided a counterbalance to the less acculturated Miami farther upstream along the Mississinewa River. The balancing of factions between more and less acculturated Miami allowed the tribe to respond more easily to changes in federal Indian policy. Whatever the new federal policy might be, there was a group of Miami who could challenge it, if necessary, and gain the support of the remainder of the tribe. This mechanism whereby one group of the tribe initiated a response, then gathered full tribal support, was to become vital to the preservation of the Indiana Miami as a tribe in the future.

Establishing Legal Rights as a Tribe

In the spring and summer of 1854 the postremoval leadership in Indiana faced its first major test when it was called to Washington, D.C., to renegotiate the terms of older treaties. With the rapid settlement of eastern Kansas and coming statehood for the territory, Commissioner of Indian Affairs George W. Manypenny was ready to reduce the size of reservations and to allot the land to individuals, a forerunner of later federal allotment policy. Commissioner Manypenny's goal for the Western Miami was to reduce the five hundred thousand-acre reservation to a fraction of its former size and to allot the remaining land to individual Miami in two hundred-acre tracts. The Indiana Miami were invited to the negotiations because the commissioner wanted to end treaty payments of $26,400 a year after a few years.[14] By now the Western Miami tribe was much smaller than the Eastern Miami tribe and in far worse shape, decimated by alcohol and besieged by violent land seekers who had been told the reservation was open to settlement.[15] The Western Miami tribe was in no condition to resist the demands of development radiating from Kansas City across the plains.

At the new treaty negotiations Commissioner Manypenny took the proper European-American legal stance that the Miami tribe was in Kansas, while the Indiana Miami were no more than residents of Indiana who were expected to agree with the results. The Indiana Miami, on the other hand, had reestablished a tribal government of a quality not seen for forty years and were not inclined to be pushed around. Meshingomesia led the delegation that included his oldest son Pecongeoh, Pimyotamah, Peter Bondy, and Keahcotwah (Buffalo) and strongly objected to ending permanent annuities. Manypenny replied through the interpreter that whatever the Western Miami decided would be binding on the Eastern Miami. He pointed to Article 4 of the 1826 treaty, which clearly stated that annuities were meant to be permanent only as long as there was a tribe.[16] The bargaining position of the red-faced commissioner was weakened when tribal delegates forced him to admit that the 500,000-acre reservation promised the Western Miami contained less than 370,000 acres. When surveyed it was even smaller, 324,796 acres, less than two-thirds the size stipulated in the 1840 treaty.[17]

Manypenny's offer to capitalize the annuities—that is, set up a fund whose interest payments would equal current annuities—likewise made a mockery of simple arithmetic. He said he could go no higher than $400,000 at 5 percent interest to replace annuities. When the tribe sued years later the finding indicated the capital fund should have been $530,800.[18] The commissioner's tone throughout the negotiations was patronizing and peremptory. Since only a few of the Indiana Miami delegates spoke English or had some formal education, there is no evidence in the minutes that they understood the meaning of capitalization of annuities and their commutation, which they eventually accepted.[19]

The Indiana delegation was determined not to give in to demands beyond ending annuities. Commissioner Manypenny shamelessly pressured Meshingomesia to privatize the small reservation held in his trust, saying he should sell most of it and cut up the remainder into farms for the young men. The stolid Miami replied that he did not come to Washington to sell the land—it was for "his women and young men, & children now growing up" and that it was not to be divided. When sale of the land was brought up the next day, Meshingomesia sat silent.[20] The reservation would not be broken up.

The greatest concern of Meshingomesia and his fellow delegates was control of enrollment in the tribe and purging the mixed bloods from Fort Wayne and southwestern Michigan who were not part of the tribe from the annuity rolls. On this point he was on secure ground, as Article 6 of the 1838 treaty granted the tribal council the right to control enrollment of those who happened to live on Miami land or intermarry into the tribe. If the tribe did not have this prerogative, outsiders could get themselves placed on tribal rolls by Congress and share in tribal assets.

Despite treaty language spelling out tribal control of membership, annuities had been paid to some forty distant relatives of Chief Richardville who were descendants of his half-sister Josetta Beaubien Roubidoux. This group had gained access to Miami annuities in 1851 with the help of Allen Hamilton and George Ewing, acting in concert with the Fort Wayne paymaster Smallwood Noel, Ewing's brother-in-law. Annuities also had been paid to a group of Miami led by Flatbelly (Papakeechi), who had moved from their village near Lake Wawasee to live among the Pokagon Potawatomi of southwestern Michigan. The Mississinewa council still resented the part the Michigan Potawatomi played in trying to force the 1809 treaty and was determined to end the diversion of annuities that undercut its authority and impoverished the tribal community.

The treaty negotiations concluded 5 June 1854 fell far short of the goals of the Indiana Miami. Meshingomesia and his colleagues went home and called a general council to discuss the issues. A smaller delegation led by Pecongeoh (Meshingomesia's oldest son), Pimyotamah, and Peter Bondy returned to Washington in August to negotiate further changes in the treaty with the Senate. Pimyotamah's father had been a captive from Kentucky, and his sister was the younger wife of Francis Godfroy. Pimyotamah had been a member of delegations to Presidents John Tyler and James Polk and also had been among the group of "best hunters and fishermen" who had investigated the new reservation in Kansas. Bondy was the husband of Ozahshinquah, the daughter of Shepaconah (Deaf Man) and Frances Slocum. Meshingomesia trusted all three men for their skills in dealing with white officials.

A critical goal for the Indiana Miami, beyond control of tribal enrollment, was federal recognition of their tribal government. Commissioner Manypenny refused to acknowledge the separate legal status of the Eastern Miami tribe, but the Senate did so in the second round of negotiations by allowing the original delegation to consult with the tribe in a general meeting and to return three members in August as "a fully authorized deputation" without the attendance of the Western Miami to suggest amendments to the 5 June treaty. The Senate agreed that enrollment with the Indiana Miami consisted only of those people accepted by the consent of the Indiana tribal council.[21] Further, the Senate accepted a request that the Eastern Miami share of the capital fund be paid in annuities for another generation—twenty-five years—rather than in six years, in order to allow more time for their transition to a market economy and citizenship. In 1881 the Eastern Miami share of the capital fund of $231,004 would be divided among legitimate members of the tribe.[22]

James Lindsay, a clerk with the Office of Indian Affairs, was authorized to compile a tribal roll acceptable to the Miami council. When completed the roll contained 302 names. When some duplications and deceased heads of family are eliminated, the Miami population was 278. This did not include the approximately 20 Eel River Miami living among the tribe. Tiny though the Eel River group was, it retained separate legal status from the Miami.[23]

The ink was hardly dry on the 1854 treaty when sixty-eight people who were placed on the tribal roll in 1851 and who were rejected by the tribal council again attempted to be enrolled as Miami. In his working papers for the roll Lindsay noted that many of these people had one-eighth or one-sixteenth Miami blood, meaning one Miami great-grandparent or one great-great-grandparent. Nearly half of the sixty-eight were in the latter category.[24] The Richardville descendants with the surnames Bowers, Creditor, De Rome, Funk, Harris, Minnie, and Roubidoux were culturally European American and lived in Fort Wayne, not among the Miami. Unlike the métis who were culturally Indian and lived among the Miami, these descendants were opportunists seeking financial gain at the expense of the tribe. They had been successful in doing so from time to time since the 1830s.[25] The Potawatomi and other midwestern tribes were plagued by similar groups, often comparatively well educated and seeking financial advantage from an Indian connection with the help of influential attorneys and politicians.

The rejected claimants gathered the support of former agents Allen Hamilton and Joseph Sinclair and the unstoppable George Ewing to lobby Congress, which passed legislation in 1858 adding 73 "Miamis at large" to the Indiana annuity rolls.[26] These privileged "Miamis" were also permitted 200-acre allotments from the breakup of the Western Miami reservation. In a short time they had helped themselves to 12,733 acres of Kansas farmland.[27] The Miami council protested, saying the legislation was "contrary to our Treaty . . . that no other persons shall be added to the payroll list, with out the consent of the Miami Tribe of Indians of Indiana."[28] More names were added in 1862, and the group ballooned from 68 to 119 individuals who diverted over a third of the tribal annuities to themselves.

The tribal government petitioned Congress and hired attorneys to overcome the legislation, spending over $5,700. In

February 1867 the matter was debated during discussion of the Indian appropriations bill in the House. Cong. John A. Kasson of Iowa called the 1858 bill a "legislative outrage." He amended the appropriations bill with the treaty language on enrollment, effectively cutting off the "bogus Miami" as they came to be known.[29] On 20 September 1867 United States Attorney General Henry Stanbery affirmed the status of the Indiana Miami tribal government before federal law, writing, "The rights of these persons are fixed, not merely on the footing of law, but of solemn contract, and should not be changed or disturbed except by their consent."[30]

The last challenge to the status of the tribal government came in the late 1860s when the state of Indiana tried to tax Miami treaty reserves. Commissioner of Indian Affairs Ely S. Parker ruled that so long as the tribal government was recognized by the federal government "their property is withdrawn from the operation of state laws."[31] Despite this advisory the state attempted to tax the land. When Meshingomesia sued to block taxation the local circuit court ruled in favor of the state. The decision, however, was overturned on appeal to the state supreme court. The high court ruled that while the Miami's "ancient customs are considerably broken in upon by the manners and customs of the whites," their "tribal organization still remains." The Miami did not vote in elections, pay road or poll taxes, or resort to the courts for settling intratribal disputes, and their children did not attend county schools. The court concluded by citing Article III of the Northwest Ordinance and asked rhetorically, "Is [taxation] not taking from them their property without their consent? Is this the manner in which the utmost good faith shall always be observed toward them?"[32]

By 1870 the Miami had gained legal recognition of their tribal government, protection against unwanted additions to their tribal membership, and exemption from local taxes. The great majority of the tribe lived near each other in familiar haunts where they could continue a variety of subsistence activities that were balanced with cash annuities of from twenty-five to thirty dollars a year per person. They had well-seasoned leaders who had overcome a variety of challenges so that once again the Miami people could acculturate at their own pace and perhaps recover from some of the violence and disruption that had afflicted them for two generations prior to removal.

Persistence and Change among the Miami, 1847–1872

By 1847 the Miami tribe, though small, was a complex mixture of subgroups of greatly varying acculturation. A few Miami were Catholic, lived in brick or frame houses, sent their children to boarding school in Fort Wayne, and lived in a manner hardly distinguishable from the white population. At the other end of the scale was a much larger group of Miami who were landless, had no formal education, spoke only Miami or limited English, and lived in bark or log houses that they left when they departed for long winter hunts. Somewhere between the extremes were the tribal leaders, living in the manner of Frances Slocum and her daughters, owning extensive tracts of land that they shared as a commons with the landless, and often counting their wealth in horses. This elite group usually had white advisers, could sell timber from their reserves, and contracted to have building construction and farming done. They met as a tribal council and handled the overall direction of the tribe.

The white actors around the edges of the Miami drama were as varied as the Indians. At the top of the heap were national figures like the Ewings, Hamilton, and Coquillard who could manipulate federal Indian policy and who had made fortunes in their dealings with the Miami and Potawatomi. After removal these men by and large lost interest in the Miami as they turned their interests westward. They were replaced by local merchants, attorneys, and land speculators who tried to feed on the smaller pickings of a less wealthy tribe. At the bottom of the scale were poor Scots-Irish and European immigrants who were pioneer neighbors of the Miami and who farmed and performed other tasks for tribespeople. Each of these groups interacted with the Miami in different ways, influencing the direction of acculturation and, among the poorer group, often becoming assimilated into the tribe themselves.

In 1846 George Slocum, a nephew of Frances Slocum, came to the Mississinewa to demonstrate horse-plow agriculture for the Miami. Slocum, who was a devout Baptist, made little progress in teaching the Miami European-style farming, but he made major progress as a missionary. By the 1850s he had converted Peter Bondy and J. B. Brouillette to the Baptist faith, and both became ministers to the Miami. Through Slocum's influence or that of others, Pimyotamah and Wahcaconah also became Baptist ministers. Thomas Richardville, who lived in the area until 1860, apparently was converted by Isaac McCoy at Carey Mission and also became a Baptist minister. Through the efforts of these five ministers many Miami became Baptists, including Meshingomesia, and two churches were built on the Meshingomesia reserve. The close relationship among ministers who were also tribal leaders made communication over many issues easier and strengthened tribal leadership.

The eight-and-a-half-mile-long and roughly one-mile-wide Meshingomesia reserve along the north bank of the Mississinewa was an area the Miami had moved in and out of since the late eighteenth century. Located a few miles northwest of the fledgling town of Marion, it was connected by trails to the Ozahshinquah and Godfroy reserves but was comparatively isolated from Peru, the center of Miami trade just before removal. Metocina, father of Meshingomesia, had a village on the southeastern end of the reserve as early as 1790. The other Miami villages on the Mississinewa were beyond the boundaries of the reserve, nearer Peru. The area around the Meshingomesia reserve had little white settlement until 1840, the year the Miami National Reserve was ceded. After 1840 more Miami began moving onto the Meshingomesia reserve, which became a refuge from encroaching pioneer settlement. Meshingomesia, his six brothers and sister, and their families formed the core group. (See map on p. 120.) After 1840 the reservation community gathered a complicated mixture of people typical of many midwestern Indian communities of the time: Meshingomesia's brothers moved in, as did the family of Mecatamungwah (Black Loon) after his death, Sam Bundy, whose parents were Ottawa, "Mollie," whose mother was Kickapoo, and John Newman, who was Delaware. Chapendoceah's two wives were half Potawatomi, and they invited their brother Wahcaconah, whose wife was Wea. Susan Dixon and a few of the landless Eel River Miami moved in as well, and there was a white captive in the group, Kimquatah (Hannah Thorpe), who was married to Capt. Dixon (Metocquasah), one of Meshingomesia's brothers. Meshingomesia invited the drunken Sasaquasyah, a Wea Indian, to move from the hunting areas along Wildcat Creek near Kokomo to make his own improvements, do what he could for himself, and stop going into debt.[33]

Photo believed to be of Kimquatah (Hannah Thorpe), taken captive as a child from the Whitewater River valley north of Richmond, Indiana, during the the War of 1812. This photograph is the only one known of a Miami captive.

LaMoine Marks

Meshingomesia's efforts to offer refuge and to encourage abstinence from alcohol and adaptation to new ways were central to the role of an Eastern Woodland civil chief. He asked Richardville and Hamilton to have the reserve set aside in common ownership in the 1840 treaty because his brothers were drinking heavily and he did not want the land lost. The fact that he asked that the land be granted in common reflected the less acculturated status of the Meshingomesia Miami.[34]

The Godfroy reserve down the Mississinewa near Peru gathered a similar collection of refugees. Cabins were built around Godfroy's former trading house to accommodate nearly all sixty Miami who returned from Kansas. Smaller numbers sought refuge on the nearby Ozahshinquah reserve, on Lafontaine's reserve near Huntington, and on Richardville's home reserve near Fort Wayne. White authorities did their best to uproot such collections of refugees because they frustrated Indian removal and perpetuated Indian values, which favored sharing, subsistence activities, and continuity of tribal culture. They believed that Indians would not take up individual farming, Christianity, and a market economy unless such communities were broken up. In the case of the Miami, strong leadership and the small size of the tribe, along with the efforts of traders to gain more money from treaty payments, ultimately delayed removal and permitted refugee communities to develop.

The violence before removal was reflected clearly on James Lindsay's tribal roll made in 1854. At that time females outnumbered males three to two, or by 50 percent. The large majority of women meant that some had to marry outside the tribe or not marry at all. Among sixty-eight marriages of Miami women born from 1810 to 1837 ten were to white men, while among forty-six marriages of Miami men born in the same years only two were to white women. The fact that so many more women than men married non-Indians suggests that Indian women were more acceptable marriage partners for non-Indians than Indian men. Miami men continued to marry non-Indians far less frequently than women, and the trend became extreme toward the end of the nineteenth century.[35]

Until 1870 nearly all marriages were conducted by Indian custom, except among the small minority of Catholic Miami. Meshingomesia performed several marriages, sometimes picking the wife for a young man and giving a pony to the wife's family.[36] It was the custom before marriage for the young man to stay at the home of the bride for a few weeks and then take her to his home. In that case she would belong to his band, as the extended Miami families were loosely called. Frequently the groom would choose to stay with the bride's family, in which case he would belong to her band or extended family group.[37] This custom was observed by all the Miami by the 1850s and would lead to some confusion later, as surnames were no sure indication of the group to which one belonged.

Plural marriages continued after removal. Two of Meshingomesia's brothers had two wives, as did three or four other men. Local whites seemed to accept this Miami custom and even incorporated it into legal practices. When William Godfroy sold a parcel of land in 1868, for example, the Miami County recorder duly requested the "X" marks of both Godfroy's wives.[38] The old custom of marrying the sister of a deceased wife continued as well.

The marriage age had become quite young by the time of removal. Of those born from 1810 to 1837 the average marriage age for men and women was twenty-two. The youngest male marriage was seventeen, and three young women were married at age sixteen. Families did not have large numbers of children. The sixty-six families formed by those born from 1810 to 1837 that could be reconstructed had an average of four children. Only five families—less than one in ten—had over seven children.[39] This number is consistent with the small number of children Agent Benjamin Stickney reported in Miami families compared with white families in 1817.[40]

The most important rule of marriage among the Miami was the taboo against marrying within a family lineage or tribal group. An echo of earlier clan rules, the practice lent stability to extended families and fostered close and complex kinship ties among all the Miami groups in the generation after removal. Such exogamy, or marrying outside one's kin group, was observed strictly in Miami marriages throughout the nineteenth century.

In the midnineteenth century children were usually named by women. The names often were those of an ancestor, although names could reflect some personal characteristic as well. Some people acquired nicknames. Frances Godfroy was Lendonakisumquah (Shadows on Treetops at Sunset), but was often called Mahchequeah (Bad Woman). Gabriel Godfroy was Wapanakekapwah (White Blossoms) to his family. Others called him Kapia (Overseer), the name for a tribal steward or crier who might later become chief. By the midnineteenth century names were in flux, reflecting the unsettled conditions of the tribe and the disappearance of the clan system. New names appeared such as Kekenakushwa (Cut Finger) for Frances Slocum's older daughter, and Ozahshinquah (Yellow Leaf) for her younger daughter. These new names were then used in the Bondy family until well into the twentieth century. Leaders just as often as not were named for an earlier leader.[41]

The Indian custom of divorce was practiced as well, meaning that a dissatisfied husband or wife could simply walk out on the marriage. Divorce was as common as death, meaning that people often had three or more spouses during the course of their life. Ozahshinquah, the younger daughter of Frances Slocum, was a notable example of multiple marriages and the practice of group exogamy. Born about 1810 Ozahshinquah lost four husbands in quick succession to disease or violence by the mid-1840s. She had two children by her first marriage and one child by each of her next three husbands before settling into a long-term marriage to Peter Bondy in the 1840s and having seven more children. Bondy had at least one and perhaps two children of his own when he married Ozahshinquah. After her death in 1877 Bondy married Frances Godfroy, Gabriel Godfroy's half-sister, in 1881. Frances Godfroy had five grown children by two previous marriages, and one of her grown daughters was married to one of Bondy's sons. This complex cycle of marriage, death, and remarriage ended when Frances Bondy died in 1895 and Peter Bondy died in 1897. Peter Bondy and his two known wives had a total of eleven spouses over their lifetimes.[42]

Children who lost parents were informally adopted by close relatives, and children could be taken from parents who did not care for them. Meshingomesia removed the seven-year-old daughter of a woman who was alcoholic and placed her with a brother's family. Two years later he took the youngest son from the same woman and placed him with another family.[43]

Adoptions for the dead were still held in the Indiana Miami community after removal in a modified form. Pecongeoh testified in 1873 that the Miami believed the spirit of a deceased person remained at the house until an adoption was made. If an adoption was not made, the rest of the family kept dying. The person who was to replace the deceased was invited into a home and was offered a new set of clothing. After this ceremonial dressing the spirit of the departed was free to leave. The

Gabriel Godfroy (1834–1910) as a young man, about 1860. A son of Francis Godfroy, he was a respected leader among the Miami living near Peru, Indiana, until his death.

Louise Hay

Peter Bondy (1817–1897) in the early 1850s. A signatory of the treaty of 1854 and a Miami Baptist minister, he led the Miami descendants of Deaf Man and Frances Slocum.

Anonymous owner

Ozahshinquah (ca. 1810–1877) in the early 1850s near the time of her marriage to her fifth and last husband, Peter Bondy. She counted her wealth in land and horses, retaining 805 acres to the end of her life.

Anonymous owner

one who was adopted did not take the place of the one who died—he or she merely freed the spirit to walk the spirit path. After the adoption the person who was given the new clothing returned with gifts for the family sponsoring the adoption. If this was not done he or she might die as well. A ritual dance was held as part of the ceremony.[44]

At the burial, food, tobacco, and other items to facilitate travel to the spirit world were buried with the dead, as well as some things the person enjoyed in life. When Francis Wildcat (Pinjewa) died near Peru in 1855, a favorite horse was killed at his grave. The Miami ate after his burial and placed food on all the graves. Someone then stood at the foot of his grave and made an address to his departed spirit. These customs continued well after the Miami affiliated themselves with various churches.[45]

As the Miami settled on particular reserves and lost their mobility they established graveyards that have been kept in use up to the present. The Godfroy graveyard south of the trading house probably had its first burials in the late 1820s. Francis Godfroy was buried there in 1840. The Mongosa or Whitewolf family has a separate section of the same cemetery. The Bundy or Frances Slocum cemetery was opened by 1832, while the Meshingomesia cemetery dates to the building of the Miami Union Baptist Church in the mid-1860s. It replaced a nearby burial site at the lower village along the Mississinewa River. When Francis Lafontaine (Topeah) died in 1847 he was buried in Mount Calvary Cemetery north of Huntington. His many descendants have continued to use the plot up to the present.

The Miami Are Asked to Speak: The 1873 Testimony

In November 1867 the Meshingomesia Miami council petitioned the secretary of the Interior Department to allot their reservation equally among the members. It is difficult to assess from documents how much influence white advisers like Samuel McClure of Marion had in the decision. McClure, who had worked for George Ewing, had on his own initiative written the commissioner of Indian Affairs many times since 1848 asking for division of the land, but was ignored. The immediate cause of Meshingomesia's decision was extensive theft of prime timber and the reluctance of state courts to handle a matter on land to which no single person had title.

In 1872 Congress finally passed legislation for the allotment or division of the Meshingomesia reserve into "farms" for eligible Miami.[46] In the summer of 1873 extensive testimony was taken from many Miami to establish who had a claim to the land of the reserve. The changeover to private property was to become a critical test of acculturation among the Miami because this was the last land held in common by the tribe. Although the questions were focused on family relationships and movements in and out of the reservation area, the testimony allowed a broad spectrum of the Miami an opportunity to comment on many topics. The testimony also gives a perspective on Miami values, lifeways, and beliefs as well as family relations, housing, and subsistence activities over a period of two generations. The testimony allowed the Miami to reconstruct their lives as Indians and offers a look at attitudes that were often not self-conscious. For the first time many ordinary Miami entered the historic record with their hopes, fears, and beliefs.

Many of the depositions taken in 1873 concerned the reconstruction of families to establish a kinship connection to the heirs of Metocina and thereby a claim to reservation land. Pecongeoh, Meshingomesia's eldest son, was able to explain relationships among seventy people. The task was complicated by plural marriages (two uncles each had two wives) and frequent remarriage. Pecongeoh himself had been married three times. Pecongeoh was able to name all the spouses in remarriages and could name nearly all of the children and cases of adoption. In later testimony Meshingomesia was able to duplicate Pecongeoh's list. Both men demonstrated an important role of a chief, that of knowing kinship ties in an extended family. Such knowledge was necessary to avoid breaking taboos against marriage within a group and to assure every tribesperson a secure place within the group.

The Miami statements give a well-rounded picture of the powers of a civil chief. Meshingomesia was widely known for his capable oversight of his small community, and the testimony bears this out. Meshingomesia sometimes arranged marriages, performed marriage rites, removed children from parents who were neglectful or abusive, suggested adoptions, and ousted troublemakers from the village community. Meshingomesia most likely played an important part in the death and adoption ceremonies mentioned in the testimony as well. He also invited homeless Indians to the reservation and encouraged them to make a new, sober life for themselves. He worked to maintain tribal rights, attended treaty negotiations and, in the days immediately after removal, disbursed the payment of annuities to each family. Finally he encouraged acculturation by permitting a school and church to be built on the reservation and made the decision to have the reservation converted from common to private ownership. Despite his power, decisions were discussed in the all-male village council and were by consensus.[47]

The witnesses called in 1873 gave direct evidence of the fear occasioned by removal of an Indian group. Many people were not sure of their status, that is, whether or not they were to be removed. One man testified that "several went to the woods to keep from being taken west" in 1846.[48] When Alexis Coquillard combed the Miami villages for "skulkers" in 1847, fear again spread through the community. In the spring of that year Coquillard came to collect Miami who had escaped removal the previous fall. Word had spread of Coquillard's search some time before his arrival. The refugees made preparations to escape and ran miles into the extensive woods, successfully avoiding the collection.[49] Meshingomesia aided the escapees by refusing to tell Coquillard who they were or where they were hiding. The escapees stayed away nearly a month.[50]

The 1873 affidavits reveal that violence continued long after removal, though not on the same scale as earlier. Wahcaconah became outraged when Meshingomesia would not let him lease land on the reservation to whites and threatened to kill the chief. He carried a pistol and on various occasions shot at several of Meshingomesia's family and one time killed several of his horses.[51] In another incident two of Meshingomesia's brothers were killed, and Mrs. Dixon, the white captive who was the wife of one of the men, Metocquasah, jumped from a limestone bluff into the river and killed herself in 1850. The surest sign that violence and disease had lessened was a natural increase in tribal population for the first time in perhaps forty years. From 1854 to 1870 the Miami population, excluding the small Eel River group, rose from 278 to 330, an increase of 52 people or nearly 20 percent.[52]

Acculturation in the Generation after Removal

As the Meshingomesia reserve population grew after removal, a few contracts were let for housing, clearing, and fencing. The earliest known lease was granted to John Marks by Chapendoceah on 10 January 1862:

> Shap has this day leased to said Markes thirty acres of land . . . the said Mark[s] is to have six crops off of the Thirty acres fer which he is to fence said Thirty acres in three ten acre fields & leave said fields with a good nine rail fence at the expiration of his term of lease said Marks to clear the land to suit himself & make such Buildings theron as may suit his convenience.[53]

The following year Ahtawatah leased twenty acres to George Koontz, who was to clear the land and to fence it in two ten-acre lots, build a sixteen-by-twenty-foot log stable, an eight-by-twenty-foot corncrib, and a log house, sixteen-by-eighteen feet.[54] The lessees generally received two-thirds of the crops for five years for their work.

Such leases were uncommon, suggesting little need to bring in farmers and the small income they provided. Rather, the Miami clustered about the lower, or southern, half of the reservation in Grant County near the old village, where the women kept small fields, leaving the northern half for maple sugaring and other subsistence activities. A similar scarceness of leases in Wabash and Miami Counties suggests that the small Miami communities there tended to continue female agriculture and subsistence activities and felt no need to clear land for the added income from horse-plow agriculture. The agricultural census for 1850 supports this view. In that year only about 10 percent of Miami treaty grants for which there is data were cleared for agriculture (or, "improved," as the census puts it), whereas 40 to 50 percent of non-Indian land in the same townships was cleared. In 1860 about 20 percent of tribal lands was cleared, and in 1870 only about 27 percent.[55] If white contractors did most of the clearing and farming, there was even less acculturation to horse-plow agriculture than the cleared land would indicate.

Meshingomesia encouraged male agriculture, but the model was the small, static landholding of the yeoman farmer of fifty years earlier, who supplemented farming with subsistence activities, not the market agriculture that was rapidly developing after the Civil War with improvements in local roads, the draining of wetlands, and new types of farm machinery. Wahcaconah, the reservation rogue, forced a clarification of the degree of acculturation acceptable to the elderly chief. In trying to settle the violent outsider, Meshingomesia sent him five miles away to a portion of the reserve called the "Hogback." He instructed Wahcaconah to clear no more than seventy-five acres. Not long after the move Wahcaconah was signing leases with whites for clearing valuable timber and building a two-story double log house. In all, two to three hundred acres were cleared. Sometime after that Wahcaconah built a church, apparently with money from the leases. Meshingomesia was appalled when he learned of the extensive clearing, saying that he did not tell him to make a big farm. The largest area cleared at the time was thirty to forty acres at the old village where the women worked. Wahcaconah's "improvements" were far too large and destroyed a great deal of timber that would be valuable to the coming generation. Further, Meshingomesia felt that a second church was not needed.[56]

Wahcaconah did not stop with clearing land, building the biggest house on the reserve, and an unnecessary church. By the end of the 1850s he was attempting to get the reservation itself subdivided into individual properties. Meshingomesia warned the commissioner of Indian Affairs not to have anything to do with him, "as he is a very wild and foolish Indian and disposed to make disturbance without cause."[57] The real problem was that Wahcaconah functioned as an enterprising individual, acting without group approval through the local council. Neither he nor his wife were blood relatives of the band, and when he came to council he was disruptive. Excluded not only from the council but also from the local Indian community itself, he took steps on his own initiative and was too much like the aggressive, individualistic whites who tried to take advantage of the commons.

The rest of the reservation was cleared slowly and modest cabins were built. The five houses for which contracts exist on Miami land built from 1845 to 1870 were invariably log, ranging from sixteen-by-eighteen feet to twenty-by-twenty feet. They were the same size as most eighteenth-century rural housing in the eastern United States (the most common size was eighteen-by-twenty feet), usually containing less than 450 square feet and surprisingly similar in size to a typical Miami summer house of the century before. This size dwelling was typically used by people who spent the majority of their time outside or away from the house in subsistence activities rather than a more sedentary family that was accumulating household goods and furnishings.[58]

A modern archaeological survey of a Miami housing site on the Meshingomesia reserve suggests a mixed economy of hunting and animal husbandry. Three-fourths of the bones in the refuse pit derived from wild animals—deer, opossum, bear, raccoon, skunk, squirrel, rabbit, and beaver—and one-fourth from domestic animals: cattle and hogs. Bear bones were scarcest, not surprising as the last bear in the area was killed by Miami in 1847. Other remains, ceramic items, and nails suggested the site was occupied from the late 1820s until the late 1850s.[59] The Miami had raised cattle and hogs since the late eighteenth century, and agricultural census records from 1850 to 1870 show from three to one hundred hogs and one to seven cattle on Indian farms. Most likely the hogs were free ranging. Fencing was placed around small fields to keep foraging animals out and was not used to enclose an entire farm.

In 1861 Adam Parker opened a general store in La Fontaine, a mile and a half east of the center of the reserve. No part of the Indian lands was over five miles from the store, and the

Mississinewa River limited access to the west. A majority of the local Miami bought store goods from Parker, who extended small amounts of credit. Parker's daybooks have survived and give some idea of the nature of the Miami trade and some hints of daily life. From 1861 to 1866 Miami trade was extremely slow, with no more than forty trades in a year, and $107 in total trade. The small amount of trade suggests the local Miami had little cash for purchases and were largely self-sufficient. At that time they could not borrow money against the land and had little or no access to credit.[60]

Beginning in 1867, when the band's council petitioned for allotment of the reservation, trade spurted to about $250 and rose quickly to $1,200 in 1872. Anticipating private ownership of the reservation, local merchants extended credit to the Miami even though there would be no legal basis for doing so until 1881. At the height of the trade there was one purchase every weekday that averaged from three to four dollars.[61] Fully three-fourths of the items purchased from 1861 to 1873 were items already in Miami trade at the Fort Wayne factory from 1802 to 1811 or were on a trading list of 1827. Many of the newer items were farm or construction goods that could have been purchased on account for white contractors, although there were three Miami men who were doing some farming at the time. The other items in Miami trade were mostly common household items such as baking powder and soda, tablecloths and teapots, washboards, flatirons, starch, fruit cans and stone jars, and clothing items such as women's skirts, hoops, hats, gloves, men's pants, suspenders, neckties, and hair oil. The clothing purchases show that the Miami were wearing the same clothing as local whites for everyday purposes. Most photographs of the time show the Miami in "citizen" clothing as well. For ceremonies and celebrations, however, the Miami continued to wear the elaborate clothing of the fur-trade era, and some women continued elaborate appliqué work on moccasins, leggings, and blankets.[62]

Adam Parker's general store, La Fontaine, Indiana, a mile and a half east of the Meshingomesia reserve. By 1882, when the building pictured was constructed, Miami trade was declining.

Stewart Rafert

The unbroken lands of the Meshingomesia reserve clearly provided a refuge from forced acculturation for a generation after removal. Clearing of land did not begin until the mid-1850s and, with the exception of Wahcaconah's farm, the areas cleared were no more than about thirty acres each. The hundred or so Miami of the reservation lived near the southern end of the reservation in Grant County, clustered near the old village, the church, and the school. Women raised many of the small crops and gathered edible plants, while the men hunted and fished. Both sexes gathered fruits, nuts, berries, and medicinal plants.

English, by and large, remained a foreign language on the reserve. Most of the testimony taken in 1873 was in the Miami language. Two of Meshingomesia's grandsons born in the 1840s were bilingual and could act as interpreters along with Thomas Richardville. Nearly all the names used were Miami rather than the English substitutes that non-Indians sometimes used. On several occasions Miami kinship terminology was used.[63] In short, the least acculturated Miami were living on the common lands of the reserve. There was change, but it was slow.

The three local commissioners who interviewed all Miami for two months in the summer of 1873 eventually selected sixty-three Miami for "headrights" or shares of land. The allotments were made so that those who had made improvements or built houses could keep them. The individual grants, when surveyed, varied from 77 to 125 acres, depending upon the quality of the soil and the lay of the land for agriculture. The allotments were exempt from taxes, mortgages, and sale until 1 January 1881. At that time the Indian owners were made citizens and were free to dispose of their land.

The other major refuge for Miami people was the cluster of individual reserves between the Wabash and Mississinewa Rivers east of Peru. These lands were already broken up to a large degree by sales of land to whites, with the Miami clustered near the former Francis Godfroy trading house and two miles south along the Mississinewa and just upstream at the Ozahshinquah reserve on the Miami-Wabash County line. By the mid-1850s Gabriel Godfroy, the youngest son of Francis Godfroy, had begun to assert himself as a family leader. In 1855 he won a lawsuit to have a white squatter evicted from family land, and in 1859 he won restitution of 185 acres of land from a prominent local white because the sale contract was fraudulent. By 1860 he had clearly emerged as a leader in defense of Indian property in the Peru area, a role he continued until his death in 1910.[64]

The Indian lands near Peru were in a checkerboard pattern, and the Miami could find seasonal work easily with non-Indians on their farms if they wished. The Godfroy Miami had begun to move beyond earlier marriages to French traders to a pattern of marrying local whites so that surnames like Kissiman, Miller, Ward, and Walker appeared alongside Goodboo and Lavonture. Many of the marriages were to whites who had traded and worked with the Miami for years and sometimes spoke the

Miami language and were in other ways acculturated to the Miami. Acculturation was a two-way street, and whites who knew Miami ways were more acceptable as marriage partners. A step ahead of the Meshingomesia Miami in the complexities of the dominant society, the Peru-area Miami found further acculturation easier.

In the generation after removal the Eastern Miami tribal government had unified around a group of village leaders who came to maturity in the 1830s and 1840s. Freed from the influence of métis chiefs who tried to balance American demands with tribal needs, the postremoval leadership led from a tribal position and gained control of enrollment and treaty recognition of the tribal council against the wishes of the assimilationist Commissioner of Indian Affairs George Manypenny. After a long and expensive legal effort the Eastern Miami tightened the ethnic boundaries of the tribe and attained a ruling from the United States attorney general that they had tribal status. This in turn helped them overcome state efforts to tax their tribal land.

Beginning as a small collection of families in 1846, the Eastern Miami had challenged removal itself and offered refuge to more Miami, thus doubling their population. While traders such as George Ewing, James Miller, and others assisted and exploited the return of the Miami to Indiana for their own gain, these added groups of Miami increased the number of groups into which tribal members could marry, assuring the cultural viability of the tribe far into the future. With prudent leadership, the Miami turned away from debt and toward a subsistence economy, aided by small annual cash payments from the tribal capital fund. The connection between debt and forced land sales was ended, and the tribe moved sharply away from dependency and toward economic self-sufficiency for the first time in two generations. Reflecting more settled times, the tribal population began to increase for the first time in forty years.

The years from 1847 to 1872 had in general been good for the Indiana Miami, a time to consolidate their population and their leadership, as well as their legal status and economic self-sufficiency as an Indian tribe behind the frontier and east of the Mississippi. Most important of all, perhaps, they had stabilized the tribal economy. Unlike many Indian refugees who had been forced to hide from removal in swamps or mountains, they had openly confronted their situation, obtained congressional permission to remain in their homeland, and had signed a treaty recognizing their form of government. It was altogether a rare achievement.

SIX

Winds of Change
1873–1900

■

The Indians as a class of people are not a progressive tribe and are really a detriment to the country, as they work but little and rent their farms to cheap tenants that make but little for themselves or for the owners of the land. There are only a few exceptions. We will be glad when such fine farming land will be owned by a better class of farmers.

Wabash Plain Dealer, *20 July 1883*

Sir this Mr. alvah taylor of Wabash Indiana was one time my guardian and had all control of my farm & money and he recieved som money from office of Indians department And when I becam of 21 year of age and he only give me one hunder and forty dollar 140.00 that all I received from Mr. alvah taylor And I lost all my farm and all the money that he received from washington D.C.

William Bundy to W. J. Jones, commissioner of Indian Affairs, 9 March 1899[1]

THE EASTERN MIAMI ENTERED THE LAST QUARTER OF the nineteenth century with a feeling of confidence. They were a federally recognized Indian tribe, but without the intrusions of an agent making every decision for them as happened among western tribes. They were adapting to change at their own pace, and their population was slowly recovering after years of decline. Best of all, the Miami were in their home territory and had well-seasoned, sober leaders who had been in power for a generation. So far as they could tell the future would bring another generation of beneficial change. Perhaps the tribe would achieve equal economic status with their rural neighbors while retaining the protection of federal Indian law.

The American farm economy and Indian policy were at a crossroads in the early 1870s. Shortly after the end of the Civil War farm prices began to decline steadily, while new, more efficient farm machinery was quickly escalating the cost of taking up farming. Railroads opened markets for a few cash crops, and commercial agriculture was rapidly replacing the self-sufficient farmstead. As new farmland was opened overseas and ocean transport improved, the American farm economy was becoming linked to world agriculture. Careful farm management, increased capitalization, and knowledge of markets were becoming as important as raising crops.

In 1871 Congress abruptly ended the practice of negotiating treaties with Indian tribes. Commissioner of Indian Affairs Ely S. Parker, himself a well-educated Seneca, bluntly expressed the official consensus that tribes were not sovereign nations capable of managing their own affairs. Hereafter, Congress would legislate for tribes and take direct control of their destinies. Former treaties were kept in force, but within a few years Congress was overriding treaty rights and in 1887 passed legislation to allot, or divide, all Indian reservations into farms and to sell surplus land.

The Meshingomesia Miami became forerunners of federal allotment policy in 1873 when the reservation was divided into private landholdings. After eight years of exemption from mortgages and taxes, the allottees would become citizens and gain full control over their land. The success or failure of the sixty-three allotments carved from the Meshingomesia reserve would serve as a precursor to the fate of the federal allotment policy itself. The purpose of allotment was to discourage subsistence agriculture and to favor individual, male, cash crop farming. Instead of clustering small fields together, Indian farmers were encouraged to disperse in family groups over the countryside like rural whites.

During the summer of 1873 surveyors marked off the Meshingomesia reserve into sixty-three potential farms varying in size from 77 to 125 acres, depending on the quality of land for farming. The commissioners who had taken testimony from the local Miami then assigned land to each allottee. Assignments were made so that those who had built houses or made improvements could keep them. Nearly all building and clearing had been done on the southern half of the reservation by Meshingomesia and his sons. The first third of the allotments went to them. The remaining two-thirds of the allotments were in parts of the reservation that had almost no clearing of land or building of cabins. These allotments went to descendants of Meshingomesia's brothers who had died years earlier and to related families that had taken refuge on the reserve.[2]

During the 1870s the Meshingomesia Miami could not mortgage or sell their sixty-three allotments, and there is no evidence of a changeover to market farming. This is not surprising since thirty-seven of the allottees were female and, of the twenty-six males, only half were old enough to go into farming. The prohibition on mortgage lending meant to protect Indians from fraud also kept the prospective farmers from raising the roughly one thousand dollars necessary to equip a one hundred-acre farm.[3]

Just before the transition to private ownership, tuberculosis swept through the Grant County Indian community, killing the most progressive leaders designated for the transition to male agriculture. Meshingomesia and his sons Pecongeoh and Ahtawatah, as well as his grandson Nelson Tawataw, and Wahcaconah died.

The year before his death Wahcaconah had organized the Treaty and Wahcaconah Gravel Road Association with several neighboring farmers to construct a three-and-a-half-mile road north from his farm to the village of Treaty, where farm products could be shipped on the Cincinnati, Wabash, and Michigan Railroad.[4] Charlie Dixon, one of the few Miami to serve in the Civil War and an experienced farmer, died in 1885.

Younger men who could have entered farming were defrauded by guardians and left with no resources. William Bundy, who turned eighteen in 1881, had as good a chance as any to become a successful farmer. In that year he, like all Miami, received $695 as his share of the distribution of the capital fund from the 1854 treaty. His 110-acre allotment was bordered by a

William Bundy. Defrauded of his 110-acre allotment by his white guardian, he spent many years protesting to officials in the Indian Office in Washington, D.C.

Wabash County Historical Society

township road leading to the nearby village of Somerset. Alvah Taylor, a local attorney, was appointed the fatherless Bundy's guardian in 1881. From 1882 to 1884 Bundy received a total income of $1,442 from his land, but expenses were heavy: taxes, $118, legal expenses for establishing an allotment, $200, and farm costs of $330 for tile ditching and fence rails, carpentry on the cabin, and hauling crops. Bundy's personal expenses were $368. Taylor's services as guardian and adviser were high. Each day he visited Bundy's property he charged $8, as well as a 5 percent fee for managing income, a total of $238. When Bundy became twenty-one in 1884, he received a total of $244 from his guardian. He was on his own as a farmer.[5]

Bundy's land was fenced and ditched and had a dwelling. To farm, however, he needed a variety of farm implements, machinery, and tools, as well as livestock, costing about a thousand dollars. Bundy's income did not cover living expenses, and within a year he sold twenty-nine acres of rough land along the Mississinewa River for $800. In 1887 he mortgaged the remaining eighty-one acres to a local dry goods merchant for $1,300. The next year he took an additional mortgage of $1,225. A year later he mortgaged chattels (movable property) for $150. In 1892, at the age of twenty-nine, he lost it all to creditors.[6] The mortgage holders got improved land with a cabin for $33 an acre. The going rate for such land in the area was $50 to $60 an acre.

The other young Indian males of the former reservation were caught in the same trap as Bundy: income from leasing or subsistence farming could not pay taxes and other expenses, while heavy borrowing was necessary to go into commercial farming. Bundy's older brother George, Cornelius Cotticipon, George W. Shap, and George D. Chapendoceah lost their land within two years of full ownership.[7] (See map on p. 159.)

After the death of Meshingomesia and his oldest son Pecongeoh in 1879, William Peconga, Pecongeoh's oldest son, became head of the group. He was a typical Miami civil chief, mild mannered and generous. A local newspaper reporter who knew him

William Peconga (1844–1916).
A grandson of Meshingomesia,
after allotment in 1873 he
managed 1,500 acres of land
until overwhelmed by debt in
the 1890s.

Miami County Historical Society

well wrote that though his name "Chinguasah" meant "thunderer," he was "an Indian who abstains from firewater, is well educated, very quiet, and never boisterous or rough in his demeanor."[8] Peconga attended elementary school and the Baptist Seminary at Ladoga, Indiana, for a term and was a Mason. He attempted to keep the many allotments of his family on the southern end of the reservation together, while offering refuge to landless Miami and encouraging adaptation of the ways of the dominant society. He was following in the steps of his grandfather Meshingomesia.

Peconga's job as an intermediary between the small Miami community in Grant County and outsiders was not easy. Conditions on the former reservation had changed little since the 1850s. Most people lived in comfortable circumstances in cleanly swept cabins, which were located off county roads and difficult to reach by horse and wagon. When a visitor came, children and from two to six dogs scampered out for a greeting. Visitors were expected to enter homes without knocking, an old sign of hospitality. Most conversation was still in Miami, as the women could not or would not speak English, and an outsider needed an interpreter.[9]

In 1873 the Peconga family had received nine of the sixty-three allotments. By 1884 William Peconga had managed, through inheritance or purchase, to consolidate eighteen of the original allotments, or 1,558 acres on the southern end of the former reservation. When the Miami capital fund from the 1854 treaty was paid out in 1882, the Peconga family received over $12,500. Peconga invested most of this money in land or mortgages to local whites, the reverse of the usual habit. He also invested with two of his brothers in a threshing machine that was probably used for custom harvesting on local farms.[10]

Peconga was proud of his farm. When anthropologist Albert S. Gatschet from the Smithsonian Institution visited in the early 1890s, Peconga boasted of the light, sandy soil where everything grew well. His farm and his wife's were completely fenced, and he had two houses, one for tenants, two stables, a milk house, corncrib, and wheat bins. He grew corn, wheat, potatoes, peas, beans, tobacco, barley, and rye. He had fruit trees and grew melons as well.[11]

After a brief pause farm prices resumed their post-Civil War decline in the mid-1880s, a decline that was to last until 1896. By the late 1880s Peconga was having difficulty managing such a large block of land. He was not helped by his principal adviser, Isaac Van Devanter, attorney for the Miami during allotment of the reservation, who was still attempting to milk the Miami of their funds after the manner of his mentor George W. Ewing. On one occasion Peconga stopped in Van Devanter's office in Marion for a brief consultation and was charged fifty dollars. A local man noticed the transaction and said he could not afford such high fees. Van Devanter told him his charge would be far less—Peconga had lots of money.[12] Beginning in 1888 Peconga had borrowed $17,000 from the Aetna Insurance Company against his land. By 1892 he was overwhelmed with debt, and the Wabash County sheriff seized two farms, a process that ended in 1898 when the last of his land was sold at a sheriff's sale. Peconga took refuge among the Godfroy family in neighboring Miami County and continued farming, but as a tenant.[13]

The deaths of many allottees had done its part in breaking up the reservation. Over half the owners of allotments died between 1873 and 1890. Some of the land passed to "squaw men," poor whites who married women for their farms, while creditors—local attorneys and merchants—ended up with much of the rest. By 1903, twenty years after the land was divided, three Indians owned a total of fifty-eight acres, only 1 percent of the original reservation.[14] The Miami experience was typical of private landownership by Indians nationwide after reservations were allotted. The Meshingomesia Miami crowded into poor housing in Marion and Wabash. The connection with the land, a vital source of Indian identity, was broken for the least acculturated Miami.

Only a County Away: Defending Miami Land and Rights in Butler Township near Peru

The Miami living a few miles down the Mississinewa on the Ozahshinquah reserve on the Miami-Wabash County line and east of Peru in Butler Township were a legal world apart from the Meshingomesia Miami. They had individual treaty reserves, so they had no reservation to be allotted. Nor was citizenship imposed. They received annuities from the trust fund set up under the 1854 treaty, but paid taxes and could buy and sell land freely. (See map on p. 167.)

Acculturation to the dominant society increased as one moved from the Meshingomesia reserve to the Francis Godfroy reserve. The small group of Frances Slocum descendants on the county line were more acculturated than the Meshingomesia group, but less so than the Godfroy Miami near Peru. Culturally they were headed by Ozahshinquah, Slocum's younger daughter. Politically they were led by Peter Bondy, Ozahshinquah's fifth and last husband, the adopted son of a French trader and a Miami woman. Bondy signed the 1854 treaty and was well

Meshingomesia Reserve Lands
circa 1873–1900

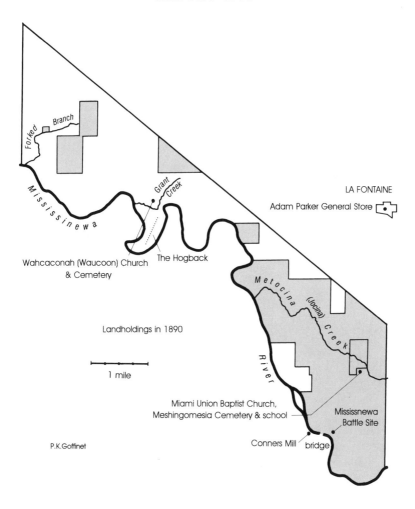

Forked Branch

Mississinewa

Grant Creek

LA FONTAINE
Adam Parker General Store

Wahcaconah (Waucoon) Church
& Cemetery

The Hogback

Metocina (Jocina) Creek

Landholdings in 1890

1 mile

River

Miami Union Baptist Church,
Meshingomesia Cemetery & school

Mississnewa
Battle Site

P.K.Goffinet

Conners Mill bridge

known among both Eastern and Western Miami. Bondy and Ozahshinquah had seven children in addition to children by previous marriages. Her eight children who reached adulthood married into both the Meshingomesia and Godfroy families, thickening kinship connections between the two larger Miami groups and strengthening connections among tribal leaders as well.

Pimyotamah led the Miami near Peru along with his nephew Gabriel Godfroy. Pim, as he was often called, was a senior leader who had met with Presidents Tyler and Polk and signed the 1854 treaty. He was head of the Mongosa or Whitewolf family, close allies of the Godfroys who were a separate political and kinship group. The Godfroys, who had been a small part of the tribe at removal, had swollen to nearly half the tribe when they took in the refugees from Kansas. The Richardville group, on the other hand, had been part of a reverse migration from Indiana to Kansas since

The Miami Indian Band in the 1880s. The three Lawson brothers, Joe Young, and the unidentified man seated on the right were non-Miami. Standing, left to right, George Godfroy, Nathan Lawson, Robert Winters, John Walters, James Winters, Frank Winters, Joe Young, Peter Peconga, and Shade Lawson. Seated, Jacob Peconga, Edward Lawson, William Winters, and an unidentified visitor.

Wabash County Historical Society

Pimyotamah (ca. 1814–1889), a prominent leader among the Miami from the 1840s until his death. The son of a white captive from Kentucky and a Miami woman, he met with two United States presidents concerning Miami affairs, signed the 1854 treaty, and was a Baptist minister and farmer as well.

Miami County Historical Society

1860 and were declining in numbers relative to the other Miami groups in Indiana. They were led by Thomas Richardville, a great-grandson of Chief J.B. Richardville. Pimyotamah, Bondy, and Richardville were all Baptist ministers. Richardville returned to Indiana frequently on tribal business, as well as to southwestern Michigan, where he had connections with the Pokagon Potawatomi.

The transition to male farming was well on its way among the leadership of the Peru-area Miami. Gabriel Godfroy was the most important Indian farmer in Indiana by the 1870s. His 220-acre farm located at the juncture of the Wabash and Mississinewa

Rivers was ideally located near markets in Peru, just a mile west. He sold timber to a brewery for making barrels, making money while increasing improved land from 68 acres in 1870 to 180 in 1880. He kept eighteen horses, forty to fifty hogs, eight to ten beef cattle, four to five milk cows, fifty or so chickens, and sheep. The value of farm production rose from $1,821 in 1870 to $2,600 in 1880. His farm was comparable to other prosperous local farms and was pictured in the county land atlas published in 1877.[15] (See map on p. 167.)

Pimyotamah, his grandson Anthony Walker, William Godfroy, and Camillus and Judson Bundy (sons of Peter) had more modest but productive farms. Most Miami males in the area were landless and did casual labor and hunting, trapping, and fishing. With the end of annuities in 1881 Gabriel Godfroy realized that farming skills would be necessary for most of the young men. In 1875 he invited Benjamin Hundley to come to the Godfroy reserve to teach farming. Hundley stayed two seasons, demonstrating plowing, harrowing, planting, cultivating, and harvesting.

When Hundley began plowing land for a potato patch one spring morning a number of young men gathered at the fence to watch. Hundley got a volunteer to try plowing, but after two rounds in which the heavy plow pulled out of the furrow or went crooked, the youth walked off without a word. When cultivating corn the Indian trainees broke and covered up the new sprouts, and when weeding they slashed many of the stalks along with the weeds. Common excuses for avoiding farmwork were "My wife, or my woman, or my squaw is sick; have some traps to set or look after; going on hunt tomorrow; must go to Peru this afternoon."[16] Hundley quit after his second season, realizing he had failed to make farmers of any of the young Miami.

The lack of interest among Miami men in commercial agriculture involving a few market crops is not difficult to explain. A complicated round of subsistence activities combined with some gardening supplied the needs of most Miami in Butler Township east of Peru. Cash came from annuities and occasional work for whites. Raising three or four different field crops, managing livestock, and repairing fences was hard, confining work compared with hunting, trapping, spearing and netting fish, gathering medicinal plants for sale to druggists, and skinning and tanning hides. There was no strong motive for exchanging a familiar way of life for a difficult and unfamiliar pattern of living.

Realizing that adaptation to European-American work was going to take more time, the Peru-area Miami leaders petitioned the secretary of the interior not to disburse the Miami capital fund and end annuities in 1881. Not only were most Miami men unprepared to farm, but alcohol also continued to be a major problem:

> a large proportion of our people are not self-sustaining, many of them very poor, intemperate, improvident, and wholly unable to [account] for the money if they had it; . . . it would be spent within six months for whiskey; . . . **We do know the wants of our people,** and we pray that our government will keep the principal and pay us the interest.[17]

Godfroy, Pimyotamah, and Bondy feared the Miami would end up as their wards if the annuities were ended.

In 1878 Gabriel Godfroy sued Miami County officials to relieve treaty grants from taxation. Godfroy asked the circuit court to mandate the return of $3,600 in local taxes, stating that he and the other treaty grantees were not United States citizens and were residing on lands set aside in treaties made between the Miami tribe and the federal government. The circuit court ruled against Godfroy, and on appeal the state supreme court also found against Godfroy on the basis that the land belonged to individuals, not to a tribe. Therefore the case did not fit the rule of nontaxability established in *Meshingomesia* v. *The State* in 1870.[18] Godfroy's attorney then sought an opinion from the commissioner of Indian Affairs. The commissioner concluded that Indians remaining "upon lands granted them by the United States from the lands of their ancestors cannot be regarded as severing their tribal relations."[19] In other words, the Miami were a tribe, with treaty rights. Although Congress had legislated citizenship for the Meshingomesia Miami, such was not the case for the remaining Miami, who were tax-exempt. The commissioner concluded that taxes Miami landowners paid should be refunded.

The 1854 treaty dictated distribution of the $221,000 capital fund to all qualified Miami despite the wishes of the tribal leaders to keep it intact. In 1881 Thad Butler, owner of the *Wabash Plain Dealer,* made a roll of 321 Miami men, women, and children who received $695 each. Butler visited every Miami family and said that the Miami in Butler Township were "ripe for a temperance movement of forty-horse power."[20] Gabriel Godfroy and Peter Bondy hoped that relief from taxation would help make up for the loss of annuities. Their hopes were strengthened when the federal district court for northern Indiana ruled that the Miami had a tribal government and that adapting to white ways did not cause the loss of "the rights incident to their tribal relation and character."[21] In 1891 the Indiana Supreme Court affirmed the nontaxation of treaty grants, and the state legislature passed legislation prohibiting taxation of treaty grants so long as the Miami were not citizens. A difficult and expensive legal battle had been won. Ongoing Miami treaty rights were recognized, as was the tribal government.[22]

The Miami community in Butler Township fared well in the 1880s. Despite lower agricultural prices, land loss was modest compared with losses in Grant County, the local land base dropping from 2,200 acres in 1880 to about 1,800 acres in 1890. (See Table 6.1.) The minor loss of land was balanced by new jobs in the Peru area from an unexpected source, circuses. In the 1860s Peru had become an important rail crossing, with the Chesapeake and Ohio, Nickel Plate, and

Pimyotamah's house, 1891. The original log structure on the right was typical of many Miami cabins of the 1870s and 1880s. For a time the addition on the left was used as an Indian Baptist church. From the left, John Roberts, a circus worker, Eclistia Mongosa, granddaughter of Pimyotamah, William Cass, a Miami who carried mail from Peru, Susan Pope, daughter of Pimyotamah, and Harvey Propeck, a Miami raised by Pimyotamah. Propeck later moved to Oklahoma.

LaMoine Marks

Wabash Railroads intersecting the town. Dog and pony shows, small circuses, and other traveling entertainment groups stopped often at the busy junction. A young man named Benjamin Wallace returned from the Civil War and bought all the local livery stables. In 1882 Wallace bought a bankrupt circus and began purchasing wild animals, which he kept in town. Seeing a large opportunity, he sold his livery stable in 1884 and opened his own circus, which he put on the railroads in 1886. He bought land in the center of the local Miami Indian community as a winter quarters, near an area called "Squawtown," so named for the Eel River Miami women who took refuge there in the 1860s. The circus would lay over in Peru from November to April before going on the road. Miami Indians were soon working as animal feeders and handlers.[23] (See map on p. 167.)

Table 6.1. Miami Landholdings, Miami and Grant Counties, 1880–1900.[24] Percentages are Losses by Decade.

Year	Miami County % Lost (Godfroy/Bundy Land)		Grant County % Lost (Meshingomesia Land)		Total % Lost	
1880	2,192		5,469		7,661	
1890	1,759	20%	2,628	52%	4,387	43%
1900	907	48%	117	96%	1,024	77%

By 1891 Wallace's circus operations had become so large that he purchased Gabriel Godfroy's 220-acre farm at the mouth of the Mississinewa River for new winter quarters for twenty-five thousand dollars. Godfroy added a large addition to his father's old trading house a half mile east and moved there with his large family. The new winter quarters were just a mile northwest of the old quarters, still within easy walking distance of the local Miami. The growth of the circus industry had a broad impact on the Miami community. Men could work as animal feeders and on the circus farm while the circus wintered over from November to April. Eventually Miami men and women moved into a variety of circus employments, some becoming performers. Circus work paid well and employed a cosmopolitan mixture of minorities and foreigners, some of whom began to marry into the Miami community. The Miami met Indians from other tribes who passed through Peru and were themselves traveling to all parts of the United States.

The large sum Wallace paid Gabriel Godfroy for his farm enabled Godfroy to pay the heavy legal expenses of defending Miami land from taxation. He could continue the generous behavior of a civil chief as well. In 1889 Pimyotamah died, and Godfroy was now considered the leader of the Peru-area Miami. In 1895 the Miami won another legal victory, this time a settlement of the claims arising from the diversion of annuities to the bogus Miami in the 1850s and 1860s. A new tribal roll was made, and 440 Miami shared in $48,528, a final annuity of about $96 each. Godfroy signed the roll as chief.

Miami Sites in Butler Township, Miami County
circa 1873–1900

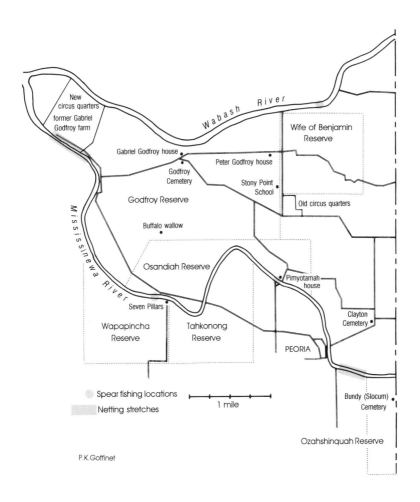

New circus quarters

former Gabriel Godfroy farm

Wabash River

Gabriel Godfroy house

Godfroy Cemetery

Peter Godfroy house

Wife of Benjamin Reserve

Stony Point School

Godfroy Reserve

Old circus quarters

Mississinewa River

Buffalo wallow

Osandiah Reserve

Pimyotamah house

Seven Pillars

Clayton Cemetery

Wapapincha Reserve

Tahkonong Reserve

PEORIA

Spear fishing locations

Netting stretches

1 mile

Bundy (Slocum) Cemetery

Ozahshinquah Reserve

P.K. Goffinet

Mary Stitt (Checonzah) and her husband Charles Nitzschke. By the 1880s some Miami were marrying European immigrants and circus workers.

Don Nitzschke

The 1895 roll of the Indiana Miami revealed changes in the tribe. Since 1881 the tribal population had shown rapid growth, increasing from 318 to 440, or 38 percent in fourteen years. The median age of children fell from nineteen on the 1881 roll to fifteen on the 1895 roll, showing that many more children were surviving. Families became much larger, with thirteen of seventy families having five or more children compared with only ten families having four or more children on the 1881 census. As a sign of decreasing violence, the proportion of men to women was 47 percent to 53 percent, almost equal.[25] The increase in family size, decrease in violence, and the overall increase in tribal population showed that a majority of the Miami (though not all) were experiencing better circumstances after 1880.

The Indiana Miami in Kansas and Indian Territory

By 1895 the Miami community had become more dispersed as well. A few lived in Michigan and Chicago, while the group living in Kansas and later in Indian Territory had grown much larger. The westward migration of Indiana Miami had begun soon after removal and was a brain drain from the Indiana tribe, as the most educated and acculturated left, nearly all of whom were from the Richardville family. These were the elite of the tribe, completely at ease in the dominant society, and frequently married into influential white families. In 1870 eighteen Indiana Miami were living in Kansas. By 1880 the group had grown to thirty-eight, and in 1895 to sixty-seven. The Eastern Miami in the West moved from Kansas to Indian Territory along with the Western Miami after the last of their reservation in Kansas was sold in 1871.[26] Thomas Richardville was the leader of the Indiana Miami in the West and was an important leader (though not a chief) of the Western Miami as well.

The Western Miami were given part of the Quapaw reservation in the northeast corner of Indian Territory after moving from Kansas. The tribe had declined to just seventy-five people in 1891. They welcomed the addition of the capable group from Indiana who had lived among them for over thirty years and equaled their group in size. Though the Eastern and Western Miami in Indian Territory lived among each other, the two groups were never legally joined. Rather, the Indiana Miami conducted their tribal business through leaders in Peru, and there were frequent and lengthy visits from both groups of Miami between Indiana and Indian Territory. After 1873 Thomas Richardville became the most important leader of the Western Miami, but he never cut his ties to the Eastern branch of the tribe. In 1891 Richardville was one of the founders of Miami, Oklahoma, which later became the seat of Ottawa County.[27]

Some Miami of Indiana were adopted as Quapaw Indians and received valuable land as well. In the late 1880s, as allotment became inevitable for the one hundred-member Quapaw tribe, the federal government questioned whether enough Quapaw lived on the 56,685-acre reservation to exist as a "nation." Believing their land to be in jeopardy, a minority of the Quapaw leadership decided to adopt other Indians in order to increase their numbers. If the tribe allotted all the land to Indians, leaders reasoned, there would be no surplus land available for non-Indians. The only requirement for adoption was that the adoptees live on the reservation.

The landless Indiana Miami who had moved into the area from Kansas fit the need of the Quapaw scheme. In 1886 and 1887 a host of "homeless Indians" were adopted, most of them from the Richardville family. The Bureau of Indian Affairs refused to permit the adoptions, being convinced there was a well-organized conspiracy to get control of Quapaw grazing land and mineral rights. At this point Abner W. Abrams entered the scene. A Stockbridge Indian who had returned from Colorado to nearby Baxter Springs, Kansas, he got himself adopted into the Quapaw tribe in 1887. Abrams's white brother-in-law was married to one of the Indiana Miami women. A gifted influence peddler (today we would say lobbyist), Abrams went directly to Washington and got the commissioner of Indian Affairs to approve the adoptions. Along with other adoptions, the size of the Quapaw tribe was nearly doubled. The tribe then allotted the reservation, keeping their land in Indian ownership.[28]

Each of the eighteen Indiana Miami adopted as Quapaw received 210 acres and continued to be eligible for any future Miami claims settlements. In 1905 one of the richest lead and zinc deposits in the tristate area was discovered on the allotment of an adopted Indiana Miami girl, Emma Gordon, near Commerce. Five mines were established on the property, and royalties in good years before World War I reached two hundred thousand dollars.[29]

Federal Indian Schools

The Miami in the Peru, Indiana, area had seemingly established their legal status by the mid-1890s. Federal court decisions and state law recognized the nontaxability of treaty reserve land. Most Miami children attended local elementary schools, while older children were attending federal Indian schools such as Haskell Institute in Lawrence, Kansas, and the Carlisle Indian Industrial School in Carlisle, Pennsylvania, in increasing numbers. The children gained a good basic education in Indian schools and returned home with a greater knowledge of the Indian world at large.

White's Manual Labor Institute, a Quaker boarding school for "poor children, white, colored and Indian," was located only five miles north of the Meshingomesia reserve, but none of the local Miami children were sent there, though there were many who qualified. Often, the major purpose of federal Indian education was to take children far from their homes so they could be more easily forced into European-American models of culture and belief. White's Institute contracted with the Office of Indian Affairs to bring in children from various Western Indian agencies from 1870 until 1895 when the contracting was ended, while nearby Miami children were sent to Kansas or Pennsylvania. Plains Indian children as young as six were sent to Indiana, often against their parents' wishes. Over twenty of the children died at White's Institute and are buried in the Indian graveyard.

None of the children from Pine Ridge, Rosebud, or the Yankton Sioux reservations are known to have seen the Miami children living a few miles away. Zitkala-Sa (Gertrude Bonnin) came to White's Institute in 1884 at the age of eight from the Yankton Sioux agency. She saw a classmate die and detested the "iron routine" of the place, trudging through each day "heavy-footed, like a dumb, sick brute." Despite her difficulties, Bonnin graduated from White's Institute and went to Earlham College in Richmond, Indiana, for a time. Illness forced her to quit (but not before she had won the college oratorical contest). Later she attended the New England Conservatory of Music. By 1902 she had returned wholly to Lakota religious beliefs, as she explained in an *Atlantic Monthly* article titled "Why I Am a Pagan." A musician, composer, and author, she later became a distinguished Indian rights activist. Years later the local Miami finally met her in Washington, D.C., seeking her help to reestablish their treaty rights.[30]

Miami students at Haskell and Carlisle seem not to have had bitter experiences such as those of Gertrude Bonnin at White's Institute. Miami pupils were older, usually in their teens, and attended school up to age twenty. They were far more acculturated than the Lakota students sent to Indiana and went with the encouragement of their parents. Many Miami were children of tribal leaders who felt they could benefit from federal Indian education at a time when there were no local rural high schools. The students who went away met young Indians from many other tribes. They gained an understanding of Indian issues and often worked for tribal rights later in their lives.

Continuing Efforts to Preserve Treaty Rights and the Loss of Federal Recognition

In the fall of 1896 the Eastern Miami drew up their first formal organization to pursue claims. Camillus Bundy was appointed attorney to contact Washington. The immediate issue was the return of taxes collected by the state of Indiana. Federal courts had ruled and the Indiana legislature had decreed in 1891 that treaty grants should not be taxed, but taxes illegally collected from 1852 to 1891 amounting to several thousand dollars had not been repaid. Bundy had elementary schooling, was extremely intelligent and well spoken, and was a successful farmer. He had taught himself Indian law, had kinship ties to most of the tribe through his many brothers and sisters, and was well regarded. He was a good choice to continue efforts to expand and consolidate Miami rights.

At Camillus Bundy's request, Commissioner of Indian Affairs Daniel Browning reported favorably upon the issue of suing the state of Indiana for the return of Miami taxes. The responsibility for pressing the matter in court then arose. Should the Miami, with their limited resources, sue in defense of their rights or should the federal government prosecute the case for the tribe? If the Indiana Miami were a tribe protected by federal Indian law the government should prosecute. In his lengthy opinion, which he sent to the assistant attorney general for the Interior Department, Browning concluded:

> That the owners of this land constitute a part of the Miami nation, and have kept up their tribal relations, is abundantly shown....They are not citizens of the United States, and, indeed, could not rid themselves of their allegiance to their nation and become citizens without the consent of the United States.[31]

The outcome of Commissioner Browning's request for clarification of the status of the Eastern Miami would have been a formality, except Indian law had shifted dramatically since 1887. In that year Congress passed the General Allotment Act, which called for the cutting up of Indian reservations into farms and the sale of surplus land. After a period of time, allotted Indians were to become citizens. The 1887 act was essentially the same as the legislation that had allotted the Meshingomesia reserve in 1872, with some refinements. This time all reservations were to be divided, surplus land sold, and Indians made over into small farmers. Upon allotment tribal governments would cease to exist. Indians would be on their own to compete in American society.

Newly appointed Assistant Attorney General Willis Van Devanter rendered his decision in regard to federal assistance for the Miami on 23 November 1897. The Indiana Miami, he ruled, had not been under the protection of federal law since legislation was passed on 3 March 1881 distributing the capital fund set up under the 1854 treaty. The Miami who owned treaty grants were the same as allotted Indians under the General Allotment Act who had full control of their land. They were citizens, not Indians under federal law. Therefore the federal government could not assist them in the return of past taxes. Van Devanter concluded by saying his ruling did not touch on taxation itself or the right to recover anything from the state.[32]

Van Devanter's opinion went far beyond the question posed by the Commissioner of Indian Affairs and administratively terminated the recognition of the Indiana Miami tribe. Nearly a century later, in 1990, the Department of the Interior stated that neither the 1872 or 1881 congressional legislation ended federal rights for the tribe. In 1910 Willis Van Devanter was appointed an associate justice of the United States Supreme Court, where he wrote the Court's opinions in several important Indian cases. In *U.S.* v. *Nice* (1915) he wrote that an Indian could be a citizen *and* a member of a tribe, contradicting his opinion in the 1897 decision. He repeated this position in 1930 in *Halbert* v. *United States.* The arguments made in these decisions were used in 1977 in the United States District Court in South Bend, Indiana, to determine that descendants of individual treaty reservees were exempt from state taxation. The 1977 opinion, however, did not restore federal legal rights to the Indiana Miami. The Department of the Interior in 1990, though admitting Van Devanter's error, used administrative guidelines to again deny legal status to the tribe.[33]

Van Devanter's family had a long association with the Miami that continued at the time he rendered his decision. Van Devanter's father, Isaac Van Devanter, clerked as a young man for the wily George W. Ewing. In 1846 the elder Van Devanter accompanied the Miami from Indiana to their Kansas reservation.[34] Later he was the attorney for the Meshingomesia Miami when the reserve was allotted and was known to overcharge the tribe for legal work. Born in Marion, Indiana, in 1859, young Willis spent many happy days on his grandfather Spencer's farm north of town on the border of the Meshingomesia reservation. There is little doubt that the fourteen-year-old boy sat in on some of the Miami testimony with his father at the reserve schoolhouse during the summer days of 1873. Later, as a young man home from Cincinnati Law School, he undoubtedly heard his father's frustration when a third of his charges against the Meshingomesia Miami were denied by the Interior Department as double billing.[35]

Isaac Van Devanter and his brother-in-law Robert J. Spencer were wealthy businessmen in Marion. During the 1880s and 1890s, Van Devanter was the attorney for the Peconga family, and Spencer loaned money on many mortgages to the same family. Beginning in 1895 Spencer began foreclosing mortgages on the land. The year following his nephew Willis Van Devanter's legal ruling on the Miami, Spencer foreclosed four mortgages. By the time Spencer finished in 1899 he owned 413 acres of land that had belonged to his brother-in-law's Indian clients.[36] While there was no direct conflict of interest, Willis Van Devanter's decision denied the Indiana Miami the protection of federal Indian law and accelerated the loss of their remaining landholdings.

The unexpected Van Devanter decision undid the hard work of two generations of Indiana Miami leaders in protecting the legal status of the tribe. In effect, the 1897 decision extinguished the tribe and, worse yet, closed off any legal recourse in the federal court system for regaining treaty rights. Within months Miami County commissioners appealed two earlier circuit court cases in favor of Gabriel Godfroy, and the state appellate court ruled that he was liable for taxes. In June 1901 Godfroy was denied a rehearing before the appellate court, and in November the state supreme court refused to hear the case. The state courts swept aside earlier federal decisions that an Indian could be a citizen and also a tribal member. Henceforth, degree of "whiteness" or acculturation would determine tax exemption or tribal status. Declaring that Godfroy had voted, paid taxes for a time, sent his children to public schools, and dressed like his white neighbors, the state supreme court decreed he had voluntarily placed himself within the legal definition of citizen. He could "not be both an Indian properly so-called and a citizen."[37]

Within two months of Van Devanter's decision, word of the changed status of the Eastern Miami had spread to federal Indian schools. In January 1898 Judson Peconga sent a typed letter to the Bureau of Indian Affairs from Lawrence, Kansas, saying that there had been talk that "we the Miami Indians of Indiana have no right to come here to school."[38] The students currently enrolled at Haskell were allowed to stay, but when two Miami wanted to enter in 1901, Commissioner of Indian Affairs W. A. Jones replied that the government had cut its connnections with the tribe and was not going to "take a backward step relative to these people." "To send them to an Indian school," Jones continued, "would be simply to perpetuate their Indian characteristics, and unquestionably would not be of advantage to the children."[39]

At the time Commissioner Jones wrote against admitting Miami to federal Indian schools, there were no high schools in the townships where most of the Miami lived, and those who went to Haskell or Carlisle came home with a far better education than the local one-room schools with a seven-month school year offered. One Miami who attended a local school tried for years to enter the Indian service but was disqualified because of low scores on civil service tests.[40] Three Miami from Indiana attended Carlisle after Jones wrote against sending members of the tribe to federal Indian schools. One pupil attended until 1908. John Godfroy, one of the three, easily got work as disciplinarian at the federal Indian school at Pipestone, Minnesota, and went on to become a Fort Wayne policeman, the only Indian police officer in Indiana.[41] It was another generation after the shutting off of federal Indian education before the Miami equaled the number of high school graduates achieved at the turn of the century. The Miami in local high schools often had to face degrading prejudice that they never encountered among other Indians in federal schools.

In April 1898 Anthony Walker, a grandson of Pimyotamah and a rising leader in the tribe, sold his farm and moved to Lincolnville,

Studio portrait of the Anthony Walker family taken in 1898, shortly before they left Indiana for better opportunities in Indian Territory. Four more children were born after the move, and seven of the children attended Haskell Institute in Lawrence, Kansas, benefiting from educational opportunities denied tribal members in the East. Standing from the left are Addison, Levi, John, Harry, and Claude. In front are Effie, Anthony, Edith, Rebecca, Myrtle, and Phillip.

Rebecca Walker

Indian Territory, with his wife and nine children. Although Walker owned his land clear of debt and was perhaps the most successful of the Indian farmers, he felt opportunities were better for an Indian family in the West. After moving to Indian Territory the Walkers had four more children. They lived in the rich corn, flax, and prairie-hay growing district of Ottawa County, between Baxter Springs, Kansas, and Miami, Oklahoma.[42] Indiana Miami children living in the West were permitted to continue attendance at federal Indian schools, though technically they should not have been. Seven of the Walker children attended Haskell Institute in Lawrence, where they received a fine education and could feel comfortable as Indian Americans.[43]

The Indiana Miami began the last quarter of the nineteenth century with high hopes of success in protecting their land, allowing another generation for adaptation to the market economy and the dominant society. Hopeful expectations were dashed by the rapid loss of the Meshingomesia land, and ultimately, the loss of all treaty protection. The Indiana Miami reached the end of the nineteenth century without any legal rights as a tribe. Before the law they were citizens of Indiana, descendants of the historic Miami tribe, equal to other citizens of the state, but with no status as Indians.

Other tribes across the United States were also losing their legal status at the same time. Liberals and conservatives joined forces to allot tribal lands and to make citizens of Indians, opening reservations to private acquisition. The Miami experience was a small example compared to the allotment of over nineteen million acres in Indian Territory to 101,506 members of the Five Civilized Tribes. Liberal reformers portrayed the destruction of tribal governments and allotment of communal landholdings nationwide as an advance toward civilization. For the Miami, as for many Indians, it was instead a descent into poverty and the destruction of tribal culture.

SEVEN

Last Years on the Land
1901–1922

■

My people, the Miamis, made peace with the whites in Washington's time and we never violated it.... The red men made their treaties and kept them, but the white men did not. Whenever they were dissatisfied they would give us a little money and make a new treaty.

Gabriel Godfroy, Speech at Tippecanoe Battle-field Site, 16 June 1907[1]

I had to give up one of my greatest desires to work and help keep up the family. My desire was an education. I graduated from public schools at the age of 13 years, and attended high school here [Marion, Indiana] until I was 14 years of age. I then went to work in a factory for $5.50 a week. That was 6 years ago but I will say that if I had a chance now I sure would go back to school and finish my education. My one ambition has always been to attend school at Carlisle, Pennsylvania.

Raleigh Felsinger to Rep. Milton Kraus, 9 March 1922[2]

AT THE BEGINNING OF THE TWENTIETH CENTURY INDIAN-apolis journalist George Cottman visited the Miami living east of

Peru in Butler Township. What he saw was an American Indian community reduced to the level of the poorest, least successful white farmers. Those who had tried farming for a time were now impoverished. William Peconga had lost his land and was working as a tenant farmer. Gabriel Godfroy, who once had appeared thrifty and prosperous, had only forty-eight hilly and sterile acres left. Cottman searched for answers to the problem. What had led these once comparatively well-off people to poverty? He felt there were two explanations. First, Indians were accustomed to satisfying immediate needs. When faced with a variety of goods and unlimited credit backed by land, the Indian spent the money and forgot the borrowing. Second, Indians were surrounded by sharp whites anxious to supply Indian wants in exchange for their land. After seventy-five years of using land for credit, nearly all the land was gone, and the Miami found themselves poor.[3]

After lamenting the condition of the Miami, Cottman unconsciously offered a deeper account of the paradox of the Miami, "the persistence of the Indian instincts despite [the] liberal admixture of [the] white man's blood." "Godfroy's boys," he wrote, "are as aboriginal in their proclivities as the Miami striplings of a century ago." The Miami cherished lore, he felt, which could explain their distinctness from the community around them, if someone took the time to study them.[4] Today we would not explain a community in terms of instincts, but Cottman was aware that communities adapt, yet keep alive memories, habits, customs, and beliefs that set them apart. In the case of the Miami the elements forming a boundary with the dominant society remained sharp.

At first glance the Miami in the Peru area appeared to be almost completely assimilated into American culture by 1900. The Miami lived in houses, almost all spoke English, the children went to public schools, and everyone dressed as "citizens" or whites. The observation of almost total assimilation was superficial, however. Gabriel Godfroy had been a favorite local example of a prosperous Indian farmer, apparently at no disadvantage with his white neighbors. Cottman, on visiting Godfroy's home, however, immediately noticed a difference. "Godfroy and his family," he observed, "are strikingly out of place in the great, barren, many-roomed house where they find shelter. The rules of living, the orderly arrangement, the convenience and ornamentation which make a house a home in any sense of the word are here missing entirely. The place is simply a refuge from outdoors, when outdoors proves unpleasant."[5]

Cottman was overly critical in his interpretation. One of Godfroy's daughters told the author that the house was a popular gathering place on weekends for dances and entertainment of whites as well as Indians. Two large downstairs rooms were used for dancing, while the large kitchen had benches that could be moved to one side to make more dancing space. There were still people living in cottages around the main house, while several of Godfroy's grown children, grandchildren, and many younger children (he had nineteen children altogether) lived in the main house.[6]

Although Miami family groups lived near Fort Wayne and Huntington, the last sizable Miami community was in Butler Township just east of Peru in Miami County. Since the return of the Miami from Kansas, the settlement had remained remarkably stable, with from 25 to 30 families and a population of from 125 to 150. Despite fifty years of rapid acculturation in everyday contact with a modern American community and much intermarriage with whites, the rural Miami remained a distinct group and were viewed as American Indian by both the local population and outsiders. The only people who emphasized the similarities of Miami to the dominant culture were those who were attempting to take Miami resources. Under this rationale, if the Miami dressed like whites, lived in houses, and spoke English, they therefore completely understood every nuance of the larger society, and if they lost their property they were clearly to blame.

The Early-Twentieth-Century Miami Community in Butler Township, Miami County

The Miami living in Butler Township were poised between well-worn folkways along the rivers and a very different world in nearby towns. They went to Peru often, but they did not want to live there, and in 1900 only one family did. Nearly all the men continued hunting and trapping for food as well as for income. Boys set traps and began some hunting and fishing as young as seven or eight and continued until they were elderly. A lively market had developed in ginseng, goldenseal (yellow-root), bloodroot, and other medicinal plants that many families gathered, dried, and sold to druggists.

As Miami landholdings shrank, foraging grew in importance. Milkweed was the most popular spring vegetable. Jerusalem artichoke and shepherd's purse were eaten often, and the young shoots of mustard, immature pokeweed, and skunk cabbage were eaten occasionally. Some families regularly visited abandoned farmsteads to gather apples, while others had their favorite wild onion patches. Persimmons and a variety of nuts were gathered, while mayapples, papaws, crab apples, and wild plums served as snack foods when in the woods. Sassafras and spicebush provided popular teas, and spicebush was also used to parboil older game to tenderize it. Honey was still gathered from trees, and the older men knew how to freshen old honey for use. There were state game laws, but they were not enforced locally with the Miami, who enjoyed fish, small game, and ducks out of season as they always had.[7]

The Wabash and Mississinewa Rivers still teamed with fish, and fish had become the most important source of protein. A Miami woman told the author that her family "ate so many fish, we almost turned into one."[8] Catfish were popular because they were easiest to spear at night, but the Miami would eat any kind of fish, from bass to sauger (pike perch) to the lowly gar. Bow and arrow fishing was done in shallow water in

Study in pauperization. Top, Gabriel Godfroy's 1822 trading post with 1893 addition on the left. Photo by Charles Worden, 1903. Middle, son Peter Godfroy's house. Bottom, grandson Oliver Godfroy's "bachelor house." Today a great-granddaughter of Francis Godfroy owns the last parcel (1.33 acres) of the 10,880 acres granted Godfroy in various treaties.

Swan Hunter, Stewart Rafert, Stewart Rafert

the spring when spawning fish "finned out" nesting areas. Men speared fish mainly in the winter when the water was cold and clear and fish were slow moving and easy to see. Gasoline torches were carried on boats for spearing at night. Netting was done in smooth water (netting stretches) where the net would not catch on obstructions. Brails held each end of the net, while tenders managed the middle, keeping a curve in it and lifting it over rocks. The net was moved downstream and from deep water to shallow. Some men were expert at feeling for fish under ledges, yanking them from the water with thumb and two fingers by mouth and gills. Sometimes hundreds of fish were stranded in ponds left by spring floods, and they could simply be gathered off the land. (See map on p. 167.)

It is probably impossible to ascertain the economic importance of subsistence activities to the Butler Township Miami. It is possible that such activities gained in importance after annuities were ended and as the loss of tribal land became more severe. The fur and herb sales brought in some money, while wild game, fish, and fowl lowered the cost of food. Subsistence activities continued to have great social as well as economic importance, since gathering wild plants, fruits, and nuts were usually group activities shared by young and old of both sexes and served to bring the Miami together frequently. Net fishing, smoking fish, butchering, and hunting (especially coon hunting) were shared male tasks. Women frequently socialized over food preparation and its storage. A few midwives still delivered nearly all the babies, and several older women and some men were healers.

There were gardens as well, and the Miami still grew the soft white corn that they had traded in the eighteenth century. Now it was dried, as in the past, on platforms and eaten mostly as hominy. Some ears were braided together by the shucks and hung over a rafter to dry for the next crop. A few chickens, pigs, and sometimes a cow were kept. Boiled beef was a weekend treat, whereas pork was a common dish. In 1900 the rural Miami were still engaged in many of the same subsistence activities that they were engaged in a century earlier.[9]

The Miami remained medically separate from the larger community in the early twentieth century. Indiana counties began keeping birth and death records in 1882 based on physicians' reports. Because midwives and medicine people attended the tribe and men still buried some of the dead, county records for the Miami are spotty. In one case nine children born to an Indian woman in Miami County from 1883 to 1899 were not in the birth records. In addition, the Indian population was omitted from records of dangerous diseases as late as 1940. County officials simply did not record the incidence of whooping cough, measles, scarlet fever, diphtheria, smallpox, typhoid, and other infectious diseases among Indian families. Although tuberculosis was a leading killer of the Miami, no cases were enumerated in local disease records until well into the twentieth century.[10]

By 1900 many Miami men were not marrying. Of the men born in the generation between the tribal rolls of 1854 and 1881, over one-third who lived to age thirty or older remained bachelors. Nearly all women continued to wed. Men bore the brunt of the pressure from the dominant society to change their ways of livelihood, while women's roles were much less changed. A rural Miami woman who married a white man experienced little change in her work of nurturing and raising children, while a Miami man married to a white woman would feel considerable pressure to adopt the prevailing male economic role as head of the family. Because of the severe shortage of men going back to the 1830s, women had been more accustomed to marrying non-Indians. With the contracting of work to whites, there had developed a community of local white men who were quite acculturated to Miami lifestyles. Many of these men hunted and fished with the Miami men as well, and some spoke the language. Culturally, they were suitable marriage candidates for the women. There was no such group of women acculturated to Miami life available for Miami men.

As a sign of the more conservative cultural role of Miami women and perhaps of their greater social isolation from the community at large, more women spoke the Miami language than men, and the older women enjoyed getting together just to talk "Indian."[11] Surprisingly, there were a few women still living in 1900 who spoke no English. Kilsoquah was one such monolingual Miami. She died in 1915. Polly Wildcat (or Mongosa) was the last person known to speak only Miami. Born about 1834, she died in 1917.

The rise of a bachelor culture among the Miami had interesting effects. Several one-room "bachelor houses" still exist in Butler Township, adding variety to the local housing stock. The Miami custom of male companionship or *kikwo* remained strong in the early twentieth century and may have fostered bachelorhood. A relic of companion warrior ties, such friends called each other *nik-ka*. This close sharing of activities strengthened the persistence of older subsistence work and raised male confidence in the face of sometimes brutal prejudice experienced in the larger community. The men helped each other get jobs with the circuses and, after 1910, on the railroads. Many unmarried Miami men worked as cooks, firemen, and engineers on the Wabash, Big Four (New York Central), Nickel Plate, and Chesapeake and Ohio in northeastern Indiana. The work paid well, and the men were readily accepted among fellow non-Indian railroaders.

Schooling in Indian Ways

By the beginning of the twentieth century all of the Miami children went to elementary school along with the neighboring white children. Most Miami children in Butler Township attended Stony Point school, located in the center of the Miami settlement. More than half of the children were Miami, and prejudice was not a problem. The longtime teacher later married a Miami man. There was no local high school until 1910.

Hunting, trapping, fishing, and plant and animal lore offered powerful competition to formal schooling, especially for boys. George Cottman observed that Miami boys were skilled in the use of the bow and liked to shoot fish from roosts in trees overhanging the rivers. Confinement in a one-room school paled in interest with the nearby woods and streams where some of the older men always had something to teach. For Miami students in general rote learning could be lifeless compared with the stories Gabriel Godfroy, James Sassaquas, John Bundy, Camillus Bundy, and others told outdoors on warm evenings of giants and little people, the sorcery of witches, the dreaded underwater panther, and ancient war parties. Some stories concerning the transformation of people and animals were shared sparingly to protect the powers they conveyed. Besides the stories there were dances, and every child received a name for some natural object or quality or for a well-respected Miami ancestor.[12] In this way the older Miami men and women modeled the intangible qualities and behaviors of being Miami, which had far greater impact than formal education because they were personal and immediate.

The older Miami also taught history as they had experienced it. The grandfathers of many of the children had met with presidents of the United States, whom the Miami called *matatsopia*, "ten heads." Some of the families had peace medals presented at treaties, a pipe tomahawk and a fifteen-star Anthony Wayne flag given at Greenville in 1795, and a few parchment copies of original treaties. Treasured also were silver trade crosses from Montreal and old Miami leggings, moccasins, shawls, a wampum belt, medicine bundles, silver gorgets, and wristbands. Although the items would furnish a small museum, they were kept among families and brought out for visitors and for special occasions.[13] In addition there were larger symbols of Miami life—the cemeteries, an ancient buffalo wallow, fishing holes and other special places with stories attached to them, and several fishing weir dams built by people preceding the Miami.

Gabriel Godfroy with his family and Miami heirlooms. Miami leaders were fond of showing visitors blouses, leggings, peace medals, silver crosses, pipe tomahawks, and other items from the eighteenth and early nineteenth centuries. In the early twentieth century many treasured items were sold to museum collectors in order to pay legal expenses and for travel to Washington, D.C., in attempts to preserve the legal status of the tribe.

Miami County Historical Society

Miami and white schoolchildren at Stony Point school about 1908. Twelve of the twenty-two children are Indian, and the teacher Mary Clark later married Clarence Godfroy, the Miami storyteller.

Swan Hunter

The stories, history, objects, special places, and older people themselves constituted a powerful context for "Miaminess" that was taught or modeled in an immediate and personal way. At the same time the inner sense of being Miami was endangered as it never had been before. With the loss of the Meshingomesia reserve in a short time, and the land in Butler Township disappearing as well, the Miami were feeling poised between two cultures. There was also a strong impression that older ways were disappearing. A sense of psychological stress and ethnic uncertainty had entered the community. Many Miami children who were to become leaders later in the twentieth century were sharply aware that their rural way of life was threatened. They were proud to be Miami, but were angry at the greed, pressure, and physical and psychological threats coming from the non-Miami world around them.[14]

Miami unease was increased by rising nationalism among the American population and a growing insensitivity to ethnic and racial differences. In Theodore Roosevelt's popular *Winning of the West* and the work of historians on the closing of the frontier, Indians were portrayed as important only because they resisted settlement, made a military training school of the frontier, and helped to develop the stalwart and rugged qualities of the frontiersman. In the melting pot of early-twentieth-century America, Indians, African Americans, and other minorities were to disappear or take a back seat. The Miami, having experienced the impact of American society and Indian policy for a century, resisted being swept under the rug. As Cottman learned, Gabriel Godfroy and other tribal leaders perceived the official version of American history as "the white man's perversion of the truth" and spoke "bitterly of wrongs done them."[15]

Acts of prejudice increased against the Miami in the early twentieth century, ranging from personal insults to some cases of violence. Camillus Bundy, sensing the need to bring an uneasy community closer together, instituted the Miami reunion in 1903. Patterned somewhat after the typical family reunion of the day, it was Indian in content. All the tribe was invited to a different location each year, usually near one of the former villages. There was a council meeting to discuss business, and at noon a *mačiani*, or "feed," at which the men ate first, then the women and children. In the afternoon there was discussion of business, footraces and other games, Indian dancing, and music. Most people came in Miami ceremonial attire. The reunion recognized the fact that over half the Miami people lived away from their old haunts, and it offered them an opportunity to come home again, to speak the language, and to visit.[16]

The Miami Community as Portrayed in the Indian Schedules of the 1900 and 1910 Federal Censuses

The Indian schedules of the 1900 and 1910 censuses give a good overview of the Miami community in Miami and Grant Counties in the first decade of the twentieth century. In 1900 the Miami of Miami County were all rural (except one family) and worked as farmers (six) or farm laborers (fifteen). Three young women were listed as servants. No other occupations were given for men or women. Most of the farm laborers worked six to ten months, so there was ample time for hunting, fishing, short-time employment at the circus's winter quarters, and other casual employment. Half of the adults over forty could not read and write, but everyone under forty could. All but two or three could speak English, and children attended school for seven months a year. Half of the twenty-six families owned their homes free of mortgage and half rented. Eight people were listed as full-blooded Miami and most of the rest half-blood or more. Two were listed as one-eighth blood. All of the people had Miami names, showing the persistence of naming. None were listed as citizens.[17]

The Miami Indians tended to disappear in other counties where they often lived in towns or cities. In Grant County most of the forty-seven Miami lived in Marion. Most families rented their homes, and the children attended city schools for nine months a year. Occupations were quite varied: box maker, tin-plate worker, street worker, laundress (two women), and a few day laborers. All were listed as citizens by allotment.[18] There were twenty-six Miami in Wabash County, all living in Wabash except one family living in the country on an eleven-acre remnant of an allotment. There were no Indian schedules. In Huntington County there was no Indian schedule either, and only one person was listed as Indian, though Mrs. Archangel Engleman, a daughter of Chief Lafontaine, lived with her large family on a treaty reserve west of Huntington, and Kilsoquah, the oldest Miami Indian, lived with her son in Roanoke after they were put out of their rural house, and it was burned.[19] Likewise, in Allen County only five people were enumerated as Indian, three on Indian schedules. This information hid a small but interesting Miami community of Richardville descendants led by John Godfroy. Godfroy, who fatally shot his father in 1894, lived with his unmarried brother George on the fifteen hundred-acre Richardville reserve southeast of Fort Wayne with fifteen or so of his children and grandchildren. George died in 1902. John died in 1904, and the land was lost. The fate of the Miami outside Miami County was the same as that of most other highly acculturated Indians of many tribes who lost tribal status. Faced with social pressure to conform and often scattered in small groups or families, it was far less stressful and even safer to keep one's identity private.

The 1910 Indian schedules showed the same number of Miami in Butler Township, just under 130, with none living in Peru. Housing conditions and decreasing ownership suggest greater poverty. Families were larger, and there were fewer households than in 1900 (twenty, down from twenty-six). Home owners had dropped from thirteen to eight while the number of renters decreased slightly from thirteen to twelve. Six men were again listed as farmers, including William Peconga, who was now renting land. Eighteen men were listed as farm laborers, up from fifteen in 1900, and five young women as servants, up from three. There were no other occupations listed for men or women. The changes were small, and the Indian community appeared surprisingly stable over the ten-year period.[20]

The Indian schedules noted that few spoke the Miami language by the beginning of the twentieth century. The last children who spoke the Miami language into adulthood were born in the 1870s, assuring the eventual death of the language. As land was lost the language-speaking community became more dispersed, and the subsistence activities and social environment that kept Miami speakers relatively separate from the larger English-speaking society were lost as well. The 1870s was a time of high death rates, and the breakup of families and a ten-year decline in population may have been factors in tipping the Miami community inexorably toward English.

Even as the Miami language was slowly dying, it exhibited some interesting features. The Miami who had gathered in the villages along the Mississinewa were from older, larger groups of Miami, and the spoken language varied. The remnant speakers in the late nineteenth century preserved some dialectical differences in their small groups so that the Miami in the Peru area tended to pronounce words differently and even to use some different words than the Meshingomesia Miami or the Bundy group. With only two or three dozen speakers left by the end of the nineteenth century, those differences made speaking and understanding the language more difficult and probably accelerated its extinction.[21]

The Miami language also became a victim of the cultural dominance of English, perhaps the most important cause of its eventual death. English was the language of the larger society and of its schools, newspapers, and employers. As the Miami became poorer and less isolated, their language lost social status, while English was the language to be learned if one wanted to advance to higher status or to integrate more thoroughly into the dominant society. The survival of the Miami language depended on residential segregation, high levels of intermarriage, and a focus on rural subsistence activities. By 1870 the Miami were quickly losing these anchors of language survival, and spoken Miami became moribund at about the same time the Miami left Indian-custom marriages for church or secular weddings and began marrying outside the tribe in much greater numbers.[22] After the 1870s parents and older Miami spoke the language, but not with children as they grew older, and the language declined quickly.

Albert S. Gatschet, a linguist with the Bureau of Ethnology at the Smithsonian Institution, began the study of the Miami language in 1890 when Thomas Richardville went to Washington on tribal business. In 1895 Gatschet traveled to Indiana where he made an extensive Miami word list. He also took down William Peconga's autobiography (*atotamané*, "I tell my life story") in Miami. Outsiders had written brief biographies of many notable Miami people, but this was the first time a Miami individual related his own life.[23] Gatschet's work is particularly valuable for field studies of poorly known and remnant languages. In the last few years of his career he was able to make notes on and compare Miami, Peoria, Kaskaskia, and Piankashaw, all closely related languages that were nearing extinction. His work was cut short by his death in 1907.[24]

In 1905 Jacob P. Dunn came from Indianapolis to continue the study of Miami begun by Gatschet. Dunn had done newspaper work in Colorado in the 1880s, where he developed a sympathetic interest in Indians and had written on the western Indian wars. Later he had begun corresponding with James Mooney, a fellow Hoosier who was by then with the Bureau of Ethnology at the Smithsonian Institution and studying the Eastern Cherokee tribe in North Carolina. By the time Dunn arrived at Gabriel Godfroy's house he was a sophisticated amateur student of Indian life. He quickly realized that Miami was an endangered language and began taking field notes. He expressed his sense of urgency to William Henry Holmes at the Smithsonian Bureau of Ethnology, writing in 1909 that Miami is more nearly extinct than any of the great languages of the Middle West. Practically, it can hardly be called a spoken language today—I think it is talked less in Oklahoma than in Indiana, and everyone I have worked with complains of forgetting words on account of disuse . . . . Whatever is done with the language must be done soon.[25]

Dunn worked closely with Godfroy and several other older Miami, making an extensive word list with notes on grammar and syntax. In the course of his work he also gathered some stories, games, and foodways that had not been described before. The 1910 Indian schedules listed only eighteen Miami-speaking residents in Butler Township. A few who lived across the county line in Wabash County also spoke Miami. Altogether there may have been thirty or so.

Gatschet and Dunn were doing what could be called "salvage linguistics," and the result was valuable. Their word lists can be used to verify the later oral history of subsistence activities and various changes in Miami economic and social life. For example, the Miami words for dollar and quarter reflected

Camillus Bundy about 1903. Son of Ozahshinquah and Peter Bondy, he inherited his mother's cultural conservatism and his father's political knowledge of the tribe. He founded the modern tribal organization in 1923 and assailed federal officials for failing to honor treaty rights.

Phyllis Miley

the fur-trade period, a dollar being *ngoti mäkwa*, one "beaver," and a quarter, *ngotiäsepana*, one "raccoon."[26] Even as the Miami language was dying, it was changing. New words were formed for circus animals, for example. An elephant was *wapingwilokia*, "white skin," a monkey *alalaciwia*, "always hunting lice," and a lion *kinozawia*, "long yellow hair." Rather than blending English words into Miami, the practice was to make compound words in Miami. Some older examples of such compounds (translated from Miami) are "makes any-thing" for carpenter, "bean liquor" for coffee, "long ears" for mule, "foaming water" for beer, "yellow money" for gold coins, and "white money" for silver coins. In this way the Miami had created words for knives, forks, guns, hoes, bug-gies, the American flag, and dozens of other items that were new to their way of life. They also gave American officials from the president down Miami names and continued, until the language died, to use the Miami names for places that later grew into modern towns and cities.[27]

Miami speakers did not simply leave their language for a generic spoken English. English possesses subtle distinctions of pronunciation and word use based on social class, region, and occupation. The long-term models of English usage for the Miami were initially frontiersmen and later poor people on the fringes of society, often of Scots-Irish origins. These people had developed a rich heritage of spoken English over many genera-tions related to hunting, fishing, and farming. The Miami hunters and rivermen and women who prepared food learned the complicated English vocabulary that went with the whole hunting-fishing-gathering complex in order to replace their own complex vocabulary for the same activities. To give a few exam-ples, they spoke in English of the men who hauled the ends of nets as "brails," an old, worn-out horse was a "bat," and of birds "nebbing" grain or seeds off the ground with their beaks. Braid-ing corn shucks was always "plaiting," and cornbread was called "hoecake." Often the pronunciation was variant. The scaffolds for drying corn were always called "scaffels," for example. Thus the rural Miami learned the English of their rural neighbors for similar activities, an English that itself was quickly dying as people moved off the land and into the cities in the early twentieth century.[28]

A New Generation of Leaders for Hard Times

By 1900 the Indiana Miami no longer had enough land to sustain their way of life along the Wabash and Mississinewa. Land along the rivers was key to the subsistence activities that sustained the Miami and underpinned their whole culture. Since the 1850s Miami leaders had realized that keeping land was crucial to the well-being of their community. As long as they had surplus land, tax exemption, and cash income from annuities, some loss of land was acceptable. For many years the most highly acculturated Miami, seeking greater opportunity, left the local community for the West, while the less acculturated and landless Miami took refuge on the Meshingomesia, Ozahshinquah, and Godfroy reserves. Tribal leaders had acted to protect these people from the harsher aspects of acculturation.

By the beginning of the new century the system of slow acculturation under the protection and guidance of a few tribal leaders had broken down. The rapid loss of the Meshingomesia reserve and heavy erosion of the remaining Miami land opened the possibility of total land loss. The Miami's attempt to regain taxes in the 1890s led instead to the complete loss of treaty rights and tax exemption, further weakening the economic base of the Miami. From 1890 to 1900 the Peru-area Miami lost 850 acres, half of their remaining land. Something had to be done. In 1903 they asked for land on the Western Miami reservation. The attempt failed because the reservation was already allotted, and even if it had not been, there was no legal means for the Indiana Miami to get allotments.[29] (See Table 7.1.)

Table 7.1. Miami Population and Landholdings, Butler Township, Miami County, 1880–1940. Includes Ozahshinquah Reserve on County Line.

Year	Families	Population	Godfroy-area	Ozahshinquah	Total	% Loss
1880	25	108	1,387	805	2,192	
1890	27	124	1,217	542	1,759	20%
1900	26	129	565	342	907	48%
1910	20	128	464	195	659	27%
1920	11	64	335	114	449	32%
1930	7	42	311		311	31%
1940	6	27	311		311	0%

In 1905 the elderly Gabriel Godfroy returned to court to press for tax exemption on his now small landholding. The *Marion News-Tribune* noted that thirteen years earlier Godfroy was worth forty thousand dollars, but he had spent it all on home and legal expenses.[30] By 1905 Godfroy also had sold most of his Miami heirlooms to museum collectors. Godfroy's lawsuit was submitted to the circuit court for trial without a jury. The court ruled that the 48 acres owned by Godfroy's children and on which he lived were to be relieved of unpaid taxes and be tax exempt until 1 January 1915. Another 121 acres Godfroy had given to his grandchildren were also relieved of unpaid taxes, but were to be taxed as of 1 January 1905.[31] The judge's ruling was a gift to Godfroy, perhaps out of sympathy for all the money he had paid the local legal profession. There was no basis in law for tax exemption after the 1901 Indiana Supreme Court ruling.

Gabriel Godfroy died on 14 August 1910. With Pimyotamah and Peter Bondy he had led the Peru-area Miami for over fifty years. In the manner of a civil chief he had given refuge to the Miami who had returned from Kansas after removal and to some Western Miami during the Civil War, as well as to landless Eel River Miami and other refugee Miami over the years. He encouraged male agriculture in the 1870s and served as the guardian of many Miami children after the Miami capital fund was paid out in 1881. Later he won tax exemption for Miami land for a time until federal recognition was administratively removed from the tribe in 1897. In his later years he helped preserve Miami culture by sharing the language with Jacob P. Dunn, who regarded him as the best speaker of both Miami and English. He was a popular story-teller among the Miami and inspired one of his grandsons to be-come a well-known storyteller. One of his stories was published in the initial volume of the *Indiana Magazine of History* a few years before his death.[32] His large home served as a kind of community center for whites and Miami, and he was a picturesque figure rid-ing into Peru on his thoroughbred horse, wearing a broad-brimmed hat with a red ribbon in his long, flowing hair.[33]

In the last years of the nineteenth century a new Indiana Miami tribal organization grew up around younger leaders. Formed the year before federal recognition was lost, it was the

Gabriel Godfroy as an old man, about 1905. He built his political power within the tribe by impoverishing himself in defense of Miami rights. He was a noted storyteller and the key informant for Jacob P. Dunn's studies of the Miami language.

Jacob P. Dunn, Indiana and Indianans, *Vol. 1*

Sarah Ward Parkhurst and Cora Ward Menefee about 1905. Both married white men who worked for the local circuses.

Swan Hunter

first formal organization of the tribe. George Godfroy was chief, Ross Bundy was secretary, and William Bundy was treasurer. Camillus Bundy acted as the local attorney, and the group consulted with Thomas Richardville who had a contract with the Bureau of Indian Affairs to pursue tribal claims. George Godfroy's Miami name was Shepaconah, the name of Deaf Man, a respected chief who died in 1832. Peter Godfroy, Gabriel's oldest son, was on the council. All of the Indiana Miami families were well represented, and both Peru and Marion were listed as tribal headquarters. Realizing that the tax exemption issue was dead after the 1897 decision and the 1901 Indiana Supreme Court decision, the leaders turned away from the focus of earlier leaders on tax exemption to tribal claims in general. (See Appendix 2.)

The most definite claim of the Eastern and Western Miami was recovery of interest on the money that was diverted to the bogus Miami from 1858 to 1867. The Interior Department reported favorably on the claim, and legislation was introduced in Congress from 1909 to 1911. Clerks in the Interior Department calculated the interest owed the Indiana Miami to be $80,715.

Kilsoquah and her son Anthony Rivarre. Kilsoquah named many Miami children and was revered for her great age, although older Miami census rolls indicate she was about 85, not 105, when she died in 1915.

Miami County Historical Society

George Godfroy (1863–1929), chief of the Miami Indians of Indiana in the first quarter of the twentieth century. The tribal council was in session when the war club that Godfroy holds was laid on the table.

Miami County Historical Society

The bill passed the Senate in 1910, but the House failed to vote on it. Richardville died before the bill was reintroduced in 1911, and it was dropped for ten years.[34]

The same year Richardville died, two brothers uncovered Little Turtle's remains while excavating a basement for their house near Fort Wayne. Many of the celebrated chief's prized belongings were carried off, including a pistol presented by Thaddeus Kosciusko and a sword given by President George Washington in 1797.[35] Eventually most of the articles became the property of the Allen County-Fort Wayne Historical Society. Grave desecration was an ongoing problem for the Miami that has continued to the present.

The death of Richardville in 1911 concluded the influence of the generation of leaders from the 1850s. Richardville had been involved in Miami lobbying most of his adult life and had come often to Indiana from Kansas or Indian Territory to testify on legal matters and to visit family. The Western Miami tribe was smaller, and Richardville's role was correspondingly larger. The Indiana leadership used his lobbying expertise but kept him at arm's length, respecting his ability to insinuate himself into tribal affairs at the expense of the local tribespeople.[36]

After Gabriel Godfroy's death the Miami community in Butler Township began to break up. Godfroy had used his property and money to offer refuge to landless Miami for sixty years, and his death hastened the end of the largest rural Miami community. The Indian population dropped from 128 to 64 by 1920, from twenty families to nine, while the Miami population of Peru increased from one family to ten and to 42 people. (See Table 7.1.) By 1920 Indian land ownership in the Peru area had declined to only 449 acres, half of the 907 acres owned in 1900, and equal in size to only one large modern farm. Some Miami from Butler Township moved to Wabash and Huntington. All of the town-dwelling men and several of the women were employed at such diverse jobs as teamster, molder in a foundry, machine operator, carpenter, laundress, and railroader.[37]

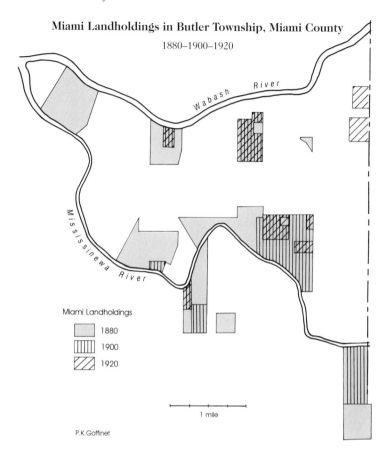

Miami Landholdings in Butler Township, Miami County
1880–1900–1920

The loss of Indian land and population in Butler Township beginning in 1890 coincided with changes in the landscape itself. Much of the Miami land had remained uncleared or only partially cleared. The Wabash floodplain or bottoms was a large wetland, home to migrating waterfowl, muskrats, and other furbearing animals, as well as some considerable dens of tiny massasauga rattlesnakes. Beginning in the 1890s the rich organic land of the bottoms was cleared and ditched for modern commercial farming. As Benjamin Wallace, the Cole family, and other wealthy families purchased and improved the land, erected white fences and large barns, and built several mansions in the countryside, the area took on the appearance of a very prosperous farm district. Several of the Miami bachelors became handymen and caretakers, living in one- or two-room "bachelor houses." By 1920 the changeover from woodsy Indian country to well-tended agricultural land was largely complete, and the few remaining Indian families on their tiny farms were hardly visible.

Most of the Miami who moved to Peru dropped their Indian identity on the 1920 census and called themselves white, even though they had been on the Indian schedules in 1910. Peru was a small city with a large foreign-born population, and it was simpler in those days of prejudice to ignore one's Miami identity before the public at large. Fewer and fewer people identified themselves as Indian across the United States on the eve of legislation in 1924 that made citizens of all Indians. In the 1920 census for Indiana, only 125 people called themselves Indian, the low point since 1850 when Indians were not officially included on the schedules.

The broad tribal coalition led by George Godfroy continued to seek help from the Bureau of Indian Affairs on a variety of problems between 1910 and 1930. Letters were written about Miami being defrauded of land, seeking aid and legal protection for the tribe, and in support of claims legislation. Doubts arose about the legality of the allotment of the Meshingomesia reserve. William Bundy and others complained that "a great many lawyers went to see Meshingomesia" and the local congressman to get legislation passed to divide the land.[38] The realization was sinking in that when non-Indians sought legislation opening access to Miami land or money, it quickly passed Congress, but when the Miami themselves sought legislation to protect their land or legal status, the Interior Department usually reported against it, and it died.

Getting claims legislation passed was becoming more difficult, as the Miami found out in 1921. They got their old bill reintroduced for paying eighty thousand dollars in interest on the annuities diverted in the 1860s, only to have the Interior

Department report to the House Committee on Indian Affairs that the statute of limitations precluded any action on the legislation.[39] If the Miami were to accomplish anything a new direction was needed.

In 1921 the Aetna Insurance Company foreclosed the mortgage on Camillus Bundy's 113-acre farm, the last land remaining from the Ozahshinquah reserve. Ten or twelve family members lived on the farm, and Bundy sued the insurance company for holding a mortgage on Indian land and lost. On 23 September 1923 Bundy called together all the Miami to discuss Miami claims in general and the future of the tribe. Sixty to eighty people attended the meeting, which is now regarded as the beginning of the modern tribal organization, the Miami Nation of Indians of Indiana. Bundy shifted the focus from tax exemption on land grants to general claims based on all the Miami treaties and the subsequent mismanagement of Miami affairs by the federal government. The Indiana Miami were a tribal organization, Bundy insisted, and the United States still had treaty obligations. It was a courageous stand to take in 1923 as it totally contradicted federal policy to assimilate Indians. The Miami served notice in hard times that they were not going to disappear.

EIGHT

Still a Tribe
1923–1945

■

Once having been recognized by the Congress and government of this union, no one has the right to dissolve us and destroy us as a race, but they have been doing so, and are doing so, and through it all we have been reduced to a plight which is a reproach upon this nation. America owes us an obligation. We appeal to you now as its head.

Camillus Bundy to President Calvin Coolidge, 8 June 1927[1]

I have seen many of my people go to their graves still professing that our government would do right by us. They never gave up hope. They were buried in poverty as they lived . . . . Isn't it about time we were recognized?

Mildred Bundy, Meshingomesia Miami, to President Franklin D. Roosevelt, 7 June 1933[2]

BY THE 1920S THE INDIANA MIAMI FACED AN UNCERTAIN future and needed a new direction. George Godfroy and the leaders who had come to power at the beginning of the century had been unable to recover tax exemption on Miami lands or to get a settlement for the interest owed from annuities diverted years earlier. In the fall of 1923, facing the loss of the last of his land and sensing the drift in tribal affairs, Camillus Bundy had sponsored a general meeting of all the Miami at his home near Peoria, Indiana. Bundy's intention was to seek redress of all the Miami grievances that had been building since removal in 1846.

The 1923 meeting is a case study in the Miami political process. Bundy, affectionately known as Kim, was well known to all the Miami, had kinship connections to most, and was asserting a new direction in tribal affairs. Each group of the tribe had to decide where it stood in relation to his initiative and to shape a response that would protect its position. The outcome of the get-together at Bundy's modest home was unexpected. The Godfroy family pulled back. They felt that pressing for a broad group of claims would jeopardize their fight for tax exemption, which they wanted to continue on the last 121 acres they owned. The Meshingomesia Miami, on the other hand, were anxious to join Bundy to push claims, even though they had been made citizens in 1881 and presumably had no legal redress as Indians. The Mongosa family, descendants of Chief Whitewolf (Mongosa), were ancient allies of the Godfroys, but could swing either way, as they had never received treaty land. They found Bundy's call for a new direction appealing. The Richardville and Lafontaine descendants in Huntington and Allen Counties had not been taxed on their lands since the 1880s and thus stood to one side.[3] (See Appendix 1.)

Miami political processes work slowly, especially when faced with major change. Word has to spread through family networks, family elders and leaders need to compare and relate the prospective change to changes made in the past, and the leader proposing the change has to be assessed in terms of staying power and ability to get something done. On a deeper level, kinship ties were important to a leader's influence in Bundy's day, as well as factors hidden from the non-Indian political process such as shamanism and the ability of a leader to communicate with ancestral leaders and perhaps animal spirits. A leader with long experience in tribal affairs, multiple kinship ties, and spiritual powers could reach to the core of the small community and inspire profound loyalty among followers, as well as fear and anger among those who chose not to follow. Camillus Bundy was such a leader.

At the time of the 1923 meeting George Godfroy and the Indiana Miami council led the tribe, but the leadership was becoming moribund. Council members did not challenge Bundy's bold new direction because they had worked with him for years and trusted him. Further, Bundy's brothers and sisters and half brothers and half sisters had married throughout the Godfroy and Meshingomesia leadership, creating close kinship ties. The Godfroy family, however, rebuked Bundy's leadership. Three grandchildren of Gabriel Godfroy owned the last 121 acres of the Godfroy reserve, and they believed that working on claims would compromise their efforts to regain tax exemption on their land. Calling themselves "Individual Miami," because they owned part of an individual treaty grant, they disassociated themselves from general claims.[4] (See Appendix 2.)

In November 1924 Camillus Bundy's farm was sold at a sheriff's sale after he refused to make payments on a mortgage to the Aetna Insurance Company. Bundy sued the company on the basis that treaty land could not be mortgaged, but he lost in circuit court. He filed an appeal in the state appellate court but lost. After refusing to surrender the land, Bundy was ejected by the Wabash County sheriff.[5] His resistance seemed foolish to local whites, but his principled stand raised his status enormously among the many landless Miami.

In order to fight on, the destitute Bundy sold his trove of Miami heirlooms to Milford Chandler, a collector and Indian hobbyist from Chicago.[6] Today they form the core of the Miami collection at the Cranbrook Institute of Science, Bloomfield Hills, Michigan, the Detroit Institute of Art, and the Museum of the American Indian in New York City. Bundy used the proceeds to lobby officials in Washington. In 1925 Bundy and his daughter Victoria ("Dooley") Brady traveled east shortly after the Miami reunion to present a petition for Miami rights to the secretary of the Interior Department. They were informed that since 1897 the Indiana Miami possessed no rights as Indians.[7] Bundy and his daughter persisted, spending every winter in Washington from 1925 to 1929, visiting the Bureau of Indian Affairs, the secretary of the Interior Department, and members of the House Committee on Indian Affairs.

In June 1927 Bundy and his daughter hand delivered a petition to the White House. Bundy took the position that the Miami were recognized under federal law, but

> We have been constantly denied these [treaty] rights by the State of Indiana, and by all the attorneys who have brought suits in every court annulling the rights vested in us by the Congress and Presidents of the United States, which no one or no state has had the warrant for doing.[8]

Commissioner of Indian Affairs Charles Burke replied for the president. Tired by Bundy's persistence, Burke reminded Bundy that he had been informed many times since 1923 that the Miami had no valid claims against the federal government. Then, in a tone of exasperation, he leveled a personal attack against Bundy and his daughter, telling them they were not Indian: "You have less of Indian than of white blood, your lifetime has been spent in a white community, you have control of your own property, and for many years have been citizens of the United States."[9] Burke was asserting the official position that outsiders, not the Indians themselves, would determine who was and who was not Native American.

In 1928 Rep. Edgar Howard of Nebraska introduced a bill in the House conferring jurisdiction on the United States Court of Claims to hear and enter judgment on any claims the Miami Indians of Indiana might have. Sen. William King of Utah, sitting on the judiciary committee, submitted a companion bill to the Senate. Similar in format to many bills introduced for tribes in the 1920s, the proposed legislation used the name "Miami

Nation" for the first time in many years. The bill set aside the statute of limitations and included any legal and equitable claims growing out of any treaty, legislation, or agreement between the United States and the Miami tribe.[10]

The Interior Department was still dominated during the 1920s by the idea that Indians should be forcibly assimilated and was profoundly intolerant of Indian ways or the notion that Indians had rights. Officials routinely took a stance against any Indian claims.[11] Although the department had seen merit in at least one Miami claim in 1910, this time it reported against any tribal claims. The director of the Bureau of the Budget seconded the Interior Department, stating that the proposed legislation was "in conflict with the financial program of the President." The legislation did not pass either house in 1928 or 1929.[12] In the meantime Victoria Brady began a one-person occupation of the Bureau of Indian Affairs. During her last visit to Washington in 1929 she trashed the office of the assistant commissioner of Indian Affairs when he did not find documents she felt would support a claim. She was evicted by security, and a memorandum was circulated through the Bureau of Indian Affairs saying, "She no doubt knows that she cannot succeed in establishing any claim for the Indians, but she likes to stay in Washington—it is so much more pleasant than to stay at home and attend to her household affairs."[13]

After losing his farm, Camillus Bundy, Victoria Brady, and several other family members had spent long periods of time living in tents at the Bundy (or Slocum) cemetery, believing the half acre to be free from seizure. In 1928 the new owner of the farm filed a suit for malicious trespass, and Bundy threatened an "Indian uprising and bloodshed" if the sheriff attempted eviction. When the sheriff showed up with armed deputies, however, Bundy and the others put down their weapons, and he was jailed. When Brady died in 1930, obituaries asserted that the fight for Miami claims was over.[14]

The Miami Community in the 1920s

The Miami economy had been in a depression since the 1870s and worsened with the loss of nearly all Indian-owned land. By 1920 the great majority of the tribespeople had taken refuge in towns and cities on the periphery of the old treaty grants along the Wabash and Mississinewa Rivers, mostly on the points of the triangle formed by Peru, Wabash, and Marion. Most Miami were now small-town or small-city Indians, and tribal social and cultural life and politics reflected their change in location.

Some Miami began moving to the Elkhart-South Bend, Indiana, and Champaign-Urbana, Illinois, areas while others were slowly moving into Fort Wayne. Usually one or two extended families moved to a new location over a period of time, so that the new settlement was a kinship group rather than a mixed group of Miami. The extended families identified closely with one of the former village communities, in this way preserving the original groupings of the tribe. Thus, the Miami in the Miami, Oklahoma, area were mainly from the Richardville-Lafontaine families, those in South Bend from the Meshingomesia reserve, and those in Champaign-Urbana from the descendants of Mazequah who had returned from Kansas after 1846. In the Miami homeland the Godfroy family formed a large majority of the Miami in Peru, while the Bundy and Meshingomesia Miami predominated in Wabash and Marion. The relocation by kin groups rather than individual families showed the continued strength of ethnic boundaries of the Miami. Only a few Miami moved to the larger outlying midwestern cities such as Indianapolis, Chicago, Toledo, or Detroit.

Although the move to nearby towns brought more educational opportunity in the form of high school education, it was an opportunity that few Miami were able to take advantage of until after World War II. Prejudice was a factor in some cases of school dropouts, but the need to help support families was perhaps more important. Butler Township did not get its first high school until 1914 and its first Miami graduate, a young woman, until 1917. The first Miami males in Miami and Wabash Counties to graduate got their diplomas in 1925, one in Butler Township, the other at Peru High School. There were a few graduates during the 1930s, but the great majority of the Miami dropped out of high school at age sixteen (the legal age for leaving school) in their sophomore or junior year.[15]

Circus work became more important to Peru-area Miami during the 1920s. In 1921 three wealthy Indiana circus owners organized the American Circus Corporation (ACC) and added the Yankee Robinson and Sells-Floto Circuses to the Howe's Great London, John Robinson, and Hagenbeck-Wallace Circuses already quartered east of Peru. The ACC bought a fleet of new railcars and sent circuses to all parts of the United States from May to October, challenging the dominance of the Ringling Brothers. The Indiana circus owners emphasized wild animal acts and spectacular street parades. They gathered what was possibly the largest collection of wild animals in the world at their winter quarters on the old Gabriel Godfroy farm—40 elephants, 125 lions and tigers, 30 camels, and numerous ostriches, llamas, zebras, monkeys, pumas, and bears.[16] Miami men and women were employed in a variety of jobs, running concessions, working on the circus farms, feeding and handling animals, and sometimes as performers. The Miami had begun working in circuses in the 1880s, but it was during the 1920s that the circuses reached their height of importance in Butler Township. Older Indians still talk of working with Clyde Beatty, Mabel Stark, Emmett Kelly, Hoot Gibson, and Tom Mix.[17]

The regrouping of Miami in towns on the edge of their former reserves made for easy communication and frequent visits and helped preserve a sense of the tribal past. The Miami reunion, begun in 1903, was an important means for members of every family to keep up with informal tribal news and visits at least once a year, as well as spreading information on legal issues. During the 1920s the reunion grew in importance as a means of unifying the tribe and expressing social and cultural identity as Miami. A tribal council and business meeting was held in the morning, and tribal members were informed of claims legislation and other tribal affairs, as well as of families in need. The reunion became one of the last places where one was likely to hear conversation in the Miami language.[18]

During the 1920s the Maconaquah Pageant was started as a new Miami institution that served several purposes. The pageant was a way of educating the public about Miami history and culture at a time when Indians were looked down upon. The general public assumed the Miami were disappearing, and the pageant was an important means of countering the idea of the "dying Indian." The pageant began about 1924 when the Miami were invited to Greenville, Ohio, for a commemoration of the treaty of 1795. It gained good publicity for the tribe, as well as earning money to pay for attorneys and to support lobbying in Washington, D.C.

On the tribal level the pageant brought old and young Miami together in performances of dances, songs, a wedding, and camp life. Costumes were a mixture of Eastern Woodland and Plains headdresses, old Miami clothing from the fur-trade era, and more modern items reflecting pan-Indian influence. The older members were tribal leaders and storytellers such as Clarence Godfroy, John and Ross Bundy, and Anna Marks. The Miami children learned tribal history and culture while performing, and many went on to become tribal leaders themselves. Up to his death in 1933 John Bundy (Wahcumoh) was an elder who undoubtedly made a strong impression on the young Miami. A gentle man who spoke fluent Miami and heavily accented English, he made bows, taught many boys hunting and fishing techniques, and shared a wealth of stories and Miami lore.

Changeover in Miami Leadership on the Eve of the Great Depression

By the time George Godfroy died in 1929 new leaders had matured, anxious to break the impass of federal law and policy

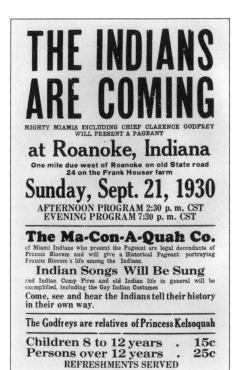

Flier for the Maconaquah Pageant, a popular entertainment and way for the Indiana Miami to "tell their history in their own way."

Stewart Rafert

that denied the existence of the Indiana Miami tribe. The new generation of Miami leaders, like older leaders, had never accepted the loss of federal recognition or treaty rights. They became more aggressive in the face of increasing dependency and social dislocation of the least educated and most conservative Miami and in the face of an increasingly hard line from Washington on claims. Camillus Bundy had set the tone with his totally uncompromising stand on Miami rights, one for which he had sacrificed his well-being.

At the onset of the Great Depression federal policies of allotment and forced assimilation were weakening. During the 1920s it was painfully evident to even the most fervent supporters of allotment that the policy was not working. R. Douglas Hurt, a modern historian of Indian agriculture, has written that allotment placed Indians not on the road of self-sufficiency, but on the road to peonage.[19] Indians were not becoming farmers or ranchers, and tribes had lost over half their land. Tribes such as the Eastern and Western Miami, whose lands were allotted earlier, had lost virtually all their land. Indians were poorer and more dependent than ever, and highly demoralized as well. Traditional tribal governments with broad support from tribespeople had been denied any legal standing and were replaced with business committees handpicked by Indian agents to rubber-stamp coal and oil leases for the Interior Department.

In 1926 the Bureau of Indian Affairs commissioned Dr. Lewis Meriam to direct an in-depth study of Indian problems. The report, which appeared in 1928 as *The Problem of Indian Administration*, provided many details on the shocking and deplorable conditions endured by Native Americans. Allotment and the resulting loss of Indian land was singled out as the main cause of Indian poverty. The land of the Miami of Indiana had been allotted, and the Miami people had been freed from federal supervision for a number of years, but they suffered many of the same economic difficulties as reservation tribes, as well as poor health and extremely low levels of formal education.

Camillus Bundy, seventy-five years old and racked with arthritis, retired from actively pursuing Miami claims after the death of his daughter in 1930. Elijah Marks was named chief and David Bondy secretary-treasurer of the Indiana Miami tribe. Marks was a grandson of Chapendoceoh, one of Meshingomesia's brothers, and as a child had received an allotment from the reserve. He bore the Miami name Mecatamungwah (Black Loon), the name of a respected Miami chief who died in the 1840s. Bondy was Camillus Bundy's son and had attended the Carlisle Indian school near Harrisburg, Pennsylvania. The tribal organization that had matured under Camillus Bundy's leadership since 1923 took over immediately when he stepped down. Regular council minutes were kept, and meetings were held frequently in Marion. The new activists were in their forties and fifties and were

Maconaquah Pageant Players, ca. 1933. A few whites joined the Miami players, portraying historic figures such as George W. Ewing.

Wabash County Historical Society

Spectators watching the Maconaquah Pageant.

Miami County Historical Society

plainspoken. Letter after letter was sent to Washington, probing various treaties, federal Indian law, Supreme Court decisions, and the allotment of the Meshingomesia reserve. The shotgun approach worked, for it forced the Bureau of Indian Affairs to go over past treatment of the tribe and, in effect, to conduct a correspondence course with the leaders, educating them on what had been done.

The professionalization of state agencies at the time the Miami were losing their land and rights had created new issues by the 1930s. Licensing of hunters in Indiana began in 1899, but game wardens exempted the Miami population along the rivers with the understanding that they were engaged in subsistence activities. In 1919 the Indiana Department of Conservation was created, and game wardens were empowered to serve warrants for the arrest of people violating fish and game laws. Although many Miami did not buy licenses they were allowed to spear and net fish and to hunt animals out of season in their customary hunting and fishing areas. By the early 1930s this informal system of Indian rights was breaking down, and the Miami themselves were beginning to openly challenge game laws that restricted treaty rights. There were some arrests, but for the time being cases were dismissed, and the skirmishes did not evolve into full-scale legal tests of Miami game rights.[20]

A more serious matter was the tightening of state adoption laws and the development of county social services. In the past, Miami children were adopted informally. By the 1920s such adoptions were not permitted, and social workers intruded on the Miami community and began removing children from family situations deemed unsuitable. Instead of being placed locally some children were sent to Chicago, southern Michigan, and other distant places. Others were placed in orphanages. The Miami did not challenge the practice at the time—there was no legal basis for doing so as a tribe—but the removal of children from their community increased the sense of powerlessness among tribespeople. Adoptees who found out

Clarence Mongosa, a Miami performer. His headdress combines the vertical feathers of Eastern Woodland tribes with trailing feathers of Plains tribes. His Miami name "Kin-no-zaz-yeah" is inscribed at the left.

Miami County Historical Society

Carmen Ryan in costume for a pageant performance, 22 August 1926.

Miami County Historical Society

years later that they were Miami reacted with rage over being taken from their cultural background and being deprived of their Indian heritage.[21]

By the early 1930s the plight of many Miami people was desperate. Cong. Glenn Griswold wrote the Bureau of Indian Affairs in early 1932 asking for relief for the Miami Indians "as there are many that are entirely destitute and in great need."[22] In September 1933 Elijah Shapp put matters more bluntly: "We the Miami Indians of Indiana want our land and money that is due us, we want action in the next regular session of Congress. My people are starving."[23]

The New Deal and the Formation of the Miami Nation

With the arrival of the New Deal, outworn and destructive federal Indian policies were quickly reversed or blunted in what has come to be known as the "Indian New Deal." President Franklin D. Roosevelt appointed Harold Ickes secretary of the Interior Department and John Collier commissioner of Indian Affairs. Both men had led the American Indian Defense Association during the 1920s and were experts on Indian affairs. They were anxious to extend reforms begun under the Herbert Hoover administration and to try new directions in Indian policy. Collier in particular believed strongly in the ability of tribes to manage their own affairs if they had control of their resources and an adequate land base. The year after Roosevelt assumed office many of the policy changes suggested in the Meriam Report of 1928 were incorporated in the landmark Wheeler-Howard or Indian Reorganization Act of 1934. The IRA, as it came to be known, was the first general reshaping of Indian law since the Omnibus Indian Act of 1834, a hundred years earlier. Under the IRA allotment of Indian land was ended and Indian policy was redirected toward stabilizing and rebuilding Indian communities.[24]

The Eastern Miami learned quickly that the Indian New Deal was restricted to federally recognized tribes. All benefits and legal protections were denied to all Native American groups not formally recognized by the Bureau of Indian Affairs as a tribe or band. Collier did not want this restriction, but it was included in order to get the IRA through Congress. Elijah Shapp wrote Secretary Ickes shortly after the inauguration in 1933 that "we [the Indiana Miami] still remain a tribe" and asked for legal protection. Ickes sent the tribe a memorandum from Collier to the effect that the previous administration had made an extensive review of Miami claims and "The affairs of these Indians, both tribal and individual, have all been definitely closed out years ago."[25] The Western Miami, who had written three times between 1911 and 1928 concerning claims

John Bundy at a pageant in the late 1920s a few years before his death. The mild-mannered Bundy was fluent in the Miami language and was a hunter, fisherman, and storyteller who was popular with all Miami people.

Miami County Historical Society

John Newman, a Delaware Indian who lived among the Miami, July 1933. Newman lived on the last 8 acres of 550 acres alloted his Miami wife and children in 1873. His propped-up cabin was a survivor of reservation days. Born about 1845, he was long known as the oldest Indian in Indiana when he died in 1939.

Wabash County Historical Society

and legislation, were likewise told that their affairs had "all been disposed of by Congress and the courts."[26]

Shapp and other angry Miami were no more deterred by Collier's denial of tribal rights than they were by earlier commissioners of Indian Affairs. "We the Miami Indians of Indiana want our land and money," wrote Shapp. "We have been swindled out of both by mismanagement of Indian affairs."[27] Mildred Bundy wrote the president, asking

> Have you ever heard of the Miami Indians? No doubt there are many there in Washington who have not. For years we have been forgotten, thrown aside as something not worth noticing.... Other Indians have their compensations—why should we be left out. For many years we have waited, trusting for a fair deal. We are poor and we shouldn't be. We were robbed.[28]

The tribe held several general meetings concerning claims during the 1930s. The general meeting evolved from what the Miami used to call a general council, an open meeting of tribal members at which business was discussed. Tribal population was estimated at about 750, with half that number living near Peru, Wabash, and Marion. Awareness of the Miami as an Indian tribe within the state rose dramatically during the 1930s, and newspapers in Indianapolis, Fort Wayne, and South Bend reprinted reports on claims meetings, fishing violations, efforts to protect cemeteries, and obituaries of prominent Miami leaders.

Living conditions for the Miami continued to deteriorate during the 1930s. Many of those who had been working in the factories of Marion, Wabash, and Peru were laid off, and there was little land on which to take refuge. A Peru-area Miami described the situation of many when he wrote in 1934, "The white man has taken our land and most of the wild game and that dont leave us Indians any way to live as they are just as clanish t[o]ward us as they ever was thoe we[']re not all full bluds."[29] By 1930 the Miami in Butler Township owned only 311 acres, most in small holdings in the eastern part of the township. (See map on p. 202.) The Bundy and the Meshingomesia Miami owned almost no land. The families who had small landholdings offered what help they could. One family had large "feeds" on Sundays, others took firewood and food into town for the elderly, and many Miami men got what they could hunting and fishing. Arrests for spearfishing became more common as the decade wore on. Families returned to foraging for greens, wild fruits, and nuts and shared what they could. Men and boys sold furs, and families gathered medicinal plants for sale to homeopathic druggists for small bits of cash. The Miami continued their own "doctoring," midwives still delivered some babies, and the Miami buried a few of their dead on their own.[30]

During the 1920s the circuses had become a major source of part-time employment for Miami near Peru, but circus work was affected by the depression as well. In 1929, on the eve of the stock market crash, John Ringling bought the Indiana circuses and by 1933 was nearly bankrupt. During the 1930s the circuses offered less employment to the Miami and sometimes had to return from the road early due to lack of business. By the end of 1938 all the big rail circuses had folded, including the upstart Cole Brothers Circus that had a highly successful run in 1937.

As members of a nonrecognized tribe, the Eastern Miami were faced with a double disability during the depression. The state of Indiana refused help because they were Indians, while the Bureau of Indian Affairs would not help because they were not Indians, legally speaking. During the 1930s the economic situation of many reservation tribes improved dramatically with the aid of the Indian New Deal, but the Miami existed in a kind of legal limbo that made their situation worse. They lived in a nearly cashless society that pushed self-reliance, even for Indians, to its limit. In one telling instance, a father was upset because his daughter had given her only pencil to a schoolmate since the father had no money to replace it.[31]

The Baptist church on the former Meshingomesia reservation as it appeared in 1936. The Miami warned off non-Indians but lacked the legal means to protect the building.

Wabash County Historical Society

Durand Godfroy wrestling a steer near Noblesville, Indiana, 1938. The Miami sometimes assumed the roles of cowboys, imitating Hoot Gibson, Tom Mix, and other stars of the Wild West shows attached to the circuses.

Swan Hunter

Camillus Bundy died in January 1935. Born in 1854, the year of the last Indiana Miami treaty, he had grown to manhood during the stable years of tribal consolidation after removal. His education in tribal rights had come from his father Peter Bondy, Pimyotamah, and Meshingomesia, men who had negotiated directly with federal officials since the 1840s. He had passed this knowledge directly to the leaders coming to power in the 1930s—his sons David and Charles Zimmerle (C. Z.) Bondy, Elijah Shapp and his brothers, and Elijah Marks. After this period of tutelage from 1925 to 1930 Bundy stepped aside.

Bundy was also a shaman, inheritor from his mother Ozahshinquah of many of the older Miami beliefs in animal spirits. His belief that he could communicate with ancestral leaders protected him from humiliation and gave him courage in the face of threats, sometimes physical, as well as a stubborn persistence and a deep sense of humor. These beliefs he shared with younger leaders as well. He was a bridge between the past and the future, lending a consistency to Miami intentions that went far beyond changes in federal policy. It was the Miami way of governing and thinking, an ethos that predated the formation of the American government itself.[32]

The Quest for Federal Recognition

Through the early 1930s the Indiana Miami employed Charles Z. Bondy to get help with various claims without success. Bondy had a difficult, if not impossible, assignment, and he was also handicapped by a nearly total lack of formal education. In 1936 the tribe found a tireless and effective lobbyist in the improbable person of Nettie B. White, a minister with her husband in a small spiritualist church in Wabash. A few Miami were in the congregation, and she took a sympathetic interest in their legal plight.

White began as many had done before, writing letters protesting the Miami situation and asking for help. Next, she was signed on as "attorney in fact," a familiar step. Unlike previous people with intentions of helping the Miami, she went a step further and filed every document with the Interior Department. She then visited Washington with an attorney from Indiana and went directly to the officials who could do the tribe the most good.

In the summer of 1937 White met with D'Arcy McNickle, a Flathead Indian anthropologist who was also John Collier's assistant in the Tribal Organization Branch of the Bureau of Indian Affairs. McNickle was the right person to see. He immediately asked for reports on the Indiana Miami tribe from J. M. Stewart, director of lands, and from the assistant solicitor for the Interior Department, Charlotte Westwood. The reports of both officials stated the familiar, that all treaty obligations to the tribe had been satisfied.[33] Despite these discouraging reports, White replied that the Indiana Miami sought federal recognition as a tribe under provisions of the IRA and wished to be placed on a reservation.[34]

White's activities after her Washington trip strongly suggest that McNickle gave her some concrete advice on the next step to take. She met with the tribal council in Marion, and plans for a formal organization and a state charter of the tribe moved quickly. On 18 July a charter and bylaws very similar to those adopted by tribes adopting provisions of the IRA were approved by the tribal council. These documents were sent to the Indiana secretary of state and were approved on 30 September 1937. In the meantime the Miami Nation of Indians of the State of Indiana, as the new formal organization was called, notified the president of the United States, the secretary of the Interior Department, and the commissioner of Indian Affairs of its activities.[35]

Both McNickle and William Zimmerman, assistant commissioner of Indian Affairs who was an Indianapolis attorney before his appointment, cautioned the Miami Nation that the incorporation itself would not convey federal recognition of the tribe without congressional legislation.[36] The Miami Nation already had a new claims bill introduced in the third session of the 75th Congress on 5 January 1938. The bill stated tribal claims as broadly as possible, along the lines of the 1928 legislation. The Interior Department prepared a report favorable to the legislation with the suggestion that the bill should be broadened "to include the so-called Western Miamis; i.e., those in Oklahoma who belong to the same tribe and have an interest in this claim founded on early treaties and negotiations with the Miami Indians."[37] The Western Miami had not presented any claims since the days of Thomas Richardville thirty years earlier. In this instance the Bureau of Indian Affairs did not want the Eastern Miami to move ahead of their western cousins in claims that would apply equally to both groups.

The 1938 legislation did not pass Congress and was reintroduced in the 76th Congress in 1939. The Interior Department asked that the claims be narrowed to the old claim of interest on money that was wrongfully paid out from 1858 to 1867 and that the Western Miami be included. At the same time the Miami tribe petitioned the Bureau of Indian Affairs for approval of an attorney's contract for representation in claims. Collier sent specific instructions explaining how to organize a meeting for selecting an attorney, along with sample tribal resolutions for designating power of attorney as a tribe. On 4 June 1939 the Miami Nation held a general meeting at Memorial Hall in Wabash that was well advertised in various newspapers and over several radio stations to discuss the matter of attorneys and to vote on a selection. Forty-seven adults attended from every Miami group.[38]

Hearings were held before the House Committee on Indian Affairs on the Miami bill, H.R. 2306, during the spring of 1939. The Interior Department reported unfavorably on Miami claims this time. Meanwhile, Zimmerman wrote the superintendent of the Quapaw Agency to inform him of the extensive claims activity of the Eastern Miami. Noting that the Indiana tribe was likely to continue to assert claims in which the Oklahoma Miami had an interest, Zimmerman suggested that the latter tribe should be given an opportunity to employ attorneys if they so desired.[39]

Harley T. Palmer had been chief of the Western Miami since 1910. The tribe had no land or tribal funds but did have limited health services after 1926. In October 1939 the tribe ratified a tribal constitution and bylaws that set up a business committee under the Oklahoma Indian Welfare Act, which brought the three hundred-person group under the provisions of the IRA as a federally recognized tribe.[40] All claims activity since the death of Thomas Richardville in 1911 had come from the Indiana tribe, and the IRA charter permitted the Oklahoma sister tribe to participate as an equal. In January 1940 the Western Miami held a meeting at which they approved the attorneys chosen by their eastern brethren. The persistence of the Indiana Miami was paying off for both tribes.[41]

The Miami claims legislation was introduced and failed to pass every year from 1938 to 1942, usually torpedoed—to use a metaphor of the time—by a small group of congressmen who sank similar legislative efforts by the Mississippi Choctaw and other tribes year in and year out.[42] When it was introduced in 1941, the Interior Department prepared a lengthy "Memorandum of Information" on both Miami tribes that for the first time was defensive in tone regarding treatment of the Indiana tribe. Regarding the treaty of 1854, whoever wrote the report stated there was no evidence it was an "unconscionable agreement or that the Miami Indians were overreached when their consent was obtained to a capitalization of their perpetual annuity." As to protection of Miami land in Indiana from loss through local taxation, the report used Willis Van Devanter's 1897 opinion as evidence that the tribe was no longer under federal Indian law. The conclusion followed that "the charge that the United States has failed to protect the Indiana Miamis from taxation or other involuntary alienation of their lands, when no duty so to do existed, is not well made."[43]

The Indiana Miami were living personally and on a daily basis with the results of the loss of their land and federal status, and denial of federal responsibility in the matter did not make their problems go away. Throughout the 1930s arrests for spearfishing and hunting out of season increased. In 1937 the Indiana legislature recodified and greatly extended the scope of all game laws. Game wardens were authorized to search the persons, vehicles, coats, and containers of hunters and fishermen and to enter private property (except dwellings) to find evidence of violation of game laws.[44] During 1939 six Miami men were charged with fishing offenses and one man with a game offense.

One such case reached federal court in South Bend. Frank Marks was arrested and convicted in 1938 for taking a wild raccoon and keeping it as a pet in violation of conservation laws. Marks was convicted and fined ten dollars, but he refused to pay the fine on the grounds that a justice of the peace did not have jurisdiction because Marks was a Miami Indian. The case was moved to federal court in South Bend. The judge did not question Miami game rights themselves, but narrowed the decision to the status of Frank Marks as an Indian. During the trial Marks dropped dead of a heart attack. The judge, however, entered an opinion because of the importance of the case to the state of Indiana. The court found that the 1872 legislation that made citizens of the Meshingomesia Miami "abrogated all former treaties affecting the Miami Indians of Indiana."[45]

The Interior Department kept an eye on the Marks decision and mentioned it in the unfavorable report on Miami claims in 1941. Federal policy toward the Indiana Miami had reached closed-system status, with Congress refusing to pass claims legislation because the Interior Department recommended against it. The Interior Department based its overall adverse stance on Miami claims on 1872 legislation that applied to only part of the tribe, the courts interpreted Miami status based on the department's negative finding on Miami legal status, and the department then used adverse decisions to buttress its negative stance. The same circuitous thinking was applied to many claims nationally. Despite the advances of many reservation tribes under the IRA and the Indian New Deal, Indian policy had reached a dead end when it came to claims.

The Indiana Miami did not gain recognition of claims or of treaty rights by the eve of World War II. Beginning with the Roosevelt administration and John Collier's Indian New Deal, however, federal Indian policy had begun to change in favor of tribal interests. The Miami tribe created a formal organization and a state charter in 1937 and succeeded in getting attorneys to prosecute claims, if the enabling legislation could be passed. The Interior Department notified the Western Miami that claims in which they would have a part could be upcoming. The fact that Miami legislation did not pass is unremarkable and does not discredit Miami efforts. Congress was not yet ready to look at Indian claims in general. When that time came after the end of the war, the Eastern and Western Miami were ready to go forward.

While Miami efforts to gain legal status as a tribe were heroic during the 1930s, the stubborn resistance of the federal government to Miami pleas left the Miami people mired, for the most part, in poverty and without hope of improvement. World War II brought an improvement in economic conditions, but the denial of tribal legitimacy left a legacy of rage among many Miami people over unfulfilled promises.

The entry of the United States into World War II in December 1941 put Indian problems on the back burner. The Bureau of Indian Affairs itself was stripped of personnel for other departments of government and was moved to Chicago for the remainder of the war. The Miami Nation passed a council resolution supporting the American war effort and ceased claims lobbying.

In 1944 Grant County officials sold the acre of land on which Meshingomesia's school and Baptist church had stood. The cemetery next to the church was subject to vandalism. The tribe had marked posted signs around the cemetery and on the church building saying, "Warning. No Trespassing. Sacred Indian Grounds." The land had always been tax exempt, and a sheriff's sale for delinquent taxes seemed highly irregular. The Miami Nation protested and was told by the Bureau of Indian Affairs that since the Miami Indians of Indiana were not a tribe, the federal government could not render assistance. A local farmer carted off the school building and turned it into a corn-crib. Despite efforts to protect it, the church succumbed to vandalism and disappeared within a few years. Vandals slipped into the Meshingomesia cemetery at some point and broke up most of the grave markers with sledgehammers.[46] While the Miami were fighting for American rights overseas the United States was not ready to acknowledge Miami rights at home.

NINE

Landless Miami and Claims
1946–1977

■

We have preserved our identity as Miamis.

Ira Sylvester "Ves" Godfroy, deposition before
Indian Claims Commission, 26 June 1954.[1]

The attorney general figures I'm old, nobody to carry on, they'll hold off as long as they can and I'll die, and it'll drop, that's what they're figurin' on.

Oliver Godfroy, concerning federal court case on
tax exemption of treaty land, 7 August 1977.[2]

DISTANT FOREIGN WARS HAVE ALWAYS HAD A MAJOR IMPACT on American Indian life, and World War II was no exception. During the war twenty-five thousand Indians from federally recognized tribes served in the armed forces as well as many more Indians from unrecognized tribes. For reservation Indians service in the military was a major break with the past, with daily competition with whites and with respect for their reputation as warriors. For nonreservation Indians like the Miami the change was similar to that of other Americans who were able to work after years of unemployment and who left small communities for the world at large. Indian fighting men were invariably called "chief" by their buddies, and the nickname was often the only reminder of the tribal community they had left behind.[3]

Support of the American war effort had not come easily for the Indiana Miami. For forty years tribal leaders had been battling to regain their treaty rights, a struggle that had grown increasingly desperate with the loss of tribal land and the pauperization of the community. In the midst of the war, land on which the Indian Village Baptist Church had stood was sold at tax auction, although the land was tax exempt. This was another vivid reminder of continuing injustices. With the end of the war in 1945 the tribal leaders were ready to resume their efforts to win awards for land claims and to reestablish their federal rights as a tribe.

The countryside along the upper Wabash to which war veterans returned was changing rapidly after World War II. The mixed farming that had absorbed Indian lands since the Civil War was giving way to corn and soybean monoculture, and farms were becoming larger. As livestock disappeared from the land fences were pulled up, fields enlarged, and barns and other outbuildings fell into disrepair. The countryside took on a more open and less tidy look. By the end of the war the Miami were virtually landless. Only about 150 acres remained in Indian ownership in a few small plots east of Peru, and the rural Miami population had dwindled to a handful of families. The last crop of the soft white Miami corn was put out to dry on platforms at the end of the war, and thus died another part of Miami culture.

The Wabash and the Mississinewa Rivers were heavily polluted by factory effluents and farm runoff, the Mississinewa so much so that by the 1950s the fish tasted bad. Both rivers had lost much of their variety of fish, while migratory birds suffered from the results of the spraying of DDT and the loss of wetlands. Furbearing animals were largely hunted out. The wildlife in the countryside had declined with the Miami, who were now town and city dwellers working in shops, factories, and on the railroads.

After World War II there was a pronounced shift in federal Indian policy. Impressed by the service of many Indians in the war, liberals and conservatives joined hands in an effort to once again forcibly assimilate Indians into American society. Settling all past claims of Indian tribes was seen as a means of ending the reservation system and breaking down the barriers between Indians and non-Indians. For nonreservation Indians, settling claims was seen as a way to close the door on past injustices.[4] Consistent with earlier reform efforts, Indians were not consulted about this major change in policy.

Tiring of New Deal reforms that had strengthened tribes, Congress responded to liberal and conservative lobbying to "mainstream" Native Americans by passing the Indian Claims Commission Act in 1946. The legislation created a three-person board to review all grievances against the federal government arising before 1946. Congress allowed the commission ten years to examine all claims against the United States and set attorneys' fees at 10 percent of settlements, for decades the traditional "cut" for Indian awards.[5]

The standards of proof for tribes were high. Indian claimants were required to prove "exclusive occupancy" of a definable territory since "time immemorial." If successful the commission would then determine a value for the land at the time it was taken and arrive at a settlement. No interest or allowance for inflation was permitted, and land could not be returned to claimants.[6] In short there was to be no encouragement of tribal sovereignty in the claims process. Rather, it was believed that a careful review of claims and the making of awards would prepare tribes to give up tribal rights, which both liberals and conservatives believed kept Indians in a separate and unequal status under American law. Better, they reasoned, that Indians should be made equal under the law with all other Americans.

The Eastern Miami were fully prepared to present claims under early-nineteenth-century treaties when the Indian Claims Commission was set up in 1946. Since the turn of the century they had been seeking interest on the annuities that had been taken wrongfully in the 1850s and 1860s. They were also anxious to reclaim taxes they felt had been levied wrongfully on treaty grants. During the 1930s the Miami had come to question the allotment of the Meshingomesia reservation and had sought to regain federal status as an Indian tribe.

The hodgepodge of Miami claims had to be adjusted to the narrow limits of the Indian Claims Commission Act, which focused on fair payment for land under various treaties. The task of defining Miami claims and presenting them to the ICC required the hiring of attorneys. In 1943 the Godfroys were again disputing the payment of taxes on the remaining eighty acres of their original treaty grant. After losing in federal court the Godfroys joined the League of Nations of North American Indians and secured the help of Frank Tom-Pee-Saw, the secretary of the organization. Tom-Pee-Saw (sometimes known as Frank Kirk), a self-taught, jack-of-all-trades activist residing in Parsons, Kansas, had previously tried to assist the Prairie Potawatomi and other tribes with various claims.[7]

With the encouragement of Frank Tom-Pee-Saw the Godfroy family formally organized a tribal council in March 1944, which they styled the "Francis Godfroy Band of Miami Indians."[8] Fond of writing multipage letters of detailed advice, Tom-Pee-Saw did not have the legal expertise to handle a complex claims case, but he could encourage the Miami and suggest attorneys. As it was he hectored and cajoled federal officials for years on behalf of the Miami, always sharing advice when the tribal council became frustrated with their expert claims attorneys.

Miami Claims Activities, 1946–1964

Federal Indian law and legislation had created a complex weave of legal precedent and legislation that often affected groups within a tribe in different ways. Hard as it is to understand, the law for people within the same tribe, even within a small tribe, often varied. In the past some land was communal, some was not; some Indians were citizens, others were not; the federal government recognized some chiefs as legal representatives, while the tribe insisted on other leaders. Although the Indiana Miami were not federally recognized, such differences in earlier treatment of groups within the tribe had created a good deal of tension and confusion. Some leaders felt that pressing for full rights would compromise the limited rights they had as owners of treaty land, while other leaders felt that nothing could be achieved without full recognition of treaty rights. Discussion of the fine points of Indian law at tribal meetings could quickly turn both abstract and acrimonious. While the following account of the claims process may strain the reader's patience, the Miami Indians involved were pushed beyond patience as frustration and anger mounted over a process that promised much and produced little, and that only after a very long wait.

The council of the Miami Nation was inactive for the duration of the Second World War. In August 1945 Ira Sylvester "Ves" Godfroy became chairman of the Godfroy council, which also referred to itself as the Indiana Miami council. A burly sixty-year-old railroader and bachelor, Ves Godfroy was well liked and respected among all branches of the Miami tribe. He had the added strength of widespread kinship ties within the tribe as well. Under Godfroy's leadership a search was begun for attorneys to prosecute Miami claims. The tribal council was well aware of the provisions of the Indian Claims Commission Act and intended to make full use of them.

In November 1947 the council voted to include all Miami on the 1895 tribal roll and their descendants in any potential award from the ICC.[9] This crucial vote was essential in securing the support of the members of the Miami Nation and in avoiding competition from the leadership of the group, even though the Nation was dormant as an organization. As it was, two council members had served on the council of the Nation during the 1930s. Leaders of the Miami Nation, trusting Godfroy's leadership of the claims process and not wishing to confuse matters, held off reactivating their charter. As had happened in the past, a portion of the tribe had let another portion of the tribe take the leadership on an issue and had cooperated so long as there were no problems.

In 1948 the Godfroy council chose Ves Godfroy, William Allola Godfroy, and John A. Owens as plaintiffs for the tribe in any claims petition. On 31 October 1949 a contract was signed by the plaintiffs with attorney Walter A. Maloney of Washington, D.C., to prosecute claims. As a further sign that the organization represented all Indiana Miami, the tribal organization was hereafter called the "Miami Indians of Indiana."[10] This was the same name Camillus Bundy had used for the tribal organization he led after 1923. The name had become defunct in 1937 when the Miami Nation was chartered and was revived by the Miami in the Peru area as a symbol of the legitimacy of their claims leadership. Though outsiders were often confused by these shifting tribal organizations, the Miami themselves never were.

In July 1950 the Western Miami, centered about Miami, Oklahoma, filed an attorney's contract for claims based on the

Ira Sylvester "Ves" Godfroy, leader of Miami claims before the Indian Claims Commission until his death in 1961.

Louise Hay

same treaties as Indiana Miami claims. The parallel Eastern and Western Miami claims based on the St. Mary's Treaty of 1818 became known as Dockets 124 and 67 before the ICC. During the five-year period allowed for the filing of claims the Eastern Miami filed eleven claims and the Western Miami nine. The ICC dismissed one claim of each tribe and consolidated some of the others to simplify the cases.[11]

The United States Department of Justice took an adversarial stand toward Indian claims in general and repeatedly sought delays and extensions of hearings. Government land experts tried to assess property at its lowest potential value, and government records were combed for every expense connected with treaties, which was then deducted as an offset to the claim. As mentioned earlier, legislation prevented the return of any land to the tribes, nor was the interest on awards allowed. Finally, no adjustment was permitted for inflation from the time of the original treaty. Such strict legal and fiscal prudence later sowed seeds of dissatisfaction among the tribes with the whole process.[12] Attorneys cautioned the Miami not to expect any awards for ten to fifteen years. As it turned out their estimates were overly optimistic.

Overlapping Indian claims in the Western Great Lakes-Ohio valley region were among the most complex faced by the ICC. As soon as the Miami claims were filed the Delaware, Potawatomi, Kickapoo, and Six Nations Iroquois filed counterclaims to Indiana land.[13] Anthropologist Erminie Wheeler-Voegelin organized the Great Lakes-Ohio Valley Project at Indiana University to assist claimants. The blending of historical research within the framework of anthropology encouraged the formation of a new field of study known as ethnohistory. Dr. Wheeler-Voegelin was the first editor of the journal of the new American Society for Ethnohistory, published at Indiana University beginning in 1954. She was fully aware of Miami history and wrote an ethnohistorical report on the tribe.[14] Her husband Carl F. Voegelin, a distinguished linguist, had edited the Jacob P. Dunn Miami dictionary for publication in the late 1930s.[15]

The claims process forced the Bureau of Indian Affairs to interact with the Indiana Miami as a tribe for the first time since 1897. The bureau was required to approve an attorney's contract with the tribe, prepare tribal rolls for the distribution of awards, and manage funds for minors. At first the Claims Commission was reluctant to recognize the Indiana Miami as a tribal group, preferring to work through the federally recognized Western Miami tribe. Indiana Miami leaders rightfully feared their interests would not be properly represented by a third party and asked for recognition of their tribal body as a legitimate plaintiff. In 1958 the ICC belatedly recognized the Miami of Indiana as an organized entity (i.e., tribe) having the capacity to present claims. In 1959 the United States Court of Claims referred to the Miami Tribe of Indiana in its decision as well, further strengthening de facto recognition of the Eastern Miami tribe.[16] While such limited recognition had no effect on de jure or legal recognition of the tribe under federal Indian law, it heightened the sense of tribal pride among the Miami.

The Indiana Miami functioned as a tribe during the claims process as it had in the two generations since loss of federal recognition in 1897. The council met regularly and sponsored at least one large general meeting a year to keep the membership informed of the progress on claims. Although the Miami were not required to prepare a tribal roll, secretary Eva Bossley did so. The first enrollment, completed in January 1964, contained 1,016 names. It was an impressive effort by a volunteer staff who paid all expenses out of pocket. The tribe also had to fend off "wanna-bes," people who thought they had a Miami ancestor and who wished to share in the claims awards. Such people were politely but firmly informed they were not Miami, testimony to the Miami awareness of their tribal identity and the maintenance of tribal boundaries. Carmen Ryan had a sophisticated knowledge of tribal history and was able to fend off the attempt of a large group of Wea descendants in Indiana to get on the claims rolls. She suggested changes in Wea claims legislation to include the descendants who had never left Indiana for Missouri and Kansas in the 1820s.[17]

In the summer of 1953 attorneys for the tribe took depositions from a number of older Miami concerning tribal life and customs. Intended to demonstrate activities on the land, the interviews also showed how the Miami perceived themselves. Born from 1868 to 1900 the interviewees had a vivid memory of county taxation of Miami land as a breach of treaty rights. They recalled the importance of earlier leaders such as Meshingomesia, Peter Bondy, and Gabriel Godfroy. Descendants of leaders easily recalled genealogy back to the late eighteenth century. Gabriel Godfroy was recalled for his hospitality to the destitute families who returned to Indiana after removal in 1846. All the deponents remembered tribal councils and social gatherings held continuously up to the present.[18]

The 1953 interviews also reflected aspects of Miami culture, though they were not asked for. Ross Bundy testified that he had spoken the Miami language until recent years, when he became one of the last people able to carry on a conversation. Ves Godfroy summed up the essence of the testimony when he said:

> We have preserved our identity as Miamis. There were and are others who joined in the work. It has been a means of keeping our people interested and has helped to preserve the traditions of our great tribe. [The Miami] have made progress and we are proud to say they are nearly all good people. A few do not yet consider themselves citizens because of their devotion to their tribe.[19]

In 1957 the Miami tribe sponsored a vote on a government offer of seventy-five cents an acre for land ceded under the St. Mary's Treaty of 1818. The ICC found the government had paid a total of only six cents an acre for the 4,291,500-acre

"New Purchase" in central Indiana. About four hundred Miami met at Peru and voted to accept the offer. Ves Godfroy insisted that this offer was not enough and, exercising his leadership, remanded the vote and asked for a new offer. The Claims Commission reevaluated its findings and on 30 June 1960 revised its offer upward to $1.15 an acre for a total increase of $1,716,600. The final Miami award was $4,935,225 which, after attorneys' fees and nineteenth-century annuities were deducted, amounted to $1,215 per person. The Miami were awarded an additional $64,739 of the total money stipulated in the treaty of 1854, which was never paid out. This small award deserves notice because in the forty years following the loss of federal recognition Miami leaders had asked many times about money remaining on account in the United States Treasury from the treaty settlement and were always told there was none. Following the award Congress appropriated funding in 1966, and distribution was held off until completion of a new tribal roll in 1969.[20]

In February 1961 Ves Godfroy died. Under his respected leadership the tribe had navigated the claims process for fifteen years and had made notable progress. His Miami name, Metocina (Indian, literally "the living"), was also the name of Meshingomesia's father, who had died in 1832. This was a factor in Godfroy's acceptance by the Meshingomesia Miami. During his tenure the Miami Nation had remained quiescent, confident in his leadership.

Immediately after Godfroy's death a leadership struggle erupted within the tribe. William F. Hale (Mongonzah) sponsored an election of himself as chief with a new council meeting in Marion while the Indiana Miami council in Peru elected Lawrence Godfroy (Lumkekumwah) as council chairman. While Hale had been active with the Miami Nation briefly in the late 1930s, he was never on the council or in a leadership position. Most of his adult life he lived in Muncie and was not generally known among tribespeople. Lawrence Godfroy, a

Ross Bundy, the last fluent speaker of Miami. A year before his death in 1963, the Bureau of Ethnology of the Smithsonian Institution invited him to make recordings of his language, but he was too ill to travel to Washington, D.C.

Herman Bundy

Clarence Godfroy, a popular storyteller. His barn near Rich Valley, Wabash County, is lettered with his Miami name, "Looking over the Top." Photo taken in 1957.

Wabash County Historical Society

younger brother of Ves Godfroy, was also less active in tribal affairs as a young man and had lived for years in Indianapolis.

With two little-known men vying for leadership, confusion resulted within the Miami membership and among the public at large. One newspaper picked up old stereotypes and declared the Miami Indians were "on [the] Warpath over Title," and told of "warring" within the tribe over the rightful chief.[21] There were now two chiefs and two councils competing with each other.

While the Miami Indians of Indiana (the Peru council) signed a new contract with claims attorneys in May 1961, William Hale declared that all Miami Indians had to register with the "Indiana Miami Tribe" in Marion within three weeks in order to be eligible for a claims award.[22] Since most Miami had already enrolled for a claim settlement in Peru, instructions to reenroll on short notice were disturbing.

Changes in leadership had always been awkward for the Miami, dependent as they were on influence within kinship networks and the ability to bring different divisions of the tribe together. Influence was best wielded by leaders who had widespread kinship ties, who were descended from earlier influential leaders, and who had worked most of their lives in Miami affairs. Without an electoral system and individual voting, leadership struggles could be prolonged and nasty if any or all of these elements were lacking.

Some of the worst fears of the older Miami were realized as tribal unity cracked in 1961. Hale sponsored general meetings on claims issues at the same time as did the Peru council, wrote letters to various authorities in Washington, and, with little knowledge, made public statements on claims matters. Worst of all for the Miami, perhaps, Hale made up a tribal membership list that included people with no Miami heritage. Attorney Walter Maloney, sensing serious problems, wrote a sharply worded letter informing Hale that his claims meetings were a "source of incorrect advice, misleading statements and trouble among the

Indians."[23] The minutes of Hale's council in Marion soon became sporadic and finally ended in late 1962. In January 1964 Hale resigned from his own council, which by that time was a dead letter.[24]

While Hale's attempt to lead the Miami tribe failed, his efforts to raise public awareness of the Indian population in Indiana were far more successful. Under the auspices of the Longhouse League of North American Indians he sponsored large intertribal powwows in Fort Wayne in 1964 and 1965, in South Bend in 1966, and in Gary in 1967.[25] The powwows received wide publicity and were the largest pantribal events in Indiana in modern times. Indiana citizens became aware that there was a Native American population in the state composed of many tribes. In 1968 Hale invited Calvin McGhee, chief of the Poarch Creek Indians of Atmore, Alabama, to an intertribal powwow at Roann, Indiana. This initial contact with Indians in the Midwest inspired the beginnings of the Poarch Creek's successful attempt at federal recognition.[26]

In his role as a popularizer of Miami "Indianness," Hale or Mongonzah caught the attention of Bert Anson, a professor at Ball State University, who was writing a history of the Miami tribe in the early 1960s. Anson, accepting Hale's virtually self-proclaimed role as a Miami chief, was influenced to portray the Miami as principally involved in claims and ceremonial activities. Failing to talk to other leaders, Anson missed the larger story of the ongoing political process of the tribe, including the political revival of the Miami Nation.[27]

A Shift in Tribal Governance

By early 1964 the membership of the Miami Nation, dormant for twenty years, was extremely concerned about feuding within the tribe and the lack of direction in tribal affairs since the death of Ves Godfroy. Some general meetings of the tribe had degenerated into shouting matches, threatening to destroy much needed tribal unity. In April 1964 several former council members reactivated the 1937 state charter of the Miami Nation at a meeting in Wabash. About seventy-five Miami adults assembled and elected officers by ballot.[28] Francis Shoemaker (Papaquan), a retired railroader then in his early fifties who had been active with the Nation for a time during the late 1930s, was elected chairman. Assertive and bluntly honest, he was able to focus anger over drift and confusion in tribal affairs on future needs and offered a strong sense of direction.[29]

The new leadership of the Miami Nation was well grounded in the kinship ties that were vital to tribal authority. The leaders were also extremely aware of tribal history. Shoemaker was a grandson of Elijah Marks, who was in turn the grandson of Chapendoceoh, one of Meshingomesia's most influential brothers. His grandfather had received an allotment from the Meshingomesia reservation, which was stolen by a guardian. Shoemaker's mother's second marriage was to David Bondy, secretary of the Nation until his death in 1943, and Camillus Bundy spent his last illness in Shoemaker's home in Wabash and died there in 1935. Bundy had shared much of the inner history and lore of the tribe with Shoemaker before his death and had radicalized Shoemaker's concept of tribal rights.[30] Shoemaker was further inspired by his grandfather's uncompromising insistence on Miami rights during the 1930s.

The leadership of the Miami Nation was further strengthened when Carmen Ryan (Checomequah, Spirit of the Lakes) joined as tribal historian. Ryan was related to the Godfroy, Mongosa, and Pimyotamah descendants. Inspired by her mother, Anna Marks, Ryan had been active in Miami affairs since childhood. She attended the 1923 meeting at Camillus Bundy's home, which was the genesis of the Miami Nation, and had participated in the Maconaquah Pageant and other Miami activities. For years she had corresponded with the Miami living outside Indiana, keeping them abreast of tribal affairs. She had also helped compile the 1964 tribal roll in cooperation with the Miami Indian council in Peru. A longtime member of the League of Nations of North American Indians, she was well aware of national Indian issues as well.

Ryan was an inveterate letter writer, and her correspondence and memoranda over the years spell out the shift in tribal governance from the council of Miami Indians of Indiana at Peru to the Miami Nation at Wabash. This shift in leadership from the Godfroy family in Peru to leadership by the Miami Nation in Wabash is of more than academic interest because the federal government later claimed that tribal governance disappeared among the Indiana Miami after the Peru council became moribund. Ryan's many letters and testimony before the ICC instead clearly show a rather smooth transition of governmental activities within the tribe from 1964 to 1967 and a consolidation and renaissance of Miami governance not seen since the 1930s.

Ryan pointed out that the Miami Nation was founded in the 1930s as "a Tribal, not a family, organization" with the intent of bypassing friction between the Godfroy and Meshingomesia Miami, the major polarities of the tribe.[31] The Nation stepped aside after World War II to let the Indiana Miami council manage affairs under the able leadership of Ves Godfroy. Leadership confusion after Godfroy's death threatened Miami unity. In a memorandum dated 29 October 1964 Ryan emphasized the importance of tribal unity during the claims process and to the continued existence of the Miami tribe itself: "We welcome all Miamis who are interested in Tribal welfare above and beyond natural family loyalty, without which the Miami Tribe would not have continued to exist."[32]

Leaders of the Miami Nation hammered home the idea that the Indiana Miami were a tribe, not a collection of families or Miami descendants who were leaving behind their Indian heritage with the settlement of claims. They did not see the death of an older generation as a loss of Miami identity, nor did older leaders view themselves as "more Indian" than younger people. The young, they felt, shared a rich heritage of tribal identity that was changing but not wasting away. Involving the young in tribal governance and activities was a way of assuring the future of the tribe.

As an inclusive tribal organization the Miami Nation wanted to bring all Miami groups together and insisted that claims awards should go to all Miami who could show ancestors on the 1889 or 1895 tribal rolls. Under the leadership of Ves Godfroy the Indiana Miami council in Peru had taken the same position. Since Godfroy's death, however, his sister, Eva Bossley, had taken the stance that claims awards should be restricted to the older Miami, whom she felt were most deserving. The Peru council went along with her, feeling claims awards should not extend beyond the fourth generation (or one-eighth Miami blood in many cases) of those included on the late-nineteenth-century rolls.[33] The Miami Nation was totally opposed to making claims awards based on blood quantum, as it would tend to cut off some younger Miami (and the tribal future) and would be time consuming and impractical as well.

The Miami Nation quickly consolidated its position as the governing body of the Indiana Miami tribe. As a sign of its appeal several council members from Hale's organization immediately joined the Nation when it organized in 1964. The Nation also reached out to the Western Miami. Shoemaker, Ryan, and others traveled to Miami, Oklahoma, to meet Chief Forest Olds of the sister tribe. During the period of confusion after 1961 rumors had spread that the Eastern and Western Miami were not getting along. After the visit from the Indiana leaders, Chief Olds wrote to Sen. Mike Monroney of Oklahoma that both tribes were cooperating fully on the matter of claims.[34]

Attempts to Regain Federal Recognition in the 1960s

Realizing that claims settlements fell far short of a full tribal agenda, the Miami Nation began pushing again for federal recognition. The Nation had made significant progress toward federal recognition in the late 1930s when World War II intervened. As far as the Nation was concerned claims and treaty rights were inseparable. The leadership was anxious to push for full federal status, although the official policy of the federal government still strongly favored termination of tribal rights. Federal status clearly would put the Eastern Miami on the same legal and administrative footing as the Western Miami and, if nothing else, would speed the payment of claims. Of greater importance was the fact that federal status would provide the legal framework within which various tribal rights could be addressed.

When the local attorney for the Nation asked if the Eastern Miami could be brought under provisions of the Indian Reorganization Act of 1934 as a federally recognized tribe, the Bureau of Indian Affairs moved with lightning speed to assure the tribal leadership that federal status was unnecessary for the distribution of claims or otherwise.[35] Pat assurances from federal bureaucrats did not reassure the Miami. They simply did not trust bureau officials to look after the best interests of the tribe. The Miami pressed ahead on federal recognition, contacting Indiana Cong. Charles Halleck, the powerful Republican chair of the Ways and Means Committee, and Indiana Sen. Vance Hartke. Early in 1965 Senator Hartke introduced a claims settlement bill, S. 1461, which would also convey federal status upon the tribe.[36]

Tribal attorney Walter Maloney also tried to get federal status for the Indiana Miami included in claims distribution bills in 1965. After the Miami and Maloney had testified and were safely out of Washington, an Interior Department official testified that federal recognition for the Indiana Miami was not useful or necessary. Maloney sharply rebutted this line of reasoning in a memorandum, pointing out that neither the Indiana nor the Oklahoma Miami could organize under the Indian Reorganization Act of 1934 because neither tribe owned tribal land nor lived on reservations. The legal status of both tribes was equal in terms of allotment of land and citizenship. The Western Miami were able to organize only as a business committee under the Oklahoma Welfare Act of 1936. This allowed them to incorporate for the purpose of getting credit, and in this way to be recognized as a tribe. The Indiana Miami, not being in Oklahoma, could not organize under this legislation. Maloney asserted that federally recognizing the Oklahoma tribe while withholding recognition from the Indiana tribe was "an act of discrimination in favor of the Miamis of Oklahoma against the interests of the similar but much larger group of Miamis in the state of Indiana."[37]

The tribal attorneys also testified that their clients did not want claims funds administered through the bureau area office in Muskogee, preferring that the central office in Washington, D.C., handle the distribution. The bureau rebuffed the request, and the claims awards were administered from Muskogee. The Indiana Miami were left to deal with the resulting chaos years later when trust funds were mismanaged and the Muskogee office took from 1979 to 1990, an incredible eleven years, to distribute one congressionally appropriated award. Payment of the same award to the Western Miami was made in two years.

The Miami Nation did its best to get federal recognition through legislation, but federal recognition was not included in the claims distribution bill that was eventually passed in 1966. Miami officials simply did not have the time or money to do the necessary lobbying in Washington at a time when the thrust of federal policy was still termination, not restoration of tribal rights. The Nation persisted with the issue anyway. Mina Brooke, the tribal secretary, wrote to Commissioner of Indian Affairs Phileo Nash in April 1965 pointing out that the Nation held three cemeteries that were included in original treaty grants and again asked for Miami recognition.[38] A year later Brooke wrote to Attorney General Ramsey Clark concerning federal recognition for the tribe. The Department of Justice informed Brooke that since the Miami were not federally recognized Indians, there was nothing the department could do.[39]

It is evident that the Miami Nation consistently sought federal status for the tribe in the mid-1960s. It is also evident that the tribal attorneys realized the great disability of nonrecognition in terms of managing claims awards in the millions of dollars. Beyond claims, tribal leaders clearly were aware of the advantages federal status held for solving a number of tribal problems. The Miami were halted by the lingering policy of termination and the fact that no tribes were being newly recognized at the time. More ominous was the hardening of the position on Miami recognition within the Interior Department. The Miami had raised the issue of treaty rights and federal status for sixty years, and the Interior Department had developed a large body of adverse information that took on a circular life of its own aside from the merits of the case. The Miami, far off in northern Indiana, did not have the time, energy, or money to correct the official mind-set, or even to get a modest hearing of their own views.

By 1965 the Miami Nation had gained de facto control of the claims process. As a sign of the shift in governance, the council of the Miami Indians of Indiana in Peru held its last general meeting of the tribe in August of that year. After 1965 there was only one set of council minutes in the Miami Indian council book. Thereafter, the organization was moribund for all practical purposes.[40]

Late in 1967 the Miami Nation asked claims attorneys if they were prepared to hold a meeting to vote on acceptance of claims. Walter Maloney had since died, and the local attorneys now managing the cases did not have Maloney's experience in Indian affairs. Early in 1968 the Nation learned the Western Miami had held their meeting and had voted unanimously to accept the claims award. Attorneys for the Indiana tribe had let the now moribund council of the Miami Indians in Peru vote on the issue without a general vote by the tribal membership. The Eastern Miami again were being shortchanged because they lacked federal status. The Nation opposed a deciding vote by a few people on such an important issue and insisted on an open meeting to discuss and vote on the same proposed settlement. On 30 March 1968, 218 adult Indiana Miami met at Bennett High School auditorium in Marion and voted 217 to 1 to accept settlement. Claims attorneys' initial resistance to this meeting showed that federal recognition did indeed make a difference to tribal participation in major decisions and in open discussion.

In May 1968 the Indian Claims Commission called hearings to close the record on the dockets relating to the St. Mary's Treaty of 1818. Chief Olds of the Western Miami tribe was invited to testify, but Chief Shoemaker of the Indiana Miami was ignored, again because of the differing legal status of the two tribes. Instead, a "token" Indiana Miami who had never been active in Miami affairs and who knew nothing of the claims history was brought to Washington. The snub to the Indiana leadership was too evident to ignore. More important, Shoemaker wanted to get the tribal status of the Eastern Miami on record. Unable to attend the hearings himself, he sent Carmen Ryan. Using her personal influence with the Western Miami attorneys she gained the witness stand. On "Washington time," Commissioner Harold Scott interrupted Ryan after less than a minute to thank her for her testimony. Unruffled and showing the well-developed stubborn streak characteristic of Miami leadership under duress, she continued, pointing out that

> we were a tribe, although the Government didn't believe it. We did not believe that the tribe was separated because they took a portion west. Our chiefs remained in Indiana. Many of those that went west later were not required [to go].[41]

Ryan was making a point that went all the way back to the treaty of 1854: the Indiana Miami had never relinquished their tribal government or status.

Although the federal government made every attempt to defeat Indiana Miami efforts to function as a tribe and consistently acted as though the tribe did not exist, the Nation just as consistently acted in the capacity of a tribal government as had its predecessors since Miami removal in 1846. The Nation also made sure such actions were part of the official record.

New Threats to the Miami Heritage

At the same time the Miami were working to redress claims they were faced with the loss of some of their little remaining land and a great deal of their rural heritage from an unexpected source. In 1961 Congress funded the construction of a dam on the Mississinewa River as part of a flood control plan for the upper Wabash River. A mile-long dam was to be constructed two miles upstream from the Seven Pillars of the Mississinewa and just downstream from the Ozahshinquah reserve, the former treaty land of the Bondy family. The reservoir would flood fourteen thousand acres when full and would leave large expanses of mudflats when lowered some twenty feet from fall to spring. In all, a twelve-mile stretch of the lower Mississinewa was to be flooded by the new reservoir. In addition to the reservoir itself, thousands of additional acres were needed to protect lands from the overflow level.

Besides the former Ozahshinquah reserve, nearly all of the former Meshingomesia reserve was to be included within the Mississinewa flood control project. In all, two-thirds of the former Miami Indian land between Peru and Marion was affected. The lower Mississinewa area had been the center of Miami population and life since the late eighteenth century, the site of at least five villages, communal fields, many burial sites, and the focus of subsistence when more distant hunting territories were settled. All the Miami reserves from Peru to Marion were connected by extensive trails and several fords across the river. It was along the Mississinewa that the Miami rebuffed the unprovoked attack of Col. John B. Campbell in 1812, and it was the Mississinewa council of the Miami that stood up to Gen. William Henry Harrison at the Fort Wayne treaty negotiations in 1809. Later two Miami churches were located in the area, as was the Indian village school, where commissioners took testimony for dividing the last reservation in 1873. Tribal councils and meetings were held in homes along the river, and during the 1920s and 1930s the Maconaquah Pageant was performed in rural parks in the area. As recently as the 1930s the rivers had been an important source of subsistence, and Miami continued to hunt and fish along the Mississinewa and Wabash.

Although the Miami had lost all but a few acres of land in the area of the reservoir, the memories of life along the river were still strong. Nearly all the mid-twentieth-century leaders had grown up between the Wabash and Mississinewa. They had participated in councils, powwows, and pageants along the river, had hunted, fished, farmed, and gathered native plants, had their children, and buried their dead there. Much Miami folklore and some older beliefs concerned the limestone bluffs, the shallow riffles, and the deep fishing holes of the Mississinewa. Ancient fishing weirs, a buffalo wallow, cabin sites, the Seven Pillars, the Hogback, Broad Riffle, spearing sites, netting stretches, and a thousand other items recalled Miami life and helped bind the tribe together in collective memory.

Of all the changes brought about by the new reservoir, none was more disturbing than the need to move several tribal cemeteries. Many Miami graves were unmarked, their location known only to elders. The relocation of the Bundy (or Frances Slocum) cemetery was the most disturbing news. During the 1920s Camillus Bundy had fought the loss of the family cemetery with every possible means. In the end he had been taken away in handcuffs and jailed for living on the burial site of his ancestors. Moving one of the largest Miami cemeteries as well as several others seemed to the Miami a new "Indian removal," again directed by the federal government and out of Miami control.

The need to find a new location for the Bundy cemetery produced a struggle between the Godfroy and Bundy families that was based on old kinship ties to Frances Slocum. Several

Godfroy family leaders were her descendants and felt the re-
mains from the Bundy cemetery should be moved next to the
Godfroy cemetery, which was outside the limits of the reservoir.
When Eva Bossley suggested joining the two cemeteries, the
Bundy family and their many kin resisted, saying the Godfroy
family wanted to make money from the historic associations.[42]
The Godfroy family felt they were offering "refuge" to more
Miami, as they had to the returnees from Kansas in the 1850s.
Bossley and her brothers were descendants of Ozahshinquah as
well, and they felt justified as heirs in speaking out. The con-
flict was at its height after Ves Godfroy died and before the
Miami Nation assumed general governance of the tribe and re-
flected drift in tribal affairs during the leadership vacuum.

In the end the Bundy cemetery was moved a mile and a half
east of its former location to higher ground. The argument over
a new location heightened tensions between Miami families at
a time when unity was needed. Corps of Engineers contractors,
impervious to Miami feelings, proceeded with the relocation.
Bulldozers shaved the ground, and local undertakers probed
and dug up remains by hand over a three-day period in early
November 1964. A relative was required to witness each disin-
terment. The human remains and burial goods were placed in
surplus army footlockers and reburied at the new site.[43] Con-
tents were photographed before reburial. Many of the older
grave markers, including that of Ozahshinquah, were stolen
from the site during the relocation.

Frances Slocum's grave contained a number of beads, a plate,
bowl, and drinking glass as well as the bones of a small animal
and a pipe whose bowl was filled with cut tobacco.[44] The Army
Corps of Engineers destroyed all the photographs of remains
and burial goods after the expiration of a seven-year waiting period. No archaeology was done at the site. One corps official told
the author that the controversy and anger expressed by the kin
of the deceased was far greater than at any relocation of non-
Indian cemeteries.[45]

After relocation, ownership of the Bundy cemetery was transferred to the Wabash County Historical Society in 1967. The state attorney general had ruled in the 1950s that the cemetery belonged to the Bundy family, but the effort to find dozens of owners was not feasible, and in the end the state accepted the property without quitclaim deeds from descendants.[46] The questions of ownership and status as a Miami Indian cemetery were to provoke further controversy years later. The impact of the relocation at the time was to severely disturb kinspeople and to enhance, once again, their feeling of powerlessness in the face of federal bureaucracy and uncaring white officials.

The flooding of several miles of the lower Mississinewa valley and the moving of several tribal cemeteries further strained the coping abilities of the small Miami community. The cemeteries that were not relocated were often vandalized. In the midst of the assault on their cultural and social identity the Miami reacted in a very old way. Accusations of witchcraft spread from some older Miami and were directed at those who appeared to be taking advantage of the situation.[47] Charges of sorcery had not been evident on such a scale since the 1870s, another time of great uncertainty for the tribe. Charges of witchcraft whispered by respected members of one clan against another further weakened tribal unity.

The loss of sites along the Mississinewa valley coincided with the deaths of a number of Miami born in the 1880s who represented an older way of Miami life. Clarence Godfroy (Kapahpwah, Looking over the Top), a popular storyteller and the author of *Miami Indian Stories*, died in 1962. Ross Bundy (Wapshingah), perhaps the last fluent speaker of the Miami language, died in 1963. Several of the men who fought for hunting and fishing rights died during the decade, as well as some of the women who had been midwives. The political renaissance of the Miami Nation was not yet sufficient to overcome the effects of time and powerful forces acting against the tribal community.

Claims Awards

The claims process proved stressful for the Miami people and their leadership. They were being asked to take money for the past misdeeds of federal officials and were treated as non-Indians by the Bureau of Indian Affairs. The Miami had a sophisticated tribal organization in terms of its knowledge of the tribal past, including complex dealings with federal officials. The Miami consistently responded as a tribe, but they were referred to in claims legislation as "Miami descendants." The award phase of the claims process came as the Miami were regrouping their leadership after the death of Ves Godfroy. The leadership vacuum from early 1961 to early 1964 took its toll as one group of the tribe verbally assaulted another over their standing. Tempers were lost and people who had grown up together and were kinspeople sometimes stopped speaking to each other.

Three years after Congress appropriated the funds, the Miami received their first claims settlement check in August 1969, amounting to $1,238 per person. The award came twenty years after the Miami signed their first attorney contract and after many of the older Miami had died. While the money was helpful it often went toward consumer goods and did not raise greatly the Miami standard of living. Reactions from non-Indians to the claims award were not helpful. Many whites wondered what paying modern Miami claims had to do with old injustices. Unaware of the tribal government and the largely hidden Miami community, whites sometimes demeaned the Miami as non-Indians. Newspapers joined the fray in the spirit of the times with headlines such as "U.S. Says We Wuz Scalped: Indiana Miamis on Wampum Warpath."[48]

The size of the Miami population receiving claims surprised some, but it was mainly a result of natural increase since 1880. In that year there were 330 Miami. The 1969 population was nine times as large, 3,066 Indians, a reasonable increase over a ninety-year period and common to a number of tribes. The Miami accepted as tribal members all who could prove they had an ancestor on the 1889 or 1895 tribal rolls. A tribal membership unrestricted by blood quantum or degree avoided bruising fights over "ins" and "outs" and made sense to most tribal members by accepting Miami who lived far from the older Miami community. The Miami tribe was still small, and leaders wanted to include children as members, not exclude some because of an abstract blood quantum limitation that reeked of older racist Bureau of Indian Affairs standards rather than those of a human community. The Miami were highly acculturated anyway, and it did not seem reasonable to exclude people on the basis of how culturally conservative they were, or on their degree of Miami blood.

The claims process was intended to settle the age-old "Indian problem" in the United States. The way the legislation and awards were structured strongly suggested that Indians should give up their identity and merge into the population. Even highly acculturated Indians such as the Indiana Miami retained powerful feelings about their identity, with a strong component of anger over past injustices. The outcome of the cash settlement degraded ancient tribal loyalties and cheapened the sense of justice being done. Worse yet, the cash settlement motivated clashes between different tribal groups or factions and fragmented rather than rebuilt tribal unity when it was most needed. The claims process also caused an overfocus on governance issues to the detriment of other projects.

The early 1960s were a low point for the Miami, as for many tribes nationally. The federal government, following a policy of termination, had stripped federal recognition from sixty tribes, forced individuals on local tax rolls, and turned over tribal assets to individuals or non-Indian corporations. The Miami Tribe of Oklahoma, along with the other seven tribes in the Quapaw Agency, had asked for termination of federal status after lengthy consultation with the Bureau of Indian Affairs officials in 1954.[49] Federal supervision was partially withdrawn, and the Western Miami were largely ignored by the bureau for a number of years.

The Western Miami tribe, while federally recognized, was hardly better off than the Indiana tribe during the 1960s. The tribe had no land, and the principal source of tribal income was donations from tribal members. Under the first appropriation for claims in 1966 the tribe was allocated $5,166, the "interest to be used for administrative expenses such as stamps, stationery, and expenses incurred in sending tribal delegations to Washington, D.C." Two-thirds of the tribal enrollment of 850 in 1969 lived outside the tribal service area in northeastern Oklahoma. In the 1969 elections for the election of tribal officials only thirty-two adults attended. A Bureau of Indian Affairs report at the time asserted that "The major, if not the only tribal business in which the members express an interest is the disposition of judgment funds [from land claims]."[50]

In 1961 the Indiana Miami were invited to send representatives to the American Indian Charter Convention in Chicago. Organized by anthropologists Sol Tax and Nancy Lurie and sponsored by the National Congress of American Indians, the Chicago conference was a turning point in American Indian activism. Over five hundred Indians from sixty-seven tribes attended. Hoping to end paternalism and to gain influence with the Kennedy administration, delegates demanded greater Indian input into the decision making affecting all tribes. The invitation to the conference came just as the Miami were preoccupied with finding a successor to Ves Godfroy, so they did not attend.[51] In 1972, however, Miami representatives attended the Eastern Indian Conference with representatives of the Wampanoag, Lumbee, Houma, Narragansett, and many other tribes that were later to seek federal recognition, several successfully.[52]

During the 1960s and 1970s various Miami claims under treaties made shortly after Indiana statehood continued. In 1965 the Claims Commission awarded $1,373,000 in Dockets 124-D, E, and F. This award concerned adjustments in the major suit over the St. Mary's 1818 Treaty. In 1969 the Eastern and Western Miami were awarded $3,826,660 for damages incurred at the treaty of Fort Wayne in 1809.[53] Congressional appropriation followed quickly. Awards were consolidated, the tribal roll updated, and the money paid out per capita in 1972. The payment per person was around $1,300.

An Old Battle Won at Last

In May 1974 Oliver Godfroy (Swimming Turtle), a great-grandson of Francis Godfroy, filed suit in federal district court in South Bend to recover "taxes wrongfully assessed and collected on Indian land" by the Miami County treasurer.[54] The land in question was 79 acres of the original 2,560-acre Francis Godfroy reserve set aside under the 1838 Miami treaty. The suit took real courage for the same court had ruled against Godfroy's grandfather on the same land in 1905 and against his older brothers and a sister in 1943. Gabriel Godfroy, in fact, had first sued Miami County for taxing the land in 1878. A previous chapter told of the fate of that suit and the effort of various Miami landowners to recover taxes.

Changes were coming to federal law that would bring a dramatic reversal in the tax status of Oliver Godfroy's treaty land. Both tribes and Indians were emerging from the legal twilight that had existed since the 1880s. The Indiana Board of Tax Commissioners and Miami County officials brought forth the time-honored arguments used in previous cases: that Godfroy was a citizen, not an Indian, and that Indiana law applied to his property, not federal Indian law. Godfroy, however, was ably represented by a local law professor, Hugo Martz, of Valparaiso University law school and by Thomas Tureen and David Crosby of Calais, Maine. The latter attorneys were backed by the Native American Rights Fund and were actively prosecuting the Penobscot and the Passamaquoddy cases in Maine for restitution of tribal land as well.

On 25 August 1977 Judge Allen Sharp ruled in favor of Oliver Godfroy, saying that he had made every effort consistent with the realities of modern society to maintain his status as an Indian.

Oliver Godfroy and his
"Indian corner."

Louise Hay

Further, Godfroy was an "Indian" as defined in Article III of the Northwest Ordinance of 1787, which exempted Miami Indian land from taxation by state or local jurisdictions. The tax-exempt status of the land was a vested right, Sharp continued, which could not be taken away without compensation.[55]

By good luck I met Oliver Godfroy at his home two weeks before the *Swimming Turtle* decision. My intention was to talk to several Miami people to see if an Indian community still existed that could serve as the subject of my doctoral work. I found Swimming Turtle to be consumed with his legal case. The gruff seventy-nine-year-old was alternately defiant and pessimistic over the outcome. He recalled the fate of taxation of his land going back to his grandfather's day, as well as Miami claims and other tribal affairs. It was a quick, personal introduction to Miami history, enough to convince me that there was indeed a community to study. At the end of the interview Swimming Turtle showed me his "Indian corner," filled with artifacts, beadwork, and pottery he had made, all presided over by a picture of Will Rogers, the Cherokee humorist.[56] A month after my visit and two weeks after the successful outcome of his case in federal court, Godfroy died quietly in his sleep.

The 1960s proved to be an important transition period for the Indiana Miami tribe. The death of older leaders left a leadership vacuum that was filled by the Miami Nation with younger, more dynamic leaders with a broader agenda. The demise of an older generation of Miami who had grown up on treaty grants along the rivers, the building of the Mississinewa Reservoir, and the residence of nearly all Miami in towns or cities caused a reevaluation of Miami identity. Younger Miami, influenced by national trends, were beginning to identify strongly as Indian while accepting the loss of the Miami language and many older folkways and beliefs. They were prepared to look to the future as Miami.

The "fish-ins" by tribes in the Northwest, the occupation of Alcatraz Island in San Francisco Bay, and the rise of Red Power were slow to have an effect on the Indiana Miami. Without a reservation there was no rural "homeland" to nurture Indian nationalism. Surprisingly few Miami lived in Chicago or Detroit where they would have contact with activists. The upper Wabash was relatively isolated from other tribes, and the Miami, while landless, were largely small-town or small-city Indians. Most had moved to the towns nearest the old treaty grants—Peru, Marion, Wabash, and Fort Wayne, with another contingent in the South Bend area and a scattering in Indianapolis. They rarely saw their kinspeople living in the northeast corner of Oklahoma.

The decade of the 1970s offered a rest from the hectic 1960s. As the pressure for American consensus and conformity of the immediate postwar years receded it became easier to identify as an American Indian. Census records show the change dramatically. In 1950 only 438 people identified themselves as Indian in Indiana. In 1960 the figure rose to 948, and in 1970 to 3,887. In the counties with the heaviest Miami Indian population

(Miami, Wabash, Grant, Huntington, and Allen) the figures for the corresponding years rose from 61 to 201 to 711.

Change would come for the Indiana Miami in the nature of past changes—slowly. The success of various claims and the *Swimming Turtle* case were encouraging. Since World War II the Miami people had focused their energies on the tedious but vital tasks of rebuilding their tribal government and pressing for rights. They had the advantage of continuing to live where they had lived for two hundred years, with leaders who remembered the highlights of their history and who insisted on full tribal rights. Success in further gains as an Indian tribe depended on convincing others of their tribal status and in complicated shifts in federal Indian policy and law. There was reason for cautious optimism.

Oliver Godfroy in regalia. Known as "Swimming Turtle," he holds an old pipe tomahawk and wears a silver peace medal awarded his great-grandfather during Andrew Jackson's presidency.

Hugo Martz

TEN

Revitalization and Recognition
1978–1994

■

Some Indians may want to become white men in their allegiance and their ways; this ought to be their right. But many Indians want to maintain their Indian values and allegiance, and many Indian communities want to maintain for their posterity an identity and heritage that were given to them. They too have this right. It is not for any white man, or Congress or the Indian Service bureaucracy, to demand that Indians stop being Indian.

> *Sol Tax and Sam Stanley,* Washington Post, *1 February 1970.*

The reality of the Miami's status has not changed. The United States Congress entered into treaties with this tribe, and in doing so, formally recognized them. Since that time, Congress has not terminated its relationship with this tribe. I urge my colleagues to join me in taking action to reaffirm the Miami's legitimate status.

> *Sen. Richard G. Lugar, statement before the U.S. Senate, 5 March 1991,* Congressional Record, *102d Cong., 1st sess., 1991, 137, pt. 37:S2621.*

THE LATE 1970S WAS A QUIET TIME FOR THE EASTERN Miami. Most claims were wound up, and the tribe had failed, through no fault of its own, to regain federal status. For the first time in many years there was no particular tribal agenda. The Red Power movement of the 1960s and Indian activism and militancy never caught on among the Miami. The tribe was small, with few members living in large cities, and those who did were by and large better educated and in middle-class circumstances. In the tribal homeland along the upper Wabash people tended to be poor, while the tribal middle class for the most part worked in factories and was blue-collar. A large number had served in the military during the Vietnam War and were loyal to the American cause. The claims awards had been spent on washers and dryers, cars, and other consumer goods and sometimes a down payment on a house or higher education for children. Strident militancy did not appeal to a largely small-town group of people who were working hard and enjoying comparative prosperity.

The Miami Nation continued to sponsor spring and fall general meetings, and the Miami reunion was well attended. A fair number of Miami traveled the midwestern powwow circuit in Indiana, Ohio, and Michigan, and most homes had an "Indian corner" where costumes, artifacts, photos, and other heirlooms were kept. During this pause after the end of the claims era, national Indian policy was changing in ways that would have a great and surprising impact on the Miami people. Liberals and conservatives began to question the effort made in the generation after World War II to assimilate American Indians. At the American Indian conference in Chicago in 1961 Indians themselves spoke out strongly for Indian involvement in the decision-making process that directly affected them. Of equal importance was preserving and holding on to a way of life, "a universe of things they knew, valued, and loved."[1]

At the time of the "Declaration of Indian Purpose" at the Chicago conference, the vast majority of Americans thought

Indian tribes were a relic of the past, if they thought about them at all. Alvin Josephy, Jr., noted at the time that Indians since 1890 had remained the "'possession' of government agents, certain sympathetic church and charitable groups, museum keepers, and students of anthropology, ethnology, and sociology."[2] He might also have noted that Indians had disappeared completely from the teaching of modern American history and made no appearance in textbooks after the closing of the frontier in 1890. Despite national indifference and ignorance of their existence, Indians did not think of themselves as disappearing or extinct. The National Congress of American Indians, founded during World War II, had resisted federal termination and relocation policies since its inception, but had little influence.

The Indian occupation of Alcatraz Island in San Francisco Bay in 1969 struck public awareness like a lightning bolt. Young Indians, better educated and often from urban settings—many of them relocated from reservations to cities by the Bureau of Indian Affairs—had found a way to get public attention. For weeks the occupation of the former federal prison was on television, while Native Americans explained a lengthy list of grievances. The American public realized Indians were not a relic of the past or a few elderly craftspeople on a dusty reservation. In 1972 Indians crossed the country in a Trail of Broken Treaties caravan, occupied the Interior Department building in Washington, D.C., and were on television daily. In 1973 and 1974 armed confrontation broke out on the Pine Ridge Reservation at Wounded Knee, South Dakota, again seizing attention in the media.

Changes in Indian policy and court interpretations occurred contemporaneously with the activism. Even though a shift away from termination of tribal rights had begun as early as 1958, activism probably accelerated the abandonment of assimilationist federal policy. President Richard Nixon pronounced the end of termination in 1970. In 1971 Congress passed the Alaska Native Claims Settlement, setting up modern corporations for many groups of Indians and Inuit preparatory to exploitation of

North Slope oil. Congress set aside both land and resources for the native groups and attempted to protect them from the corruption and despoliation of tribal resources that had impoverished Southwestern tribes earlier in the century. The Indian Finance Act of 1974 greatly enlarged revolving loan funds available to tribes and provided direct grants to tribal businesses. In 1975 Congress passed the Indian Self-Determination and Education Assistance Act, which for the first time permitted tribes to manage their own social services through contracts with the Bureau of Indian Affairs. Finally, the Indian Child Welfare Act of 1978 gave tribes power over adoption of Indian children and restricted placement of children by social agencies in non-Native American homes. Tribes were also given greater control over education and slowly began to manage school systems where Indian children were the majority.[3] Legislation was also passed to protect Native American religious freedom for the first time, but it lacked teeth and was much less effective.

The effect of the Indian activism and 1970s legislation was to lift the heavy hand of Bureau of Indian Affairs paternalism and direct control of tribal affairs, something that even John Collier had not really attempted in the heady days of the Indian New Deal. Tribes were taking over management of their own affairs and were moving toward greater independence. Federal funding of tribes rose greatly at the same time, from about $600 million in current dollars in 1960 to about $3 billion in 1980, a fivefold increase.

Changing court interpretations of Indian law greatly enhanced tribal sovereignty and legal status at the same time that Congress was restoring tribal independence. The 1974 Boldt decision, in which a Washington federal judge ruled that tribes were entitled to catch 50 percent of the salmon and steelhead trout in fishing off their reservations, was a sign of shifting legal interpretations. In that decision off-reservation fishing rights set forth in the 1855 Point Elliott Treaty were recognized. In 1980, in *Passamaquoddy* v. *Morton*, the Supreme Court ruled that tribes could sue under provisions of the Nonintercourse legislation of 1790, which prohibited state or private purchase of Indian land. The resulting settlement brought federal recognition to the Passamaquoddy and Penobscot tribes in Maine, an $81.5 million settlement, and restoration of three hundred thousand acres of land. Other tribes east of the Mississippi sued for state sale of their land, and several have achieved large claim settlements and federal recognition.

The effect of Indian militancy and the shift of federal legislation and court decisions toward enhancement of tribal sovereignty was a revolution in American Indian affairs. Tribes had gained power and status undreamed of before the 1970s, and they were quick to make use of it. The distinction between federally recognized and nonrecognized tribes became very real in terms of money, political clout, and visibility.

The Indiana Miami watched television like everybody else and were aware of all the changes affecting tribes, but they were not legally a tribe and had to sit on the sidelines. They could have taken advantage of various Organization of Economic Opportunity (OEO) programs, but the word "program" was not in the Miami vocabulary. Once having been federally recognized, the tribal leadership had a fixation on tribal rights in a narrow legal sense. Some of the Miami leaders were legal experts, educated in the school of oral history, but they were not sociologists, and there were not enough Miami with college degrees and an urban background to come home to reeducate the leadership. It is highly questionable whether the conservative older leaders would have accepted such leadership from younger, highly educated people in any case.

In 1975, following the Wounded Knee confrontation, Congress created the American Indian Policy Review Commission to examine the historical and legal background of federal-Indian relations to determine if policies and programs should be revised. Ada Deer was one of the three representatives of federally recognized tribes on the commission. A Menominee activist from

Milwaukee, Wisconsin, she had led the effort to restore recognition to her tribe. The commission concluded that the results of nonrecognition were devastating for Indian communities, leading frequently to total loss of land and deterioration of cohesive, effective tribal governments and social organizations. Most tellingly, the commission felt that budgetary considerations, not the framework of law, had frequently determined Indian policy. The commission recommended legislation for establishing criteria for recognizing nonrecognized Indian groups.[4]

The Department of the Interior had been quietly granting federal status to unrecognized Indian tribes for several years before the American Indian Policy Review Commission made its recommendations. In some cases tribes that had been terminated merely declared their need for federal status and the recognition was granted after a brief review. In other cases recognition came with court settlements.[5] The year following the expiration of the Policy Review Commission in 1977, the Bureau of Indian Affairs published regulations whereby nonrecognized groups could petition for federal status and get an administrative decision, rather than having to seek legislation or a court test. By coincidence, the regulations were published in September 1978, the same month the Indian Claims Commission issued its final report. Created to wrap up all possible Indian claims so that federal/tribal relations could be ended, the ICC's final report ended on a philosophical note, suggesting that other remedies to the unresolved problems between the government and the Indians might be found beyond simply paying money for past wrongs.[6]

Petitioning for Federal Recognition

Under the regulations published in 1978 Indian groups seeking federal recognition were asked to notify the Bureau of Indian Affairs of their intent. The petitioning groups were then asked to satisfy seven criteria to gain tribal status. Petitioners were asked to show that they:

1. have always been identified as Indian
2. inhabit a specific area and descend from a historical tribe
3. have maintained political influence over their members
4. have a governing document
5. have a current membership list and copies of former lists
6. are not members of any other Indian tribe
7. have not had federal status terminated by Congress

Guidelines for preparing the necessary documentation were published in December 1978.[7] In March 1979, less than three months later, the Indiana Miami sponsored a general meeting to discuss federal recognition and immediately notified the Bureau of Indian Affairs that they were petitioning.

The Miami political process functioned with the new opportunity for federal recognition as it had with past political challenges. Normally one of the family groups, which were often informally called clans, would learn of an issue or change in federal policy. The group would then check out the change, notify other families, and lead a coalition of tribal groups to gain whatever the goal was. In the 1920s Camillus Bundy had rallied most of the tribe behind treaty claims and federal recognition. In the 1940s the Godfroy family had provided the forum and leadership for land claims. After the death of Ves Godfroy the Miami Nation had regrouped around land claims and completed the task. In 1979 the Richardville-Lafontaine families sponsored the first meeting on petitioning for federal recognition. Before the meeting Robert Owens and other Miami from Huntington had done a background check on the issue with the Western Miami, with whom they were in close touch as distant cousins.

In September 1982 I became an employee of the Indiana Miami, a much different role than that of researcher of the tribe.[8] I was a powerful outsider, as I had brought grant money to the tribe and already knew a great deal of Miami history. Fortunately, in my guise as doctoral student, I had interviewed Chief Francis Shoemaker at his home along the Eel River near

Participants in the first workshop on federal recognition, October 1982.

Stewart Rafert

Robert Owens. Owens, a descendant of Chiefs Richardville and Lafontaine, initiated the effort of the Indiana Miami to regain federal recognition in the late 1970s.

Stewart Rafert

Roann, Indiana, on two bitterly cold days in December 1980. Shoemaker had pulled stacks of papers from his archive beneath a bed and had allowed me to use any documents I needed. He surprised me further when he talked quite honestly of tribal matters going back to the days of Meshingomesia. Years later Shoemaker laughingly told me that he had dreamed two weeks before my appearance on his doorstep that someone was coming to help the tribe.

Armed with Shoemaker's special status, I spent two years preparing the Indiana Miami petition for federal recognition. A wealth of new information was added to the four-drawer file cabinet I had filled as a student. The Miami had long ago sold the originals of treaties, peace medals, and craft items during their time of need, but they retained a wealth of letters and documents going back to the time of removal. The older leaders also had sharp memories and strong feelings about people and events going back to the 1870s, which helped me understand the documentary evidence. The Miami retained a strong allegiance to their extended families or clans as well, so I heard Miami history as it was passed down in families.

Shortly after I began petition work, the Godfroy Miami, represented by Lawrence Godfroy, then eighty-eight years old, joined the council of the Miami Nation, which now represented all Miami groups and had sixteen members to accommodate the diverse tribal constituencies. The Richardville-Lafontaine Miami, led by Robert Owens (Pehkokia) of Huntington, had joined the council in 1979. During the two years of writing the petition with the Miami, which stretched into another seven years before the Bureau of Indian Affairs rendered a decision, I was able to observe tribal governance and various Miami activities at close hand. Members of the tribal council represented large family units that derived from old village sites or old divisions of the tribe. Among the Godfroy contingent was a descendant of an Eel River Miami, a member of the group that returned from Kansas after 1846, and a direct descendant of Francis Godfroy who was also descended from Ozahshinquah. Ross Bundy's son sat on the council, as did a granddaughter of Camillus Bundy. Three members represented the intermarried Pimyotamah/Mongosa family. Four members were descendants of J. B. Richardville and Francis Lafontaine, and the Meshingomesia Miami had four members. The tribal council was the repository of family and tribal political knowledge and history. (See Appendix 1.)

Other Miami represented Miami culture. They were the storytellers, craftspeople, namers, and carriers of remembered history. They were often not involved in tribal politics. The politically active Miami and the culture bearers usually had a passionately emotional identity as Miami. They were frequently old people and defined "Miami-ness" for the rest of the tribe. The size of the passionately committed Miami group is difficult to estimate. In the course of my field research from 1977 to 1981 I interviewed nine such people. The people I was interviewing controlled the process, in one case refusing to see me for a year because I had gone into sensitive material too

Francis Shoemaker, chief of the Miami Nation. Shoemaker furnished records of the 1930s effort of the Eastern Miami to get recognition and successfully invited all Miami groups to work with the Miami Nation for federal recognition in the 1980s.

Stewart Rafert

LaMoine Marks, bearer of the knowledge of everyday life among the Miami communities along the rivers that began with his father's experiences in the 1870s.

Stewart Rafert

quickly, and in other cases setting the context and passing me on to someone else. I was told to hold off on interviewing Chief Shoemaker until later because the chief was "radical" and I did not know enough to talk to him yet. In the course of petition work I met a few more such committed people, and the total may have been twenty-five to thirty. These people handled the questions that defined Miami ethnicity, were willing to assert their Miami identity powerfully and stubbornly to outsiders, and were the ultimate arbiters of what it was to be a member of a particular Miami group and of the tribe itself.

Beyond the small core of passionately committed Miami was a much larger group of highly interested and committed people, who cared greatly about being Miami and were willing to work for the tribe and to attend meetings and reunions. They, too, usually knew lots of tribal history, had often experienced prejudice at some time in their life for being Indian, and were usually more open to outsiders in discussing Miami concerns or issues than the passionate Miami, who directed their knowledge inward toward the tribe. This second group was younger, still actively making a living, but wishing to contribute some time to the tribe. They usually reacted to outside events from a Miami perspective, with definite feelings shaped by their experience as Miami. No surveys were made, but judging by attendance at tribal events the group might number from five to seven hundred people.

The largest group consisted of people who were aware they were Miami Indians, who sometimes attended a meeting or kept up on tribal matters by checking with relatives. They often lived farther away, were perhaps better educated, and had complex commitments to family, job, or church, which competed with tribal identity. These Miami were sometimes not clear on their group identity within the tribe and did not look at the world through a Miami lens when speaking to outsiders. Their interest in the tribe was one of curiosity and of wanting to know more, if it was easily available. If they came to meetings their primary interest might concern distribution of the next claims award. Some were nostalgic about their tribal connection, while others were noncommittal. A few put their Miami connection down as unimportant. This group, which is the most difficult to assess, may have numbered half or more of the four thousand five hundred Miami enrolled in the mid-1980s.

Miami Activities during the 1980s

The existing layers of Miami identity, from a passionately committed nucleus that defined Miami identity to those who were interested in tribal affairs, allowed for great flexibility in people's responses to changes in federal policy or national attitudes toward Native Americans. In the hardest of times, the core group kept tribalism alive, while in more welcoming times a much larger group could identify with its Miami ethnicity and contribute to tribal affairs.[9] In the early 1980s the Eastern Miami were a landless tribe, the language was no longer spoken, and there was little overt evidence beyond historical markers that the Miami had ever existed in their homeland. Tribal activities centered about the spring and fall annual meetings and the August reunion in Wabash, which had met without a break since 1903. There was no tribal office and no tribal income beyond the annual dues of three dollars. In many respects it could be said that being Miami was a state of mind. At the same time it was a powerful state of mind, and under the right circumstances, Miami activities could flourish. The era of the claims commission had encouraged tribal government activities. Federal recognition and a changed national climate that encouraged tribal identity could lead to a revitalization of Miami culture.

As work on federal recognition progressed, the shape of Miami commitment began to change. The second level of commitment increased as Miami people learned more of federal recognition and a larger group of people participated in various tasks. Working toward federal recognition stimulated the start up of many new activities by the tribe and a sense of hope and looking to the future. The tribe established an office for the first time, in Peru, and within three years needed to move to larger offices. Most Miami were aware that the tribe had signed treaties and had once had federal acknowledgment. Tribespeople felt that treaty commitments were a moral obligation of the United States government, and federal status recognized the treaties. Beyond that, access to health services, preservation of tribal culture, and education were top priorities. People began to think seriously about the future and to the growth of the tribe as a meaningful institution. There was a feeling that federal recognition would bring some benefits to the tribe as well as equal status with other Indian tribes. Beyond federal benefits, and just as important, the tribe could protect the Miami cultural heritage and leave something of great value for future generations.

The Miami submitted their petition on 10 July 1984. It was well supported with documents, especially after American contact in the 1790s. There was no difficulty proving that the Miami submitting the petition were descended from the same Miami that the government had dealt with since the 1790s. The Miami commitment to regaining treaty rights after 1897 was easy to demonstrate, and the tribe was one of very few petitioners to have an Indian Reorganization Act file showing efforts to gain recognition during the 1930s. After World War II there were council minutes up to 1974, when there was a brief gap. Political influence is an abstract term, especially hard to document in the past, but council minutes are the most overt sign of a tribal government as are tribal petitions and letters to the government concerning various needs and problems, attempts to get legislation passed, and lineages of leaders, all of which were supplied. The Miami governing document dated from their state charter in 1937, and the tribe provided a current membership list with 4,387 people on it, all linked to tribal rolls made in 1889 and 1895. Less than 1 percent of the Indiana Miami were members of the Quapaw, Northern Arapaho, and some other western tribes, but this was acceptable under the regulations. Finally, Congress had not terminated the tribe in the 1950s, although it had made some Miami citizens in 1881.

Right after beginning work on federal recognition, the Miami tribe began having one annual meeting a year in Miami, Oklahoma, at the time of the Quapaw powwow over the Fourth of July weekend. The Indiana group was warmly welcomed at the powwow and was admired for some of the old costumes they wore. The powwow was an opportunity to meet with many of the three hundred Indiana Miami who had lived in the area of Miami, Oklahoma, Baxter Springs, Kansas, and Joplin, Missouri. The Carver, Walker, and Plotner families had left Indiana from 1895 to 1920 and were not far removed in time from Indiana memories. The Indiana Miami in the West frequently had attended local Indian schools as well as Haskell Institute in

Kansas and had been getting health services at Indian clinics. During federal budget tightening in the 1970s the Eastern Miami living in the above-named tristate area were denied services because they were not on federal tribal rolls. They became loyal supporters of federal recognition, and some began to attend tribal meetings in Indiana.

The Branch of Acknowledgment and Research (BAR), the unit within the Bureau of Indian Affairs that evaluated petitions, took a year and a half to review the Miami documents. In January 1985 the Bureau of Indian Affairs informed tribal officials that, "Generally speaking, all of our staff who reviewed the petition stated that it is an exceptionally well done document, and that you and all those who worked on its production . . . are to be congratulated for having done an outstanding job."[10] The letter went on to list some deficiencies, which if corrected would further strengthen the petition. Among these were more evidence for the social distinction of the Indiana Miami from

Eastern Miami participants Homer Mongosa and David Marks at the Quapaw powwow in Oklahoma, 1985. Mongosa's vest and leggings date to the early twentieth century.

Stewart Rafert

the surrounding population after 1900 and evidence of maintenance of social cohesion as a distinct group through social ties,
visits, and so on. More evidence was asked for informal
processes of leadership and decision making that went beyond
seeking redress for claims.[11] The BAR later recommended that
other petitioning groups use the Miami petition as a model for
their own petitions, which suggested that there were no major
problems with the document.[12]

The Miami submitted additional information to the Bureau
of Indian Affairs in October 1985 and began a long wait for a decision on tribal status. In the meantime, Francis Shoemaker,
chief of the Miami Nation, appointed Raymond White of
Muncie as chairman of the tribe with the unanimous approval
of the tribal council. White, who was forty-eight, stepped into
the day-to-day management of the tribe. His role clearly
derived from the Miami tradition of a *kapia* or steward who ex-
ercised day-to-day management in earlier generations.

Shoemaker's choice was both daring and astute. It was daring
because White was a Richardville descendant, from the smallest and most acculturated group of the Miami, and Chief
Richardville was sometimes a villain to the Miami communities
on the lower Mississinewa. Shoemaker realized, however, that
the tribe needed educated and effective management. White
had been active in union leadership at a General Motors plant
in Muncie and had run various small businesses. He had the
further advantage that he had grown up in Muncie, away from
the friction between Miami groups. He could sit down and
work with all of the clans without prejudice, and he was comfortable with non-Indians.

The Miami continued various activities and added some new
ones while waiting for a decision on their federal status. Floats
in parades had become the modern equivalent to the
Maconaquah Pageant of the 1920s and 1930s. Tribal floats won
several prizes in the Circus City Festival parade at Peru and at
the Three Rivers Festival in Fort Wayne. Chairman White

Raymond O. (Ray) White,
chairman (1983–93) and
chief of the Miami Nation
(1993–94).

Nick Clark

Headquarters of the
Eastern Miami tribe,
Peru, Indiana.

Stewart Rafert

encouraged the formation of a junior council of the tribe, responsible for representing the tribe in public relations events and for making recommendations to the tribal council. The Miami participated in the intertribal council of Indians of Indiana, and White lobbied with others for a state Indian commission. The tribe also worked with state officials to kill an innocently intended, but demeaning, "Injun Andy" logo and commercials for the state fair in 1981.

One of the biggest thorns in the side of Miami and Wabash County officials was the Bundy (Frances Slocum) cemetery. After relocation to make way for the Mississinewa Reservoir, the Corps of Engineers had turned ownership of the cemetery over to the Wabash County Historical Society. Difficulties arose when the county published guidelines for cemetery use that permitted burial of non-Indians. The issue came to a head in 1989 when the county wished to bury a young indigent man who was part Indian. The tribe insisted the Bundy cemetery was a Miami cemetery, still used by the Bundy family, and several carloads of Miami set up a vigil to prevent the burial. The county backed off and in 1993 returned the cemetery to the Miami Nation, helping to heal some of the tension that had existed since Camillus Bundy was evicted from the land.[13] During the early 1980s the tribe signed an agreement with the Indiana Department of Natural Resources for maintenance of the Meshingomesia cemetery and assumed protection of the Godfroy cemetery, which was also placed on the National Register of Historic Places.

In 1987 pothunters and professional grave looters destroyed a large prehistoric burial site called Slack Farm in Union County, Kentucky.[14] Ray White joined Dennis Banks and others to lobby the Kentucky and Indiana legislatures for better protection of Indian burial sites. For the first time both states passed legislation making the destruction of historic burial sites (pre-1850) a felony offense. The legislation was not passed in time to prevent the destruction of Windsor Mound a few miles east of Muncie in Randolph County, Indiana. Indian leaders and archaeologists watched helplessly as one of the last large Hopewell mounds on private land was leveled. White's work on burial issues brought him national attention and raised the visibility of the Miami tribe, even gaining a mention in the *National Geographic* magazine.[15]

While awaiting the decision for federal acknowledgment, the Miami visited other recently recognized tribes to see what programs they had and to gain an idea of the process of shifting to federal status. Visits were made to the Narragansett and Mashantucket Pequot tribes in New England, the Grand Traverse Ottawa and Chippewa in Michigan, and to the Poarch Creek tribe in Alabama. These tribes all had been recognized administratively by the Branch of Acknowledgment and Research and had comparable backgrounds to the Indiana Miami. Most had new tribal administration buildings, and all had health clinics, a food distribution program, housing rehabilitation, job training programs, low-income home energy grants, substance abuse programs, and community health services. These were the basic social programs that went with federal recognition. The tribes had begun various businesses as well to boost employment and tribal income.[16]

By the middle of the 1980s high-stakes bingo was catching on among Indian tribes. The Reagan administration did not want to increase funding for Indian tribes and encouraged Indian gaming as a means of raising tribal revenue to make up for cuts in federal funds. When the Miami visited the Mashantucket Pequots in Connecticut in October 1986 the tribe had just opened its first large bingo hall. Connecticut had challenged the tribe in federal court and had lost, as state jurisdiction does not apply on Indian trust lands. The Grand Traverse Ottawa and Chippewa near Traverse City, Michigan, had passed a federal court test of their small casino as well when the Miami visited in 1986. Indian gaming was expanding and diversifying and was increasingly well protected under federal Indian law.

Restored grave of
Meshingomesia.
Woody Snyder

The Indian Village schoolhouse in 1988. Today it is used as a farm storage shed.
Stewart Rafert

The Miami also visited some long-established tribes that were leaders in tribal development. Among these were the Oneida tribe in Green Bay, Wisconsin, and the Mississippi Choctaw tribe. By the mid-1980s these federally recognized tribes owned many businesses and had annual budgets of over a hundred million dollars. The Choctaw, located in one of the poorest states, employed large numbers of non-Indians at their large industrial park, where Boeing Aircraft, American Greeting Cards, and General Motors had facilities. These tribes had their own tribal schools, police forces, and judicial systems. The Choctaw tribe was well on its way to becoming a major employer in Mississippi and showed the positive impact a tribe could have on a state.

During the 1970s and 1980s the status and visibility of the Miami rose within Indiana. In the 1950s and early 1960s state newspapers demeaned Miami claims efforts with news headlines such as, "Palefaces Barred: Descendants of Miami Indians Powwow Over Land Wampum," or "U.S. Says We Wuz Scalped: Indiana Miamis on Wampum Warpath."[17] Beginning with the *Swimming Turtle* decision in 1977 the tone changed. In 1977 the *Prairie Farmer* did an article on the Miami titled, "Indian Country: Proud People Preserve Their Heritage and Tribal Hunting Grounds."[18] By 1987 the *Peru Daily Tribune* ran an editorial, "Reservation Site Should Be Here."[19] After the late 1980s the Miami received frequent coverage in newspapers and on television in Indiana and began to receive national coverage on PBS radio, in large urban newspapers, *The Nation*, and other national magazines.

The Decision on Federal Recognition

On 12 July 1990 Eddie Brown, the assistant secretary of the Interior Department for Indian Affairs, notified the Miami Nation of a proposed finding that the tribe did not meet two of the seven criteria for acknowledgment and therefore did "not meet the requirements necessary for a government-to-government relationship with the United States."[20] The tribe was given additional time to respond with further evidence of tribal community and a continuing political system since World War II, the two areas that were deficient.

The Miami contacted the Native American Rights Fund (NARF), a well-regarded Indian law organization staffed with Native American lawyers who worked on various tribal issues. NARF had worked with several petitioners and had success in gaining recognition in every case. The Miami were familiar with NARF's work on the *Swimming Turtle* case in 1977 and were glad to have its support at this critical juncture of their fight for status.

The four hundred-page finding against recognition was unusual in several regards. The great majority of the government's report supported Miami evidence for all seven criteria, with some hedging after World War II. The Bureau of Indian Affairs saw evidence of a tribal government up to the early 1940s, but not since, saying that claims activities did not constitute tribal governance. So far as community was concerned, the only lack was clear evidence of a contemporary Miami community.[21] The most surprising element of the government report was admission that Willis Van Devanter's 1897 decision that took away Miami recognition was wrong. The decision was based on Miami legislation in 1873 and 1881, yet "Neither act explicitly severed Miami tribal relations, or even hinted that the Government was attempting to sever those relations."[22] The findings went on to say that loss of land through taxation and loss of federal status forced the breakup of the land-based Miami communities, disrupted social relationships and economic cooperation, eroded Miami culture, and disabled the tribal government. In other words, the loss of tribal recognition was a government error that so damaged the tribal community that it did not, in 1990, meet the criteria to regain tribal status.

There was an irony to the timing of the 1990 finding against federal status for the Indiana Miami tribe. After eleven years of effort the Bureau of Indian Affairs finally approved an updated tribal roll later the same year so that the final claims award could

U. S. Says We Wuz Scalped.

Indiana Miamis on
Indiana State Library
Wampum Warpath

(NDPLA. TIMES NOV 2 1962

Times Washington Bureau

WASHINGTON, Nov. 2 — The federal government is ready to fight the Indians from Indiana again.

This time it will be Justice Department lawyers arguing a $4,650,000 judgment awarded the Miami Indians in Indiana and Oklahoma by the Indian

that the Miami Indians would agree to reduce an award of $1.15," Mr. Maloney said, "when the evidence is clear that it is worth $1.87 an acre— the minimum statutory price at that time (1818) was $2.00.

"There is no way to settle with those Miamis for less than the award already made to them."

Changing perceptions of the Miami in newspapers after World War II.

INDIAN COUNTRY

Proud people preserve their heritage and tribal hunting grounds

Peru Daily Tribune Nov. 23, 1987

Our view

Reservation site should be here

It's hard to believe that there appears to be another dispute about an Indian reservation in the area. That's a topic one would expect to hear about 150 years ago, not in 1987.

Miami Indian tribal officials claim they tried to meet almost a year ago with city officials to discuss the possibility of creating a reservation in Miami County. Tribal officials said they invited city and state representatives to meet with them. City officials said they don't remember such a meeting.

Regardless of whether the invitation was offered or not, city and chamber officials knew the Miamis were looking for a reservation site. It appears nothing was done to entice the tribe to locate here.

According to tribal officials, a reservation might mean a financial benefit to the area around it. One way would

be through the increased number of tourists, a trade th Miami County is aiming at with its Circus Hall of Fan plans.

Miami leaders, feeling snubbed by local governmen started discussions with Wabash County officials about reservation. Wabash County officials have welcomed th tribe with open arms, and it might be too late to stop the move there.

But we hope tribal officials will wait and discuss th matter with incoming Mayor Dick Blair and his new a ministration. It's possible a change in the city's leade ship might be of benefit to the tribe. Blair already ha said he would be willing to talk with tribal leaders.

Wouldn't it make sense to have the Miamis' reserv tion in Miami County?

■ 285 ■

be paid. Congress had appropriated the money in 1979, but since the tribe lacked federal recognition, amending the tribal roll was more difficult and had a lower priority. In the meantime many older tribespeople had died. Once again, lack of federal status made a very real difference to the Miami people.

Anthropologist Jack Campisi and attorney Arlinda Locklear, a Lumbee Indian qualified to practice before the United States Supreme Court, coordinated research to rebut the negative finding. Campisi had written several tribal petitions and had a reputation for innovative approaches to demonstrating the existence of modern tribal communities. The Miami Nation by 1990 had gathered one of the most complete tribal archives in the United States. Having all of the documentation in one place helped research, as did the very narrow basis for denial of recognition, which was concerned only with the period after World War II for tribal government and with additional evidence of a contemporary tribal community.

The Miami response to the proposed finding against recognition was impressive. Anthropologist Elizabeth Glenn of Ball State University mapped the location of all Miami households in Peru, Wabash, Huntington, Fort Wayne, and South Bend. The maps showed concentrated Miami populations in all the cities except Fort Wayne. In each city a single Miami group dominated the tribal population, reflecting migration from nearby village and rural locations. In Peru, 93 percent of the Miami belonged to the Godfroy lineage (or extended family). In Huntington, 79 percent of the Miami were from the Richardville-Lafontaine group, and in Marion, 72 percent were Meshingomesia Miami. Wabash, which was more centrally located to Miami lands, had a mixture, as would be expected. Nearly all the Miami in South Bend were from the Meshingomesia group and derived from three families who had moved there for jobs after World War I. Migration to the urban areas was clearly based on family lineages and was not simply a general Miami movement.[23] (See Table 10.1.) Tribal information from reunions and meetings was passed on to each extended group. Miami people knew which group they belonged to, and Campisi analyzed tribal council membership and voting patterns to show how the groups functioned as political units within the tribal government.

Table 10.1. Geographic Distribution of Largest Miami Groups in Indiana (Predominant Group Italicized)[24]

City	Godfroy	Meshingomesia	Bundy	Rich./Lafont.	Total
Total, Ind.	1,142	594	235	320	2,291
Peru	*420*	19	15	—	454
Wabash	64	80	*89*	7	240
Marion	7	*63*	18	—	88
Huntington	5	10	4	*70*	89
South Bend	15	*119*	5	1	140
Fort Wayne	*135**	58	6	78	277
Indianapolis	*68*	9	10	4	91

* Many of the Godfroy family in Fort Wayne are also descendants of Chief Richardville through his daughter Archangel, who married James R. Godfroy.

I assembled further evidence demonstrating an active tribal government since World War II. Newly discovered files clearly showed the Eastern Miami had sought federal recognition in the 1960s. More tribal council minutes were found as well, showing unbroken sessions from 1944 to 1974 and a resumption in 1979. There were thirty-five well-attended general meetings of the tribe from 1944 to 1973 and from 1979 to the present.[25] Beyond claims activities, the tribe acted to protect the interests of its members. Carmen Ryan found in 1970 that the Miami Minors' Fund was being mismanaged by the Bureau of Indian Affairs area office in Muskogee and forced changes.[26] The tribal government lobbied for changes in the first claims settlement bill and insisted on testifying on claims before the Indian Claims Commission. It was an impressive performance in the face of consistent discouragement of governance activities from the Bureau of Indian Affairs. The bureau feared an active Eastern Miami government because any recognition of such governance implied tribal rights.[27]

In February 1992 staff from the Branch of Acknowledgment and Research came to Peru to conduct field research among the Miami and to attend a general meeting at the tribal headquarters. Over eight hundred Miami attended the general meeting, which was called on one week's notice in mid-winter. During the visit bingo games went on, children attended day care, elderly people came for meals, and the officials from Washington saw a fully functioning Indian tribe similar to others in the Midwest, except it lacked the advantage of federal status.

On 9 June 1992 the Bureau of Indian Affairs made a final finding against recognition of the Indiana Miami, again based on alleged insufficient evidence of a distinct contemporary tribal community and lack of tribal political process since the early 1940s. The bureau asserted in its report that there was "virtually no social distinction between Indiana Miami members and non-Miamis with whom they interact." It went on to say that the tribal government did "not act on matters which are of sufficient importance to the membership to meet the requirements of the regulations for exercise of tribal political authority."[28] By this time the Miami had put ten years of effort and over $750,000 into regaining federal status. The tribe had also purchased thirty-five acres of land south of the Seven Pillars on the Mississinewa River and had moved to the tribal complex in Peru, had options on land near Fort Wayne, and was running two bingo halls for income to pay for legal expenses and tribal administration. At the same time the recognition was important because tribespeople knew it had been taken away without just cause, and the tribe could build on its current success with the advantages of federal Indian law.

By late 1993, after fifteen years of judging the status of Indian groups, the Branch of Acknowledgment and Research had granted federal recognition to nine tribes and had denied recognition to thirteen groups.[29] The stubborn denial of Eastern Miami recognition on the part of the Bureau of Indian Affairs is difficult to explain in terms of modern federal Indian policy. In the years since the termination policy was ended, the Bureau of Indian Affairs and Congress again recognized over sixty terminated tribes. The criteria for legislative recognition were essentially the same as those of the administrative process. The major difference was that the standards for meeting those requirements were made far higher for the Indiana Miami than they were for legislative recognition. In October 1990, for example, Congress recognized the Northern Ponca tribe of Nebraska. The tribe's 1987 charter was very similar to the Indiana Miami 1937 charter. The Ponca at the time were scattered over twenty-four different states, with half of the tribe dispersed over a large area of Nebraska, South Dakota, and Iowa. The fact that 54 percent of the Ponca lived in three states was accepted as a demonstration "that there is most certainly an identifiable community."[30]

In contrast to the Northern Ponca, the Eastern Miami supplied maps of every Miami community showing the location of households clustered near each other, particularly in towns, but the Branch of Acknowledgment and Research did not accept the maps and information on daily communication among the Miami as evidence of an identifiable community. The geographic breakdown of Miami subgroups supplied by the Branch of Acknowledgment and Research itself showed clear groupings of the Miami in Indiana near old village locations. Most of the Godfroy group, for instance, still lived in the area of Peru, while the Bundy lineage lived near Wabash. The Meshingomesia Miami, who had experienced the greatest disruption through rapid loss of land, lived in approximately equal numbers in Wabash, Marion, and Fort Wayne (10 percent in each area), while the largest group lived in the South Bend area, where they had migrated for jobs after World War I. The Richardville-Lafontaine lineage was the smallest Miami group and was grouped in the Fort Wayne and Huntington areas, as expected, as well as in Oklahoma, where many had migrated since 1860.[31] (See Table 10.1.)

Like the Miami, three-fourths of the Northern Ponca population lived in cities or small towns.[32] A Miami needs assessment conducted in 1987 indicated difficulties with access to health care, income, and housing similar to those of the Ponca, although figures cannot be directly compared.[33] The major difference between the Ponca of Nebraska and the Indiana Miami was size. The Ponca counted four hundred members, while the Miami population was over four thousand. Thus, federal services would cost ten times as much if the Miami were recognized, and many felt this was the real stumbling block, not the ability of the tribe to meet the standards of recognition.

Administrative recognition of the Snoqualmie tribe of Washington in April 1993 was particularly frustrating for the Indiana Miami because much of the evidence for Snoqualmie governance and a tribal community seemed weaker than the Miami case. From 1859 to 1915 there was no evidence of leaders among various scattered Snoqualmie settlements.[34] In 1929 the tribe had organized to regain rights from the 1855 Point Elliott Treaty. In 1955 the local director of the Bureau of Indian Affairs reported that the only activity of the landless Snoqualmie was settlement of claims, a focus of tribal activity that was held against Miami recognition.[35] After the death of a chief in 1956 the tribe had no leader until 1986, a period of thirty years. From the 1950s until the 1980s there was one annual council meeting a year, and minutes for several meetings were missing. Meetings in the 1960s were often poorly attended.[36] The Snoqualmie tribal membership lived scattered in various towns in western Washington State. There are no current marriages between members of the tribe, and marriages within the tribe had ceased around 1920.[37] While tribal members regarded general council meetings as a place for making tribal decisions, one individual characterized the 1987 general meeting as "like past ones, nothing but yelling and screaming matches."[38]

The Miami evidence for recognition seemed, on review, far better documented over a far longer period of time than that of the Snoqualmie tribe. Again, the major difference (aside from substantially better evidence for the Miami) was size of the tribes, 313 Snoqualmie compared to over 5,000 Miami currently. The largest tribe to be administratively acknowledged had 1,470 members.[39] After a careful comparison of the Ponca of Nebraska and the Snoqualmie cases, it appeared to experts on federal recognition that budgetary considerations, not tribal qualifications, had been the problem for Miami recognition.

The forces arrayed against Miami recognition were fairly visible and obvious and were acting out of their own well-developed sense of self-interest. The executive branch had no desire to expand the number of Indians entitled to federal services while the federal deficit was ballooning. The Office of Management and Budget had quietly recommended against Miami recognition from the beginning.[40] So far as the Bureau of Indian Affairs was concerned, the Miami tribe *was* recognized and existed in Oklahoma. The Indiana legislature had passed a joint resolution supporting federal recognition in 1980, but in the fall of 1989 had begun a state lottery and did not wish competition from an Indian tribe that could sponsor large-stakes bingo. Though several neighboring federally recognized tribes supported Miami recognition, reservation tribes did not want competition for federal dollars from a new tribe that they regarded as highly acculturated.[41] Tim Giago, editor of the *Lakota Times*, expressed such resistance succinctly when he said, "If there's tribes sitting out there [in Indiana], they have been totally acculturated and assimilated. We haven't."[42]

Long before the adverse proposal was made, tribal chairman Ray White had been meeting with Reps. Jim Jontz and Phil Sharp and with Sen. Richard Lugar's staff, keeping them up to date on the petition and preparing to submit legislation for recognition if the petition failed. White also testified several times on the slowness and expense of the petitioning process before Sen. Daniel Inouye's Select Committee on Indian Affairs.

In the spring of 1991 Senator Lugar sponsored S.R. 538, a bill to confer federal recognition on the Eastern Miami. In his floor speech Lugar stated the bill

> would rectify an injustice imposed upon thousands of my constituents for over 90 years.... The legislation I have introduced today seeks to correct this injustice by restoring the Miamis' legitimate status and directing the Department of the Interior to make available to the tribe all rights and privileges enjoyed by other federally recognized Indian tribes.[43]

After the negative finding in June, NARF staff and tribal chairman Ray White began working closely with the offices of Senator Lugar and Representative Jontz to introduce legislation for Miami recognition.

In November 1992 Senator Inouye of Hawaii scheduled hearings on the Miami legislation before the Select Committee on Indian Affairs. Three days before hearings were to begin, however, Senator Lugar suddenly withdrew his support, citing a 1991 Supreme Court decision that unanimously backed the powers of Indian tribes under the Indian Gaming Regulatory Act of 1988 to conduct casino gambling free of state regulation if they were in a state that allowed nonprofit organizations to hold "Las Vegas nights." Indiana had legalized "Las Vegas nights" in 1990, which opened the way for the Miami tribe to sponsor casino gambling, if it chose to. Senator Lugar noted that the legislature had debated and rejected casino gambling over the past two years and that federal recognition for the Miami tribe could allow such gaming.[44] If the Miami had been in a state with other federally recognized tribes, gaming would not have been an issue. The Pokagon Potawatomi tribe just

Chief Ray White speaking to Miami people who marched from Peru to South Bend in September 1992 to support a lawsuit against the Interior Department for denying Miami recognition. Native American Rights Fund attorney Henry Sockbeson and tribal attorney Arlinda Locklear stand in the right foreground.

Nick Clark

north of South Bend, but in Michigan, did not have to struggle with the issue of gaming because other tribes already sponsored casino gambling.

On 11 September 1992 the Miami filed a lawsuit against the United States on the basis that only Congress could terminate recognition of a tribe.[45] A large number of Miami marched the seventy-five miles from Peru to South Bend in support of the case. Judge Robert Miller ruled on 26 July 1993 that the Miami were recognized as a tribe in the 1854 treaty and that the government had no authority to strip recognition from the tribe in 1897. However, Judge Miller also ruled that the tribe had waited too long to sue and was blocked by the statute of limitations.[46] Indian tribes are especially vulnerable to arguments based on statutes of limitation because tribal government powers have often been dormant, especially during the twilight years of tribalism from the 1890s to the 1960s. Judge Allen

Sharp was able to overcome these disabilities in the *Swimming Turtle* case in 1977. By and large, the Supreme Court has refused to find that Indian tribes are prejudiced in legal actions by a lack of tribal activity or acquiescence in state jurisdiction.[47] Again, the Miami seemed to suffer for their location, since federal courts in Indiana and the seventh judicial district did not have a body of Indian law or case histories as background for tribal litigation. The tribe could have filed its lawsuit in the District of Columbia, but chose not to because of the heavy case load and the inconvenience of distance.

The Miami accepted Judge Miller's ruling as another problem in the battle for recognition. On 14 February 1993 Chief Francis Shoemaker retired, and Ray White was appointed the new chief of the tribe at a large public ceremony held at Grissom Air Force Base.[48] The Twigh Twee Drum sang an honor song as did the Yellow River Singers and the Pokagon Potawatomi Drum from southwestern Michigan. Floyd Leonard, chief of the Oklahoma Miami, conducted an Eagle Feather Ceremony, and the Eastern Shawnee, Moraviantown Delaware from Ontario, Canada, and other tribes acknowledged the transition in leadership. For several years the Indiana Miami had been leading various activities along with the Minnetrista Council for Great Lakes Native American Studies, located in Muncie. The Minnetrista Council sponsored conferences, craft workshops, and many other activities that brought the Eastern Miami into a closer working relationship with the Western Miami and other tribes throughout the Midwest and the eastern Plains. Such contacts greatly increased the spread of pan-Indian culture among the Indiana tribe and helped give members a strong sense of connection to the modern Native American world.

The 26 July 1993 court ruling was only the first of four findings in the Miami case, which was continued into 1995. Some tribes and Indian rights organizations were beginning to realize that as "so go the Miami, so go the Indian nations," in other words, actions in court detrimental to the Miami could rebound on other tribes, including those with federal acknowledgment.[49]

The Miami Future

In 1996 the Miami will have continued in Indiana, despite many predictions of their demise, for 150 years after removal. The tribe's persistence under adversity is remarkable and is a testimony of its ability to adapt to changed circumstances and to set itself apart as a distinct group, although acculturation is nearly complete. Judgments on ethnic identity, however, are highly questionable. Ethnicity is not quantifiable, nor does it progress in one direction toward disappearance. Like learning, it can zigzag, moving toward or away from the dominant society. Nonethnic peoples are most likely to pronounce the death of ethnicity, since they are not inside those boundaries from which the ethnically bounded person views the larger world. Thus, there are always opposing judgments on the future of ethnicity in American society.

The Indiana Miami are presently reconstituting their self-identity, selecting from the past of their own culture, and adding elements from modern pan-Indian culture. This phenomenon was evident in the summer of 1993, when an elderly Miami man who had grown up in Butler Township returned to the Miami longhouse to dance before a crowd at a midnight ceremony. Some, including an anthropologist, had judged that the man no longer cared about being Miami—in fact, he sometimes seemed angry and almost anti-Miami when asked about his memories. In the longhouse that summer night he danced alone for the crowd and brought tears to all the observers. Without using words, he said "I am Miami."

The Miami Indians of Indiana are approaching the centenary of the loss of their federal status as an Indian tribe. Whether or not they have federal status on 23 November 1997 they will probably make note of the day and stage a vigil—or a celebration, as they did when they commemorated the two hundredth anniversary of St. Clair's defeat on 4 November 1991. In the days of claims cases the Miami tended to look backward with a sense of loss and nostalgia, some feeling that perhaps it was time to close the books on the past. Beginning in the 1960s they began a slow revitalization and began to look to the future. No longer a land-based, rural Indian group, they realized that an Indian heritage could be kept alive in a different context. In a way, they were freed from the land and a very narrow definition of being Indian. Now the Miami could look beyond their immediate past and painful memories to an enlarged view of their past and from that build a future.

AFTERWORD

■

THE PAST FIFTEEN YEARS HAVE BROUGHT UN-
precedented positive change and revitalization to the Indiana
Miami tribe. Although efforts to attain federal status took
great energy and were expensive, the tribe was able to coor-
dinate the work of many volunteers, hire highly qualified
experts, and to do much else as well. The Miami are reno-
vating and expanding their tribal headquarters in Peru
and have purchased thirty-five acres of land south of
the Seven Pillars of the Mississinewa for a longhouse and various cultural activities.

The Minnetrista Council for Great Lakes Native American
Studies in Muncie has sponsored frequent meetings and workshops in the past few years where the Indiana Miami and other
Great Lakes tribes have worked and shared together on a regular basis. The meetings have included the Western Miami, the
Peoria, Shawnee, Ottawa, and Delaware of Oklahoma as well as
other tribes in Oklahoma, Kansas, and Nebraska that were removed in the 1830s and 1840s. These exchanges have increased
contacts between the tribes, and the Indiana Miami tribe is
accepted as an equal.

In 1992 Gov. Evan Bayh created a state Indian Commission, recognizing the need to facilitate communication among the citizens and various Indian constituencies in Indiana. The commission serves as a clearinghouse for the state's Native Americans to express their needs and concerns. The American Indian Council of Lebanon has for a number of years sponsored intertribal powwows and gatherings of all the Native American people in Indiana. Tribal diversity in Indiana continues to increase, with members of Great Plains and Southwestern tribes moving into the state in greater numbers. The Miami constitute about one-fifth of Indiana's Indian population, as they have for many years. Because they are not as well known as larger reservation tribes, the Miami have had to educate other Native Americans, particularly in urban areas, concerning their history and identity. This is not an easy task.

The growing influence of the Miami tribe has affected the appearance of the countryside in Butler Township and in other former village sites. When I began research in the late 1970s there was almost no evidence of the existence of the Miami beyond a few cemeteries. The contrast was striking when in the fall of 1993 I drove to various sites on the former Meshingomesia Reserve and through Butler Township with a Miami man who had spent his whole life hunting, fishing, and trapping along the rivers. In Butler Township my friend told me the old buffalo wallow had been filled in, but we saw the historic Miami sites were well marked and protected. A nonprofit land trust had purchased over a hundred acres adjoining the Miami land to the west of the Seven Pillars and would allow it to revert to its natural state. We saw several Miami people on our tour, and it seemed the land was again becoming "Indian country."

The Mississinewa Reservoir project has encouraged the growth of "Indian country" along the Mississinewa River as well. Farms in the flood control plain were purchased in the 1960s and turned over to the Indiana Department of Natural Resources for game management. The federal land, which includes most of the former Meshingomesia Reserve, is growing back into forest and beginning to resemble its appearance before it was cleared for modern farms. Wild turkeys, the sandhill crane, beaver, and deer are returning after an absence of many years. Mink and muskrat are increasing in numbers. The closing of older factories and smelteries upstream, along with increased control of pollution, has improved the water quality of the Wabash and Mississinewa. Fish have returned in large numbers, though some older species such as the buffalo fish are still rare or nonexistent.[1]

The "hidden community" I described in my doctoral dissertation has emerged. As Chief Francis Shoemaker said to me, using the old language of metaphor, "We have come out from under a rock, and we are going to stay out." Today most people in Indiana and many people nationally are aware that the Eastern Miami tribe exists. People seeking information on the Miami now start inquiries at the tribal office, and the Miami people now have a primary role in shaping their public image, not outsiders.

The Miami remain as diverse as ever, meeting and sharing information as extended families, which they often call clans. The point of reference within the tribe is still that of the Godfroy, Bundy, Meshingomesia, Richardville/Lafontaine, Mongosa, and other key families. The differing alignments within the tribe often slow down decisions, but the decisions that emerge are shaped by a long history and are "Miami," not necessarily what an outsider would recommend.

The Indiana Miami still have not solved their century-old problem with the United States government. Their position is that a treaty is a moral obligation and that they have never given up their rights as a tribe. The government position is that a treaty is a legal instrument and that the Miami do not meet the legal requirements of a government-to-government relationship. The Miami are angry that the federal government will not live up to its obligations. They feel that regaining legal status as a tribe would close the circle of their existence as Indian Americans and allow them to regain ground lost when they were orphaned from their treaty rights. What historian Bert Anson wrote in 1970 remains true today: "The Miamis' attitude toward their national history seems securely fixed. It is one of pride in their place in past Indian history, combined with determination that their tribal existence must continue."[2]

APPENDIX 1

Miami Leaders by Generation, Tribal Group, and Location, 1830–1994

■

1. Deaf Man's Village, later Bondy or Bundy Lineage:

(1) Shepaconah ("Deaf Man"), died 1832. (2) J.B. Brouillette, died 1867. (3) Peter Bondy, died 1895. (4) Camillus Bundy, died 1935. (5) David Bondy, died 1943. (6) Phyllis Miley, treasurer and Frances Dunnagan, council member. Original treaty grant was on the Miami/Wabash County line. Members now concentrated in Wabash.

2. Meshingomesia Miami:

(1) Metocina, died 1832. (2) Meshingomesia, died 1879. (3) William Peconga, died 1916. (4) Elijah Marks, died 1948. (5) Francis Shoemaker, retired as chief 1993. George Dorrin, council member. Reservation was in Wabash and Grant Counties. Most members now live in Wabash, Marion, and South Bend areas.

3. Godfroy Miami:

(1) Francis Godfroy, died 1840. (2) Gabriel Godfroy, died 1910. (3) Peter Godfroy, died 1928. (4) Frank Godfroy, died 1938. (5) Ira Sylvester Godfroy, died 1961. (6) Lawrence Godfroy (brother of Ira Sylvester), died 1986. (7) Louise Hay, council member. Treaty grants were east of Peru. Most live now in Peru.

4. Pimyotamah/Mongosa lineage:

(1) Chief Whitewolf, died ? (2) Pimyotamah, died 1889. (3) Mary Mongosa, died 1904. (4) Anna Marks, died 1934. (5) Joe Mongosa

(brother of Anna Marks), died 1949. (6) Carmen Ryan, died 1985. (7) Lora Siders (sister of Ryan), tribal secretary. Originally lived on Godfroy treaty grants. Most now live in Peru.

5. Richardville/Lafontaine lineage:

(1) Jean Baptiste Richardville, died 1841. (2) Francis Lafontaine, died 1847. (3) Thomas Richardville, died 1911. (4) John Owens, died ca. 1968. (5) Robert Owens (brother of John), died 1989. (6) Ray White, Jr., died 1994. Treaty grants were near Fort Wayne and Huntington. Most now live in Huntington and Fort Wayne.

Note: This list of leaders is based on current leaders and omits some leaders who were the last of their generation. For specific populations and locations of Miami groups, see Table 10.1, page 287. Because of marriages between lineages (often called clans within the tribe), most Miami share more than one lineage.

APPENDIX 2

Miami Tribal Organizations in the Twentieth Century

■

ca. 1900–ca. 1929:

"Headquarters" of the Miami Indians of Indiana. Composed of all Miami groups, this organization primarily attempted to regain federal recognition for the tribe, which was terminated in 1897.

ca. 1921–ca. 1967:

The Miami Indians of Indiana. Focused on nontaxation of treaty grant land until the late 1930s, then pursued Eastern Miami claims before the Indian Claims Commission until the late 1960s.

1923–present:

Miami Nation of Indians of Indiana. Pursued all potential claims the Eastern Miami tribe might have. In the 1930s the Miami Nation actively sought federal recognition for the tribe. Incorporated in the state of Indiana 30 September 1937. Dormant during World War II, the Miami Nation was reactivated in 1964 and again asserted broad tribal rights and federal recognition.

1978–1982:

Reorganization Council of the Miami Indians of Indiana. Formed in Huntington, Indiana, to pursue federal recognition, this organization was included in the Miami Nation after 1982.

NOTES

■

Introduction

1. Carmen Ryan to the author, 20 Aug. 1983.

2. Francis Shoemaker to the author, 6 July 1985.

3. John B. Dillon, *The National Decline of the Miami Indians*, Indiana Historical Society *Publications*, vol. 1, no. 4 (Indianapolis: Indiana Historical Society, 1897), 140–41.

4. Elizabeth J. Glenn, "Miami Heritage: Continuity and Change," speech delivered at Indiana Historical Society Annual Meeting, 7 Nov. 1987.

5. Brian S. Vargus and Jennie Lengacher with the assistance of Sheila Sego, "Needs and Goals of the Miami Indian Nation," Public Opinion Laboratory, Indiana University, Indianapolis, 1987, Miami Nation Tribal Archives, Peru, Ind.

Chapter 1

1. Reuben Gold Thwaites, ed., *The French Regime in Wisconsin, 1634–1727*, vol. 16 of *Collections of the State Historical Society of Wisconsin* (Madison, Wis.: Published by the Society, 1902), 45.

2. James A. Clifton, *The Prairie People: Continuity and Change in Potawatomi Indian Culture, 1665–1965* (Lawrence: Regents Press of Kansas, 1977), 37–40.

3. Ray Allen Billington, *Westward Expansion: A History of the American Frontier*, 5th ed. (New York: Macmillan Publishing Co., Inc., 1982), 114.

4. George R. Stewart, *American Place-Names: A Concise and Selective Dictionary for the Continental United States of America* (New York: Oxford University Press, 1970), 285, 293.

5. C. C. Trowbridge, *Meearmeear Traditions*, ed. Vernon Kinietz (Ann Arbor: University of Michigan Press, 1938), 6.

6. Alfred W. Crosby, Jr., *The Columbian Exchange: Biological and Cultural Consequences of 1492* (Westport, Conn.: Greenwood Pub. Co., 1972), 48, 52–53; Henry F. Dobyns, *Their Number Become Thinned: Native-American Population Dynamics in Eastern North America* (Knoxville: University of Tennessee Press in cooperation with the Newberry Library Center for the History of the American Indian, 1983), 25.

7. Crosby, *Columbian Exchange*, 47, 49, 56.

8. Dobyns, *Their Number Become Thinned*, 16–17.

9. Ibid., 25–26.

10. Louise Phelps Kellogg, *The French Régime in Wisconsin and the Northwest* (New York: Cooper Square Publishers, 1968), 130.

11. Emma Helen Blair, *The Indian Tribes of the Upper Mississippi Valley and Region of the Great Lakes...*, 2 vols. (Cleveland, Ohio: The Arthur H. Clark Co., 1911), 2:117.

12. Bert Anson, *The Miami Indians* (Norman: University of Oklahoma Press, 1970), 14.

13. Clifton, *Prairie People*, 68.

14. Kellogg, *French Régime*, 129.

15. R. David Edmunds, *The Potawatomis: Keepers of the Fire* (Norman: University of Oklahoma Press, 1978), x.

16. Richard White, *The Middle Ground: Indians, Empires, and Republics in the Great Lakes Region, 1650–1815* (New York: Cambridge University Press, 1991), 50–53.

17. W. Vernon Kinietz, *The Indians of the Western Great Lakes, 1615–1760* (Ann Arbor: University of Michigan Press, 1965), 180.

18. C. F. Voegelin, *Shawnee Stems and the Jacob P. Dunn Miami Dictionary*, vol. 1, nos. 3, 5, 8, 9, 10 of *Prehistory Research Series* (Indianapolis: Indiana Historical Society, 1938–40), 148.

19. Bruce Trigger, ed., *Northeast*, vol. 15 of *Handbook of North American Indians* (Washington, D.C.: Smithsonian Institution, 1978), 681.

20. Reuben Gold Thwaites, ed., *Jesuit Relations and Allied Documents*, 73 vols. (Cleveland: Burrows Bros. Co., 1896–1901), 44:247.

21. James Mooney, *The Aboriginal Population of America North of Mexico*, vol. 80, no. 7 of *Smithsonian Miscellaneous Collections* (Washington, D.C.: Smithsonian Institution, 1928), 33.

22. Blair, *Indian Tribes of the Upper Mississippi Valley*, 2:117.

23. Henry Dobyns challenges Alfred Kroeber and James Mooney's figures set forth in the 1920s by estimating population densities and

possible losses through disease caused by various sixteenth- and seventeenth-century epidemics which he lists. Dobyns's "Essay Two," in *Their Number Become Thinned* includes a discussion of pre-Columbian populations in the present American Midwest.

24. Anson, *Miami Indians*, 7.

25. Kellogg, *French Régime*, 215.

26. Clifton, *Prairie People*, 70.

27. Billington, *Westward Expansion*, 120.

28. Trowbridge, *Meearmeear Traditions*, 75–77.

29. Thwaites, ed., *The French Regime in Wisconsin*, 375.

30. Kinietz, *Indians of the Western Great Lakes*, 172, 174.

31. Henry Rowe Schoolcraft, *Information Respecting the History, Condition and Prospects of the Indian Tribes of the United States*, 6 vols. (Philadelphia: J. B. Lippincott, 1853–57), 5:194–95.

32. Voegelin, *Shawnee Stems*, 143.

33. Jacob P. Dunn Notebook, 4:75, Jacob P. Dunn Papers, Indiana Division, Indiana State Library, Indianapolis.

34. Melvin R. Gilmore, *Uses of Plants by the Indians of the Missouri River Region* (Lincoln: University of Nebraska Press, 1977), 84.

35. Kinietz, *Indians of the Western Great Lakes*, 223–25; Virgil J. Vogel, *American Indian Medicine*, vol. 95 of The Civilization of the American Indian Series (Norman: University of Oklahoma Press, 1970), lists fifteen uses for medicinal plants, most before 1760.

36. Kinietz, *Indians of the Western Great Lakes*, 173–74.

37. Jacob P. Dunn, *Indiana and Indianans: A History of Aboriginal and Territorial Indiana and the Century of Statehood*, 5 vols. (Chicago and New York: American Historical Society, 1919), 1:75.

38. Kinietz, *Indians of the Western Great Lakes*, 174.

39. Dunn, *Indiana and Indianans*, 1:75–76.

40. Cornelius J. Jaenen, *Friend and Foe: Aspects of French-American Cultural Contact in the Sixteenth and Seventeenth Centuries* (New York: Columbia University Press, 1976), 90.

41. Voegelin, *Shawnee Stems*, 417.

42. Robert E. Ritzenthaler and Pat Ritzenthaler, *The Woodland Indians of the Western Great Lakes* (Garden City, N.Y.: Natural History Press, 1970), 60–61.

43. Ibid., 61–62.

44. Kinietz, *Indians of the Western Great Lakes*, 171; Voegelin, *Shawnee Stems*, 443; Ritzenthaler and Ritzenthaler, *Woodland Indians*, 63.

45. Kinietz, *Indians of the Western Great Lakes*, 167–68.

46. Dunn, *Indiana and Indianans*, 1:61–63.

47. Ibid., 64–65; Trowbridge, *Meearmeear Traditions*, 56.

48. Ibid., 44–45.

49. Kinietz, *Indians of the Western Great Lakes*, 202–3.

50. Ibid., 203.

51. Ibid., 203–4.

52. Trowbridge, *Meearmeear Traditions*, 44.

53. Kinietz, *Indians of the Western Great Lakes*, 205–6.

54. Trowbridge, *Meearmeear Traditions*, 44.

55. George Irving Quimby, *Indian Life in the Upper Great Lakes, 11,000 B.C. to A.D. 1800* (Chicago: University of Chicago Press, 1960), 136.

56. Ibid.

57. Trowbridge, *Meearmeear Traditions*, 40.

58. Jacob P. Dunn interview with Sarah Wadsworth, 14 Jan. 1911, Dunn Notebook.

59. Trowbridge, *Meearmeear Traditions*, 30–33.

60. Ibid., 34–36.

61. Ibid., 60.

62. Clifton, *Prairie People*, 125.

63. Ibid., 264.

64. Anson, *Miami Indians*, 25.

65. Voegelin, *Shawnee Stems*, 376.

66. Trowbridge, *Meearmeear Traditions*, 68.

67. Raymond E. Hauser, "The *Berdache* and the Illinois Indian Tribe during the Last Half of the Seventeenth Century," *Ethnohistory* 37, no. 1 (1990): 58.

68. Voegelin, *Shawnee Stems*, 414.

69. Ibid., 323, 357.

70. Dunn Notebook, 1.

71. Trowbridge, *Meearmeear Traditions*, 61–63.

72. Ibid.

73. Ibid., 63–64.

74. Clifton, *Prairie People*, 56.

75. Trowbridge, *Meearmeear Traditions*, 14.

76. Ibid., 14–15.

77. Ibid., 14.

78. Ibid., 19.

79. Ibid., 19, 25.

80. Ibid., 19–21.

81. Ibid., 26.

82. Ibid., 21–23.

Chapter 2

1. Wallace A. Brice, *History of Fort Wayne* (Fort Wayne, Ind.: D. W. Jones and Son, 1868), 38.

2. Henry Rowe Schoolcraft, *Information Respecting the History, Condition and Prospects of the Indian Tribes of the United States*, 6 vols. (Philadelphia: J. B. Lippincott Co., 1853–57), 5:192.

3. Ibid., 29–30.

4. Ibid., 30–31.

5. Reuben Gold Thwaites, ed., *The French Regime in Wisconsin, 1634–1727*, vol. 16 of *Collections of the State Historical Society of Wisconsin* (Madison, Wis.: Published by the Society, 1902), 323, 375.

6. John D. Barnhart and Dorothy L. Riker, *Indiana to 1816: The Colonial Period* (Indianapolis: Indiana Historical Bureau and Indiana Historical Society, 1971), 84.

7. Richard White, *The Middle Ground: Indians, Empires, and Republics in the Great Lakes Region, 1650–1815* (New York: Cambridge University Press, 1991), 217; Reuben Gold Thwaites, ed., *The French Regime in Wisconsin, 1727–1748*, vol. 17 of *Collections of the State Historical Society of Wisconsin* (Madison, Wis.: Published by the Society, 1906), 175.

8. White, *Middle Ground*, 120–21.

9. Ray Allen Billington, *Westward Expansion: A History of the American Frontier*, 5th ed. (New York: Macmillan Publishing Co., Inc., 1982), 132.

10. Ibid., 132–33; Barnhart and Riker, *Indiana to 1816*, p. 97.

11. Thwaites, *French Regime in Wisconsin, 1727–1748*, pp. 482 n. 2, 484–85, 503–4; Harvey Lewis Carter, *The Life and Times of Little Turtle: First Sagamore of the Wabash* (Urbana: University of Illinois Press, 1987), 31–33.

12. Theodore Calvin Pease and Ernestine Jenison, eds., *Illinois on the Eve of the Seven Years' War, 1747–1755*, vol. 29 of Illinois State Historical Library *Collections* (Springfield, 1940), 149, 166, 169.

13. White, *Middle Ground*, 230–32.

14. Ibid., 216–17.

15. Ibid., 219.

16. Louise Phelps Kellogg, *The French Régime in Wisconsin and the Northwest* (New York: Cooper Square Publishers, 1968), 425, 428–29.

17. Barnhart and Riker, *Indiana to 1816*, pp. 120–21; Carter, *Little Turtle*, 35–36.

18. Billington, *Westward Expansion*, 139–40.

19. Adapted from Elizabeth J. Glenn, "Miami and Delaware Trade Routes and Relationships in Northern Indiana," in Ronald Hicks, *Native American Cultures in Indiana: Proceedings of the First Minnetrista Council for Great Lakes Native American Studies* (Muncie, Ind.: Minnetrista Cultural Center and Ball State University, 1992), 63.

20. Helen Hornbeck Tanner, *Atlas of Great Lakes Indian History* (Norman: Published for the Newberry Library by the University of Oklahoma Press, 1987), 80.

21. Donald J. Berthrong, *Indians of Northern Indiana and Southern Michigan* (New York: Garland Publishing, Inc., 1974), 210–11.

22. White, *Middle Ground*, 495–96; Carter, *Little Turtle*, 76.

23. Tanner, *Atlas of Great Lakes Indian History*, 89.

24. Glenn, "Miami and Delaware Trade Routes," 64.

25. C. C. Trowbridge, *Meearmeear Traditions*, ed. Vernon Kinietz (Ann Arbor: University of Michigan Press, 1938).

26. Billington, *Westward Expansion*, 147.

27. Howard H. Peckham, *Pontiac and the Indian Uprising* (Princeton, N.J.: Princeton University Press, 1947), 160–61.

28. Reuben Gold Thwaites, ed., *Early Western Travels, 1748–1846*, 32 vols. (Cleveland: Arthur H. Clark Co., 1904–7), 308, 313–18.

29. Clarence Walworth Alvord and Clarence Edwin Carter, eds., *The New Regimé, 1765–1767*, vol. 11 of Illinois State Historical Library *Collections* (Springfield, 1916), 35–36.

30. Billington, *Westward Expansion*, 153.

31. Ibid., 173–75; Anthony F. C. Wallace, *The Death and Rebirth of the Seneca* (New York: Alfred A. Knopf, 1970), 122–23.

32. White, *Middle Ground*, 381.

33. John D. Barnhart, ed., *Henry Hamilton and George Rogers Clark in the American Revolution* (Crawfordsville, Ind.: R. E. Banta, 1951), 189; *The French, the Indians, and George Rogers Clark in the Illinois Country*, Proceedings of an American Revolution Bicentennial Symposium (Indianapolis: Indiana Historical Society, 1977), 53.

34. Barnhart, ed., *Henry Hamilton and George Rogers Clark*, 102–6; Billington, *Westward Expansion*, 197.

35. John F. Meginness, *Biography of Frances Slocum, the Lost Sister of Wyoming* (Williamsport, Pa.: Heller Bros. Printing House, 1891), 19–20.

36. Ibid., 38.

37. Louis Houck, ed., *The Spanish Regime in Missouri*, 2 vols. (Chicago: R. R. Donnelly, 1909), 1:44.

38. Carter, *Little Turtle*, 72–74; Anson, *Miami Indians*, 91.

39. Wallace, *Death and Rebirth of the Seneca*, 151–53, 158–59.

40. Ibid., 154–55.

41. Billington, *Westward Expansion*, 211–13, 215, 219.

42. Wallace, *Death and Rebirth of the Seneca*, 156.

43. Robert M. Taylor, Jr., ed., *The Northwest Ordinance, 1787: A Bicentennial Handbook* (Indianapolis: Indiana Historical Society, 1987), 61–62.

44. Lawrence Kinnaird, ed., *Spain in the Mississippi Valley, 1765–1794: Translations of Materials from the Spanish Archives in the Bancroft Library*, 4 vols. (Washington, D.C.: U.S. Government Printing Office, 1949), 3:179–80.

45. Gayle Thornbrough, ed., *Outpost on the Wabash, 1787–1791*, Indiana Historical Society *Publications*, vol. 19 (Indianapolis: Indiana Historical Society, 1957), 115–17.

46. Kinnaird, ed., *Spain in the Mississippi Valley*, 3:292.

47. M. M. Quaife, *Fort Wayne in 1790*, Indiana Historical Society *Publications*, vol. 7, no. 7 (Indianapolis: Indiana Historical Society, 1921), 299–300; White, *Middle Ground*, 449–50.

48. Carter, *Little Turtle*, 76.

49. Brice, *History of Fort Wayne*, 285 n.

50. Quaife, *Fort Wayne in 1790*, pp. 311–12.

51. Ibid., 320, 324.

52. Ibid., 359.

53. Wiley Sword, *President Washington's Indian War: The Struggle for the Old Northwest, 1790–1795* (Norman: University of Oklahoma Press, 1985), 75.

54. *American State Papers: Indian Affairs*, 2 vols. (Washington, D.C.: Gales and Seaton, 1832–34), 1:94.

55. Sword, *President Washington's Indian War*, 85.

56. Ibid., 87.

57. Francis Paul Prucha, *American Indian Policy in the Formative Years: The Indian Trade and Intercourse Acts, 1780–1834* (Boston: Harvard University Press, 1962), 45–46.

58. Sword, *President Washington's Indian War*, 88.

59. Carter, *Little Turtle*, 90.

60. Ibid., 90–91.

61. *American State Papers: Indian Affairs*, 1:104.

62. Billington, *Westward Expansion*, 225; Carter, *Little Turtle*, 94–95.

63. Trowbridge, *Meearmeear Traditions*, 10.

64. Carter, *Little Turtle*, 95.

65. Sword, *President Washington's Indian War*, 168; Carter, *Little Turtle*, 104–5.

66. Carter, *Little Turtle*, 107–8.

67. Ibid., 108–9; Sword, *President Washington's Indian War*, 195.

68. Sword, *President Washington's Indian War*, 206–7.

69. Ibid., 232, 234.

70. Anson, *Miami Indians*, 126–27; Sword, *President Washington's Indian War*, 278.

71. Carter, *Little Turtle*, 112.

72. *American State Papers: Indian Affairs*, 1:490.

73. Anson, *Miami Indians*, 128–29.

74. Billington, *Westward Expansion*, 227–28; Anson, *Miami Indians*, 129–30.

75. Richard B. Morris, ed., *Encyclopedia of American History* (New York: Harper and Row, 1970), 126–27.

Chapter 3

1. Bernard W. Sheehan, *Seeds of Extinction: Jeffersonian Philanthropy and the American Indian* (Chapel Hill: University of North Carolina Press, 1973), 169.

2. Nellie Armstrong Robertson and Dorothy Riker, eds., *The John Tipton Papers*, 3 vols. (Indianapolis: Indiana Historical Bureau, 1942), 1:83.

3. Several scholars have studied the phenomenon of American notions of the Indian. These ideas have become so ingrained that the particular existence of Indian groups often has been ignored or distorted, frequently with serious negative impact for the Indians. Major works describing the process are Robert F. Berkhofer, *The White Man's Indian: Images of the American Indian from Columbus to the Present* (New York: Alfred A. Knopf, 1978) and James A. Clifton, *The Invented Indian: Cultural Fictions and Government Policies* (New Brunswick, N.J.: Transactions Publishers, 1990). Non-Indian myths and creations of Native American identity often are patronizing and denigrate the Indian people's sense of who they are.

4. R. David Edmunds, "National Expansion from the Indian Perspective," in *Indians in American History*, ed. Frederick E. Hoxie (Arlington Heights, Ill.: Harlan Davidson, Inc., 1988), 167–69.

5. Ibid., 159–60.

6. *American State Papers: Indian Affairs*, 2 vols. (Washington, D.C.: Gales and Seaton, 1832–34), 1:570.

7. Wiley Sword, *President Washington's Indian War: The Struggle for the Old Northwest, 1790–1795* (Norman: University of Oklahoma Press, 1985), 328.

8. Charles J. Kappler, ed., *Indian Affairs: Laws and Treaties*, 2d ed., 2 vols. (Washington, D.C.: Government Printing Office, 1904), 2:44.

9. Wilcomb Washburn, ed., *History of Indian-White Relations*, vol. 4 of *Handbook of North American Indians* (Washington, D.C.: Smithsonian Institution, 1988), 195. The United States government concluded 370 treaties with Indian tribes before treaty making was ended in 1871. This figure includes the eight treaties concluded during the period of the confederation from 1778 to 1789.

10. Kappler, ed., *Indian Affairs*, 2:39–44.

11. Samuel Flagg Bemis, *Jay's Treaty: A Study in Commerce and Diplomacy* (New Haven, Conn.: Yale University Press, 1962), 393–94.

12. Ibid., 42.

13. C. F. Volney, *A View of the Climate and Soil of the United States of America* (London: Printed for J. Johnson, 1804), 399–408, 493–503 (word list).

14. Virgil J. Vogel, *American Indian Medicine*, vol. 95 of The Civilization of the American Indian Series (Norman: University of Oklahoma Press,

1970) lists about fifteen medicinal plants used by the Miami. The author has supplemented Vogel with interviews with Miami, particularly LaMoine Marks, 7 Nov. 1989.

15. Jacob P. Dunn, *Indiana and Indianans: A History of Aboriginal and Territorial Indiana in the Century of Statehood,* 5 vols. (Chicago: The American Historical Society, 1919), 1:74–80; Swan Hunter and Eva Bossley, interview with the author, 10 Aug. 1978; Marks interview, 7 Nov. 1989.

16. R. David Edmunds, *Tecumseh and the Quest for Indian Leadership* (Boston: Little, Brown, 1984), 63–64.

17. Elizabeth J. Glenn, B. K. Swartz, Jr., and Russell E. Lewis, *Archaeological Reports, Number 14* (Muncie, Ind.: Ball State University, 1977), 49, mentions that beaver traps were in demand before the War of 1812 and that the Mississinewa was good beaver country. Dunn, *Indiana and Indianans,* 1:75; Herman and Wyneeta Bundy, interview with the author, 24 Nov. 1980; LaMoine Marks, interview with the author, 24–25 Aug. 1989.

18. Dunn, *Indiana and Indianans,* 1:75; Marks interview, 24–25 Aug. 1989.

19. Wallace A. Brice, *History of Fort Wayne* (Fort Wayne, Ind.: D. W. Jones and Son, 1868), 23.

20. Logan Esarey, ed., *Messages and Letters of William Henry Harrison,* 2 vols. (Indianapolis: Indiana Historical Commission, 1922), 2:138.

21. Brice, *History of Fort Wayne,* 291.

22. Bert Anson, *The Miami Indians* (Norman: University of Oklahoma Press, 1970), 149.

23. Ray Allen Billington, *Westward Expansion,* 5th ed. (New York: Macmillan, 1982), 263–65.

24. Clarence E. Carter, *Territorial Papers of the United States,* 27 vols. (Washington, D.C.: Government Printing Office, 1934–69), 7:86–87.

25. Dorothy Goebel, *William Henry Harrison: A Political Biography* (Indianapolis: Indiana Library and Historical Department, 1926), 101–2.

26. Ibid., 101.

27. James A. Clifton, *The Prairie People: Continuity and Change in Potawatomi Indian Culture, 1665–1965* (Lawrence: Regents Press of Kansas, 1977), 186–87.

28. Carter, *Territorial Papers,* 7:88–92.

29. Ibid.

30. Sheehan, *Seeds of Extinction,* 174.

31. Carter, *Territorial Papers,* 7:90–92.

32. C. A. Weslager, *The Delaware Indians: A History* (New Brunswick, N.J.: Rutgers University Press, 1989), 339.

33. Goebel, *William Henry Harrison,* 103.

34. Kappler, ed., *Indian Affairs,* 2:81.

35. Edmunds, *Tecumseh,* 69–70.

36. Gayle Thornbrough, ed., *Letter Book of the Indian Agency at Fort Wayne, 1809–1815*, Indiana Historical Society *Publications*, vol. 21 (Indianapolis: Indiana Historical Society, 1961), 18.

37. Charles C. Royce, comp., *Indian Land Cessions in the United States* (New York: Arno Press and The New York Times, 1971), 662–69; Anson, *Miami Indians*, 148.

38. Reginald Horsman, *Expansion and American Indian Policy, 1783–1812* (East Lansing: Michigan State University Press, 1967), 149–51, 154.

39. Anson, *Miami Indians*, 150–51.

40. Harrison to Secretary of War, 15 July 1801, in Esarey, ed., *Messages and Letters*, 1:28–30; Anson, *Miami Indians*, 150–51.

41. Erminie Wheeler-Voegelin, Emily J. Blasingham, and Dorothy R. Libby, *Miami, Wea, and Eel-River Indians of Southern Indiana* (New York: Garland Publishing, Inc., 1974), 344–64, 422–24; Clifton, *Prairie People*, 187, 197.

42. Esarey, ed., *Messages and Letters*, 1:375.

43. Kappler, ed., *Indian Affairs*, 2:102. Silver Heels's native name and marriage are mentioned in Jacob P. Dunn Notebook 1, p. 207, Indiana State Library, Indianapolis. Mrs. Sarah Wadsworth said in an interview in 1909 that Silver Heels went west with the Miami at the time of removal and later settled in the Cherokee Nation near Chetopa, Kansas.

44. Clifton, *Prairie People*, 198.

45. Esarey, ed., *Messages and Letters*, 1:577–79.

46. Thornbrough, ed., *Letter Book*, 172–73 n.

47. Elizabeth J. Glenn, B. K. Swartz, Jr., and Russell E. Lewis, *Archaeological Reports. Number 14. Ethnohistorical and Archaeological Descriptive Accounts of the War of 1812. Mississinewa Campaign and Aftermath: Project Report*, edited by B. K. Swartz, Jr. (Muncie: Ball State University, 1977), 3-4; Esarey, ed., *Messages and Letters*, 2:138.

48. Esarey, ed., *Messages and Letters*, 2:229.

49. Anson, *Miami Indians*, 169–70.

50. Ibid., 173.

51. Ibid., 174; Kappler, ed., *Indian Affairs*, 2:105.

Chapter 4

1. Nellie Armstrong Robertson and Dorothy Riker, eds., *The John Tipton Papers*, 3 vols. (Indianapolis: Indiana Historical Bureau, 1942), 1:588.

2. Ibid., 2:116.

3. Benjamin Stickney, Indian agent at Fort Wayne, to Thomas L. McKenney, superintendent of Indian Affairs, 27 Aug. 1817, quoted in Wallace A. Brice, *History of Fort Wayne* (Fort Wayne, Ind.: D. W. Jones and Son, 1868), 291.

4. Ibid.

5. Ibid. See also John B. Dillon, *The National Decline of the Miami Indians*, Indiana Historical Society *Publications*, vol. 1, no. 4 (Indianapolis: Indiana Historical Society, 1897), 139, 140.

6. George A. Schultz, *An Indian Canaan* (Norman: University of Oklahoma Press, 1972), 37–38, 58–59; Bert Anson, *The Miami Indians* (Norman: University of Oklahoma Press, 1970), 25.

7. Anson, *Miami Indians*, 284; Charles J. Kappler, ed., *Indian Affairs: Laws and Treaties*, 2 vols. (Washington, D.C.: Government Printing Office, 1904), 2:172.

8. Kappler, ed., *Indian Affairs*, 2:172–73; Bernard W. Sheehan, *Seeds of Extinction: Jeffersonian Philanthropy and the American Indian* (Chapel Hill: University of North Carolina Press, 1973), 169.

9. Robert A. Trennert, Jr., *Indian Traders on the Middle Border: The House of Ewing, 1827–54* (Lincoln: University of Nebraska Press, 1981), 7.

10. Kappler, ed., *Indian Affairs*, 2:171–74.

11. Trennert, *Indian Traders on the Middle Border*, 7–8.

12. Robertson and Riker, eds., *Tipton Papers*, 1:10–11, 351n, 360–61n.

13. Ibid., 1:446–47n.

14. R. David Edmunds, "National Expansion from the Indian Perspective," in *Indians in American History: An Introduction*, ed. Frederick E. Hoxie (Arlington Heights, Ill.: Harlan Davidson, Inc., 1988), 167–69.

15. James A. Clifton, *The Prairie People: Continuity and Change in Potawatomi Indian Culture, 1665–1965* (Lawrence: Regents Press of Kansas, 1977), 275–76.

16. Anson, *Miami Indians*, 210–11; Jacob P. Dunn, *True Indian Stories: With Glossary of Indiana Indian Names* (Indianapolis: Sentinel Printing Co., 1909), 197–212. Jessamyn West wrote a historical novel, *The Massacre at Fall Creek* (New York: Harcourt Brace Jovanovich, 1975), based on the episode.

17. Brice, *History of Fort Wayne*, 35–37.

18. Ibid., 291; Robertson and Riker, eds., *Tipton Papers*, 1:475.

19. C. A. Weslager, *The Delaware Indian Westward Migration* (Wallingford, Pa.: Middle Atlantic Press, 1978), 85, 160.

20. C. C. Trowbridge, *Meearmeear Traditions*, ed. Vernon Kinietz (Ann Arbor: University of Michigan Press, 1938), 39.

21. Ibid., 46–47, 63, 87–88.

22. Robertson and Riker, eds., *Tipton Papers*, 1:307n.

23. Ibid., 1:307–8; Sheehan, *Seeds of Extinction*, 122–23.

24. Robertson and Riker, eds., *Tipton Papers*, 1:358.

25. Ibid., 1:664; Anson, *Miami Indians*, 189 n.20.

26. In the long run, Methodist, Catholic, Episcopalian, and other denominational missionaries to midwestern tribes had a positive impact on tribal survival and the preservation of tribal rights.

27. Sheehan, *Seeds of Extinction*, 254.

28. Ibid., 254–55.

29. Robertson and Riker, eds., *Tipton Papers*, 1:3–8.

30. Ronald N. Satz, *American Indian Policy in the Jacksonian Era* (Lincoln: University of Nebraska Press, 1975), 182, 184–85.

31. Robertson and Riker, eds., *Tipton Papers*, 1:10–11.

32. Trennert, *Indian Traders on the Middle Border*, 9–13, 16.

33. Robertson and Riker, eds., *Tipton Papers*, 1:11, 353, 380.

34. Ibid., 1:12.

35. Ibid., 1:578–79.

36. Ibid., 1:583–84.

37. Ibid., 1:15–16.

38. Ibid., 1:603–5.

39. Ibid., 1:17–18.

40. Kappler, ed., *Indian Affairs*, 2:280.

41. Ibid., 2:279.

42. Robertson and Riker, eds., *Tipton Papers*, 1:19–21.

43. Erminie Wheeler-Voegelin, Emily J. Blasingham, and Dorothy R. Libby, *Miami, Wea, and Eel-River Indians of Southern Indiana* (New York: Garland Publishing, Inc., 1974), 151–52.

44. Allen Hamilton to T. Hartley Crawford, 13 Aug. 1842, RG 75, M234, roll 418, National Archives, Washington, D.C.

45. John Tipton gave the landholding and population figures to Secretary of War John Eaton in a report dated 5 Apr. 1831, in Robertson and Riker, eds., *Tipton Papers*, 2:399. His estimate for Miami landholdings is too small, considering the land ceded during the 1830s that is listed in Charles C. Royce, comp., *Indian Land Cessions in the United States* (New York: Arno Press and The New York Times, 1971). The estimate for land still in Indian hands in 1840 is based on the small reservations existing at that time. A careful search of land transactions in several counties would be necessary to ascertain a more precise figure. The Miami population of eight hundred in 1840 is a rough estimate based on Agent Samuel Milroy's comments in the *Annual Report, Commissioner of Indian Affairs* (Washington, D.C.: J. Gideon, Jr., 1840), 127–28.

46. Elfrieda Lang, "An Analysis of Northern Indiana's Population in 1850," *Indiana Magazine of History* 49 (Mar. 1953): 17–18; Charles R. Poinsatte, *Fort Wayne during the Canal Era, 1828–1855: A Study of a Western Community in the Middle Period of American History* (Indianapolis: Indiana Historical Bureau, 1969), 104.

47. Steven L. Johnson, *Guide to American Indian Documents in the Congressional Serial Set, 1817–1899: A Project of the Institute for the Development of Indian Law* (New York: Clearwater Publishing Co., Inc., 1977), 22–25, 26.

48. Robertson and Riker, eds., *Tipton Papers*, 1:42–43.

49. Ibid., 2:400.

50. Clifton, *Prairie People*, 298–99. See R. David Edmunds, *The Potawatomis: Keepers of the Fire* (Norman: University of Oklahoma Press, 1978), 267–68, for a detailed account. Irving McKee, *The Trail of Death: Letters of Benjamin Marie Petit*, Indiana Historical Society *Publications*, vol. 14, no. 1 (Indianapolis: Indiana Historical Society, 1941), contains Father Petit's description of the event.

51. Robertson and Riker, eds., *Tipton Papers*, 1:47.

52. Kappler, ed., *Indian Affairs*, 2:521.

53. Ibid.

54. Ibid., 2:520; Robertson and Riker, eds., *Tipton Papers*, 1:47–48.

55. Trennert, *Indian Traders on the Middle Border*, 85; Anson, *Miami Indians*, 204–5.

56. Trennert, *Indian Traders on the Middle Border*, 84.

57. Kappler, ed., *Indian Affairs*, 2:531.

58. Ibid., 2:533.

59. Trennert, *Indian Traders on the Middle Border*, 85–87.

60. John F. Meginness, *Biography of Frances Slocum, the Lost Sister of Wyoming* (Williamsport, Pa.: Heller Bros. Printing House, 1891), 206.

61. Robertson and Riker, eds., *Tipton Papers*, 1:49; Brice, *Fort Wayne*, 315n.

62. Trennert, *Indian Traders on the Middle Border*, 98, 121, 126.

63. Senate Document, No. 164, 26th Cong., 1st sess., 4–5.

64. *Annual Report, Commissioner of Indian Affairs*, 127–28.

65. Meginness, *Frances Slocum*, 69.

66. Ibid., 110–11.

67. *The Journals and Indian Paintings of George Winter, 1837–1839* (Indianapolis: Indiana Historical Society, 1948), 164–67.

68. Meginness, *Frances Slocum*, 111.

69. *Indians and a Changing Frontier: The Art of George Winter* (Indianapolis: Indiana Historical Society, 1993), 27.

70. Ibid., 28.

71. Meginness, *Frances Slocum*, 111.

72. Anson, *Miami Indians*, 220–21.

73. Clifton, *Prairie People*, 299–300, 315, 330–31.

74. *History of St. Joseph County, Indiana* (Chicago: Charles C. Chapman and Co., 1880), 467.

75. National Archives, Record Group 75, Office of Indian Affairs, Letters Received, M234, roll 418, frames 85–86 (hereafter cited as RG 75, OIA LR).

76. George W. Ewing to Commissioner of Indian Affairs, 24 Nov. 1846, RG 75, OIA LR, M234, roll 418, frame 86.

77. Bert Anson, "Chief Francis Lafontaine and the Miami Emigration from Indiana," *Indiana Magazine of History* 60 (Sept. 1964): 255–56.

78. Ewing to Commissioner of Indian Affairs William Medill, 12 Mar. 1846, RG 75, OIA LR, M234, roll 418, frames 72–73.

79. Trennert, *Indian Traders on the Middle Border,* 130.

80. Allen Hamilton and Father Julian Benoit to Commissioner of Indian Affairs William Medill, 31 Aug. 1846, RG 75, OIA LR, M234, roll 418, frames 63–64.

81. RG 75, OIA LR, M234, roll 418, frames 56–59, and Anson, *Miami Indians,* 224.

82. Anson, *Miami Indians,* 224.

83. Ibid., 225–26.

84. George W. Ewing to Commissioner of Indian Affairs William Medill, 24 Nov. 1846, RG 75, OIA LR, M234, roll 418, frame 83.

85. Ibid., frame 84.

Chapter 5

1. "Testimony Pursuant to Congressional Legislation of June 1, 1872, taken before the commission appointed by the Secretary of the Interior to make partition of the reserve granted to Me-shin-go-me-sia in trust for his band by the seventh article of the treaty of November 28th 1840 between the United States and the Miami Tribe of Indians," pp. 72–74, 160, RG 75, ISP Shelf 8, Item 310, National Archives, Washington, D.C. Page numbers are those from lower left of document (hereafter cited as "1873 Testimony").

2. Bert Anson, *The Miami Indians* (Norman: University of Oklahoma Press, 1970), 229.

3. Robert A. Trennert, Jr., *Alternative to Extinction: Federal Indian Policy and the Beginnings of the Reservation System, 1846–51* (Philadelphia: Temple University Press, 1975), 30–31, 40–42, 56.

4. H. Craig Miner and William E. Unrau, *The End of Indian Kansas: A Study of Cultural Revolution, 1854–1871* (Lawrence: Regents Press of Kansas, 1978), 18–19, 100.

5. This estimate is based on a search of land transfers in Miami, Grant, and Wabash Counties and an examination of published transfers for Allen and Huntington Counties. As Miami landholdings declined in the late nineteenth century the figures became more precise.

6. *Statistics of Population, Ninth Census of the United States* (Washington, D.C.: Government Printing Office, 1872), Table 3.

7. *Wabash Weekly Intelligencer,* 16 Dec. 1857.

8. Anson, *Miami Indians,* 229; James Aveline to Judge Albert Cole, 28 July 1847, M586, box 4, folder 6, A. A. Cole Papers, Indiana Historical Society Library, Indianapolis.

9. Alphonso A. Cole to William Medill, 10 Apr. 1848, box 4, folder 7, ibid.

10. George W. Ewing to A. A. Cole, 24 Jan. 1851, box 4, folder 10, ibid.

11. George W. Ewing to A. A. Cole, 9 July 1851, box 4, folder 10, and Daniel Bearss to Commissioner of Indian Affairs Luke Lea, 26 Sept. 1850, ibid.

12. *U.S. Statutes at Large* 9 (1857): 806; House Report, No. 281, 31st Cong., 1st sess., 24 Apr. 1850, 2:584.

13. Oliver P. Morton and Thomas A. Hendricks to Office of Indian Affairs, Washington, D.C., 17 July 1868, RG 75.

14. William T. Hagan, *American Indians* (Chicago: University of Chicago Press, 1979), 97–98.

15. Miner and Unrau, *End of Indian Kansas*, 16, 100.

16. "Minutes of Conference with Miami Delegation, May 23–June 5, 1854," p. 2, RG 75, Treaty File, Microcopy T494, roll 5.

17. Anson, *Miami Indians*, 263.

18. U.S. Court of Claims, Appeal No. 2-59, decided 15 July 1960.

19. Anson, *Miami Indians*, 270.

20. "Minutes of Conference with Miami Delegation," 6, 8.

21. Charles J. Kappler, ed., *Indian Affairs: Laws and Treaties*, 2d ed., 2 vols. (Washington, D.C.: Government Printing Office, 1904), 2:644.

22. Ibid.

23. Lindsay's instructions dated 13 Jan. 1854 are on page 309 of RG 75, Office of Indian Affairs, Letters Sent, M21, roll 48, RG 75, Osage River L295, Civilization File. This is the original of Lindsay's roll, which includes extensive family information that was not included on the final roll.

24. Ibid.

25. Anson, *Miami Indians*, 271–73.

26. *U.S. Statutes at Large* 11 (1863): 332.

27. House Executive Document, No. 23, 49th Cong., 1st sess., 6 Jan. 1886, 25:4, 5, 26.

28. Council Book, Miami Nation of Indians, 1937–42, Miami Nation Tribal Archives, Peru, Ind.

29. *Congressional Globe*, 39th Cong., 2d sess., 1867, vol. 37, pt. 3: 1647–50.

30. *Opinions of the Attorney General* (Washington, D.C.: Government Printing Office, 1898), 12:236.

31. Ely S. Parker to Commissioner of the General Land Office, 21 Feb. 1870, RG 75, Letterbook, Meshingomesia Reserve Entry 310, ISP Shelf 8.

32. *Me-shing-go-me-sia and Another v. The State and Another*, 36 Ind. 310, 313, 315, 317–18 (1871).

33. "1873 Testimony," 64.

34. Ibid., 255.

35. Stewart J. Rafert, "The Hidden Community: The Miami Indians of Indiana, 1846–1940" (Ph.D. diss., University of Delaware, 1982), 172.

36. "1873 Testimony," 144, 186.

37. Ibid., 55, 191–92.

38. Miami County, Ind., Deed Book V, 530.

39. Rafert, "Hidden Community," 174. Families were reconstructed by using annuity rolls.

40. John B. Dillon, *National Decline of the Miami Indians*, Indiana Historical Society *Publications*, vol. 1, no. 4 (Indianapolis: Indiana Historical Society, 1897), 139.

41. Dunn Notebook 1, Jacob P. Dunn Papers, Indiana Division, Indiana State Library, Indianapolis.

42. This constellation of marriages was reconstructed by family members of the three individuals, using the author's Individual Survey Forms 49, 128, and 131.

43. "1873 Testimony," divorce, 332, adoption, 106.

44. Ibid., 154, 411–12.

45. Jacob P. Dunn interview with Sarah Wadsworth, Miami, Okla., 10 Oct. 1909, Dunn Notebook 1, p. 222.

46. *U.S. Statutes at Large* 17 (1872): 213.

47. "1873 Testimony," 72, 82, 85, 105–6, 135, 148–50, 158, 160, 206–7, 384.

48. Ibid., 300.

49. Ibid., 278.

50. Ibid., 291, 382, 423.

51. Ibid., 395–405.

52. The numbers are from the 1854 treaty roll and the 1870 annuity roll, RG 75.

53. Grant County, Ind., Deed Records T, 358.

54. Grant County, Ind., Miscellaneous Records, 1:31.

55. These figures are aggregates developed from the spotty reporting of Miami landholdings on the U.S. Census, Agricultural Returns, Indiana, 1850, 1860, and 1870 for Miami, Grant, Wabash, Huntington, and Allen Counties. The original agricultural census returns are held by the Archives Division, Indiana Commission on Public Records, Indiana State Library.

56. "1873 Testimony," 423–25, 428.

57. Meshingomesia to Commissioner of Indian Affairs, 8 Dec. 1859, RG 75, Letterbook Meshingomesia Reserve.

58. Bernard L. Herman, *The Stolen House* (Charlottesville: University Press of Virginia, 1992), 183, 186.

59. Mark Rose, "A Nineteenth Century Miami House on the Mississinewa" (Honors thesis, Ball State University, 1979), 22, 26.

60. Rafert, "Hidden Community," 125.
61. Ibid.
62. Ibid., 115–16.
63. "1873 Testimony," 202, 254.
64. *Godfroy v. Poe*, Miami Circuit Court, spring session, 1855 and *Godfroy v. Loveland*, Miami Circuit Court, fall session, 1859. James R. Godfroy, an older half brother, was married to Archangel Richardville and lived near Fort Wayne. He was never deeply involved in tribal affairs.

Chapter 6

1. RG 75, OIA LR 1899:11762, National Archives, Washington, D.C.
2. "Report of Commission appointed by the Secretary of the Interior to make partition of the Reserve to Me-shin-go-me-sia," RG 75, Entry 310, ISP Shelf 8, Item 95.
3. Clarence Danhof, "Farm-Making Costs and the 'Safety Valve': 1850–60," *Journal of Political Economy* 49 (June 1941): 317–59.
4. Wabash County, Indiana, Recorder's Office, Miscellaneous Record H, 155–56.
5. Wabash County Clerk's Office, guardianship box 88, packet 20.
6. The history of Bundy's property is from the Wabash County Recorder's Office, Deed Record 41, 117; Mortgage Record 4, 405; Mortgage Record 1–3, 448; and Chattel Record, 193.
7. Stewart Rafert, "The Hidden Community: The Miami Indians, 1846–1940" (Ph.D. diss., University of Delaware, 1982), 39–40.
8. Peru *Miami County Sentinel*, 30 Dec. 1880.
9. Ibid.
10. Rafert, "Hidden Community," 42–44.
11. "Pikanga's Life, as told by himself," translated by Jacob P. Dunn, Jacob P. Dunn Papers, Indiana State Library, Indianapolis.
12. Otho Winger, *The Frances Slocum Trail* (North Manchester, Ind.: The News-Journal, 1943), 72–73.
13. Rafert, "Hidden Community," 44–45.
14. This total was compiled from the 1903–7 property transfer books in the Grant and Wabash Counties auditors' offices. John and Jane Newman owned 10.74 acres, Lucy Peconga 15.2 acres, and Emma Walters 31.9 acres. The author was able to compile a history of every land transfer of the Meshingomesia Reserve.
15. Ninth and tenth censuses of the United States, 1870 and 1880, Agricultural Schedules, Indiana, Miami County, 1, 21; *Combination Atlas Map of Miami County* (N. p.: Kingman Brothers, 1877), 87.
16. Will M. Hundley, *Squawtown: My Boyhood among the Last Miami Indians* (Caldwell, Idaho: Caxton Printers, Ltd., 1939), 55–56, 58, 128.
17. Peru *Miami County Sentinel*, Jan. [?] 1880.

18. *The State, ex. rel. Godfroy v. The Board of Commissioners of Miami County*, 63 Ind. 497, 499–500 (1878).

19. RG 75, BIA Report Book 37:51, 55, 70.

20. Peru *Miami County Sentinel*, 30 Dec. 1880.

21. *Wau-pe-man-qua v. Aldrich*, 28 F. 489, 494 (1886).

22. *Board of Commissioners of Allen County v. Simons*, 28 N.E. 420; *Acts of Indiana*, 57th regular sess., Indiana General Assembly, 1891, p. 115.

23. *Miami County Historical Bulletin*, vol. 14, no. 7, July 1988, p. 8; George L. Chindahl, *History of the Circus in America* (Caldwell, Idaho: Caxton Printers, 1959), 127.

24. Compiled from land transactions in recorders' offices, Miami, Grant, and Wabash Counties.

25. Rafert, "Hidden Community," 188–89.

26. Annuity Payroll, Miami Indians of Indiana, 27 Oct. 1880 and 12 June 1895, prepared by M. D. Shelby, RG 75; Bert Anson, *The Miami Indians* (Norman: University of Oklahoma Press, 1970), 247–48.

27. Velma Nieberding, *The History of Ottawa County (Okla.)* (Miami, Okla.: Walsworth Pub. Co., 1983), 25–26.

28. W. David Baird, *The Quapaw Indians: A History of the Downstream People*, vol. 125 of the Civilization of the American Indian Series (Norman: University of Oklahoma Press, 1980), 130–48.

29. Nieberding, *History of Ottawa County*, 475–76.

30. Peter Iverson, *Carlos Montezuma and the Changing World of American Indians* (Albuquerque: University of New Mexico Press, 1982), 33–34; *Atlantic Monthly* 90 (1902): 801–3.

31. RG 75 BIA, Correspondence, Land Division, vol. 176, 411–23.

32. *Decisions Relating to the Public Lands* (Washington, D.C.: Government Printing Office, 1881–1921), 25:426–32.

33. "Summary Under the Criteria and Evidence for Proposed Finding Against Federal Acknowledgment of the Miami Nation of Indians of the State of Indiana, Inc.," 12 July 1990, Assistant Secretary Eddie L. Brown, U.S. Department of the Interior. (Copy in author's possession.)

34. "Testimony Pursuant to Congressional Legislation of June 1, 1872, taken before the commission appointed by the Secretary of the Interior to make partition of the reserve granted to Me-shin-go-me-sia in trust for his band by the seventh article of the treaty of November 28th 1840 between the United States and the Miami Tribe of Indians," p. 188, RG 75, ISP Shelf 8, Item 310.

35. M. Paul Holsinger, "Willis Van Devanter: The Early Years, 1859–1911" (Ph.D. diss., University of Denver, 1964); RG 75, ISP Shelf 8, Item 95, Claim of Van Devanter & McDowell, Secretary of Interior to Commissioner of Indian Affairs, 11 Jan. 1882.

36. Grant County, Indiana, Recorder's Office, Deed Book, vol. 2, p. 550; Deed Book, vol. 3, pp. 8, 13; Deed Book, vol. W, 11, 482; Sheriff's Decree Book, vol. 5, pp. 103, 562.

37. *Board of Commissioners of Miami County v. Godfroy*, 60 N.E. 177–80.

38. Judson Peconga to Office of Indian Affairs, RG 75, OIA LR 4378, 22 Jan. 1898.

39. W. A. Jones to James Stutesman, 23 Nov. 1901, OIA LS 46376.

40. RG 75, OIA LR 32952, 26 Apr. 1905; OIA LS 27244E, 3 May 1906.

41. Carlisle Indian School Student Files, RG 75. "Local Police Department Has Only Indian Officer in State," undated press clipping, *Fort Wayne Journal Gazette*.

42. Nieberding, *History of Ottawa County*, 37.

43. Personal communication with Rebecca Walker, 17 May 1990.

Chapter 7

1. Lawrence W. Schultz, "Godfroy Family Genealogy," Miami County Historical Society, Peru, Ind.

2. Raleigh Felsinger to Rep. Milton Kraus, 9 Mar. 1922, RG 75, Central Classified Files, 1907–36.

3. George S. Cottman, "The Last of the Miamis," *Indianapolis Sunday Journal*, 7 Jan. 1900.

4. Ibid.

5. Ibid.

6. Swan Godfroy Hunter and Eva Godfroy Bossley, interview with the author, 10 Aug. 1978.

7. Ibid.; LaMoine Marks, interview with the author, 24–25 Aug. 1989.

8. Hunter and Bossley interview.

9. Marks interview.

10. The author examined all birth and death records for Miami, Wabash, and Grant Counties from 1882 to 1960 and dangerous disease records for Miami and Wabash Counties from 1880 to 1940.

11. Hunter and Bossley interview.

12. Cottman, "Last of the Miamis."

13. Most of the objects listed were later purchased by museum collectors and are now at the Cranbrook Institute of Science, Bloomfield Hills, Michigan, the Detroit Institute of Art, the Museum of the American Indian, New York, and the Wyoming Historical and Geological Society, Wilkes-Barre, Pennsylvania. The history of the Miami collections is given in David W. Penney, ed., *Art of the American Indian Frontier* (Seattle: University of Washington Press, 1991), 299–322. Peter Godfroy spoke about the Anthony Wayne flag in an interview before his death in 1924.

14. Oliver Godfroy, interview with the author, 7 Aug. 1977. Godfroy was born in 1897.

15. Cottman, "Last of the Miamis."

16. *Huntington Press*, 30 Aug., 1 Sept. 1925.

17. Twelfth Census of the United States, 1900, Indian Population, Butler Twp., Miami Co., Ind.

18. Ibid., Marion, Grant Co., Ind.

19. Millie Rivarre to Commissioner of Indian Affairs, RG 75, LR OIA, 3 Jan. 1898: 1155.

20. Thirteenth Census of the United States, 1910, Population and Indian Population, Butler Twp., Miami Co., Ind.

21. Though there were no Miami speakers by the time the author did field research in the late 1970s older people remembered words and phrases; differences in pronunciation between Miami groups were obvious even to a nonlinguist.

22. This analysis is based on Nancy C. Dorian's field research on the decline of Gaelic among fishermen in East Sunderland, Scotland, set forth in *Language Death* (Philadelphia: University of Pennsylvania Press, 1981), 42–73.

23. Albert S. Gatschet, Notebook 1, item 3025, National Anthropological Archives, Smithsonian Institution, Washington, D.C., 198–203.

24. Wilcomb E. Washburn, ed., *History of Indian-White Relations*, vol. 4 of *Handbook of North American Indians* (Washington, D.C.: Smithsonian Institution, 1988), 646.

25. Caroline Dunn, *Jacob Piatt Dunn: His Miami Language Studies and Indian Manuscript Collection*, vol. 1, no. 2 of *Prehistory Research Series* (Indianapolis: Indiana Historical Society, 1937), 31–32, 38.

26. Gatschet, Notebook 1, p. 27.

27. Jacob P. Dunn Papers, alphabetical notecards unpaginated, Indiana Division, Indiana State Library, Indianapolis.

28. Marks interviews, 24–25 and 7–8 Nov. 1989.

29. T. W. Annabal to William A. Jones, RG 75, LR OIA, 24 Feb. 1903: 13221L; Reply OIA, LS 11262L, 6 Mar. 1903.

30. *Marion News-Tribune*, 14 Feb. 1905.

31. Miami Co., Ind. Circuit Court, Order Book No. 51: 411.

32. Gabriel Godfroy, "An Indian Story," *Indiana Magazine of History* 1 (1905): 19–21.

33. Hunter and Bossley interview.

34. Richard A. Ballenger to Rep. John H. Stephens, 25 Feb. 1911, RG 75, Miami Claims and Legislation File, 1492-1910-Seneca-073.

35. Wiley Sword, *President Washington's Indian War: The Struggle for the Old Northwest, 1790–1795* (Norman: University of Oklahoma Press, 1985), 335–36; Bruce Trigger, ed., *Northeast*, vol. 15 of *Handbook of*

North American Indians (Washington, D.C.: Smithsonian Institution, 1978), 684.

36. In 1873 Richardville testified that he was related to Meshingomesia and raised by his brother Chapendoceah in an effort to get an allotment from the reservation.

37. Federal census, Peru City, 1920.

38. William Bundy to COIA, 9 Aug. 1925, RG 75, Central Classified Files, 112065-1916-053, General Service, National Archives, Washington, D.C.

39. E. C. Finney, Acting Secretary of Interior, to Rep. Homer Snyder, 6 May 1921, RG 75, File 1492-1910-Seneca-073.

Chapter 8

1. Camillus Bundy to President Calvin Coolidge, 8 June 1927, RG 75, OIA LR 28876.

2. Mildred Bundy to President Franklin D. Roosevelt, 7 June 1933, RG 75, 38901-1923-General Service-File 302.

3. Carmen Ryan memorandum of 23 Sept. 1923 meeting, Miami Nation Tribal Archives.

4. Clarence Godfroy to the Secretary of the Interior, 5 Feb. 1924, RG 75, OIA LR 10387.

5. *Charles Z. Bondy v. Aetna Life Insurance Co.*, No. 310, Northern District of Indiana, South Bend Division, 4–7, Recorder's Office, Wabash Co., Ind.

6. The history of the collection is given in David W. Penney, ed., *Art of the American Indian Frontier* (Seattle: University of Washington Press, 1992), 299–322.

7. Hubert Work to Victoria Brady, undated 1925, RG 75, 38901-1923-General Service-File 302.

8. Camillus Bundy to President Calvin Coolidge, 8 June 1927, RG 75, OIA LR 28876.

9. Charles Burke to Camillus Bundy, 20 June 1927, OIA LS 28876, ibid.

10. H.R. 12101 and S. 3750, 70th Cong., 1st sess., 15 Mar. 1928, RG 75, 1492-1910-Seneca-013.

11. Both Commissioner of Indian Affairs Charles Burke and Secretary of the Interior Hubert Work refused to listen to Bundy's complaints on several occasions. Both officials set the tone at Bundy's first meeting with them. Their refusal to listen to grievances was directed at all allotted Indians, not just the Miami. Shortly after Bundy returned from Washington in Nov. 1925 he told his experiences to Hal C. Phelps, a Peru attorney sympathetic to the Miami. Phelps wrote that Burke and Work both walked out on Bundy and his daughter after telling them they were

white, not Indian, and citizens with no tribal rights. Later, the two Miami attended a discussion with several other Indian chiefs attempting to present complaints. A Ute and Ojibwa chief from Oklahoma offered to meet the same officials to see how he was treated and would report to them when he returned. Later the chief returned in an agitated state. He reported that when he called on Secretary Work with his interpreter, he was told about the same things that Bundy was told. When the chief saw he was getting nowhere, "he began to chew his tobacco hard and spit in Mr. Work's face." The chief then told Work, "You will not remember what I have said and the wrongs I am telling you that we have suffered . . . but there is one thing that you will remember and that is that I spit in your face." The chief told Bundy that all of the visiting Indians were treated with little respect. Hal C. Phelps Papers, Miami County (Ind.) Historical Society, 14 Nov. 1925, Item VIII-E-20.

12. E. C. Finney to H. M. Lord, 6 Apr. 1928 and E. B. Meritt to Charles Milton Shapp, 2 Nov. 1928, ibid.

13. Unknown to Dr. Marschalk, 22 May 1929, RG 75, 38901-1923-General Service-File 302.

14. *Indianapolis Star,* 17 Feb. 1930; *The Vidette-Messenger* (Valparaiso), 18 Feb. 1930.

15. Nongraduates File, 1924–59, Principal's Office, Wabash High School, Wabash, Ind.; Peru High School Yearbooks, 1920–40, Peru High School Archives, Peru, Ind.; Butler Township High School Records, Maconaquah School District, Miami Co., Ind.

16. Joanne Carol Joys, *The Wild Animal Trainer in America* (Boulder, Colo.: Pruett Publishing Co., 1983), 88.

17. LaMoine Marks, interviews with the author, 25 July and 11 Oct. 1991.

18. *Huntington Press*, 30 Aug. 1925.

19. R. Douglas Hurt, *Indian Agriculture in America: Prehistory to the Present* (Lawrence: University Press of Kansas, 1987), 153.

20. *Huntington Herald-Press*, 12, 13 May 1931; Miami Co., Ind., Clerk's Office, Fee Book, Criminal, No. 10, Cause 4000.

21. Chris Boyer and Paul Galbreath, Jr., interview with the author, 10 Feb. 1992.

22. Glenn Griswold to Bureau of Indian Affairs, 11 Feb. 1932, OIA LR 7791, RG 75, 1492-1910-Seneca-013.

23. Elijah Shapp to Harold L. Ickes, 12 Sept. 1933, ibid.

24. James S. Olson and Raymond Wilson, *Native Americans in the Twentieth Century* (Provo, Utah: Brigham Young University Press, 1984), 107–9.

25. Elijah Shapp to Harold L. Ickes, 27 Mar. 1933, OIA LR 13420 and Ickes to Shapp, 26 May 1933, RG 75, 1492-1910-Seneca-013.

26. C. J. Rhoads to Louise Leonard, 1 Nov. 1932, ibid.

27. Elijah Shapp to Harold L. Ickes, 15 June 1933, OIA LR 26420, ibid.

28. Bundy to Roosevelt, 7 June 1933, RG 75, 38901-1923-General Service-File 302.

29. Kinnozazyeah [Clarence] Mongosa to John Collier, [?] Dec. 1934, RG 75, 1492-1910-Seneca-013.

30. Lora Siders, interview with the author, 9 July 1985.

31. LaMoine Marks, interview with the author, 6 July 1979.

32. Francis Shoemaker, interviews with the author, 9–10 Dec. 1980. One of Bundy's stories concerning Miami leadership and spiritual powers is printed as "The Miami War Pipe" in Penney, ed., *Art of the American Indian Frontier*, 295–98.

33. J. M. Stewart to D'Arcy McNickle, 12 July 1937 and Charlotte Westwood to D'Arcy McNickle, 14 July 1937, RG 75, 41706-1937-066.

34. Nettie B. White to Secretary of the Interior, 21 July 1937, OIA LR 47296, ibid.

35. Miami Nation to President Franklin D. Roosevelt, 3 Dec. 1937, Nettie B. White to Secretary of the Interior, 23 Dec. 1937, and H. H. Evans to John Collier, 31 Dec. 1937, OIA LR 77154, 79210, 1938:285, ibid.

36. D'Arcy McNickle, Memorandum to Tribal Organization Branch, Bureau of Indian Affairs, 14 Jan. 1938 and William Zimmerman, Jr., to Evans and DeWitt, 1 Feb. 1938, RG 75, 1492-1910-Seneca-013.

37. Undated handwritten memorandum from Dodd to John Collier and memorandum, 31 Mar. 1938 from G. M. Paulus, Jr., ibid.

38. Miami Nation to John Collier, 26 Apr. 1939, OIA LR 26106; Collier to David Bondy, 12 May 1939; and undated affidavits and report on 4 June meeting, RG 75, 26106-1939-174.

39. William Zimmerman, Jr., to H. A. Andrews, 3 Nov. 1939, ibid.

40. Bert Anson, *The Miami Indians* (Norman: University of Oklahoma Press, 1970), 260–61.

41. Minutes of Special Meeting, Miami Tribe of Oklahoma, 12 Jan. 1940 and H. A. Andrews to Commissioner of the Office of Indian Affairs, OIA LR 3463, RG 75, 26106-1939-174.

42. *Indianapolis Star*, 22 Nov. 1940.

43. "Memorandum of Information Regarding the Claims of the Miami Indians of Indiana and Oklahoma," [undated] 1941, pp. 4–6, RG 75, 1492-1910-Seneca-013.

44. *Acts of the Indiana General Assembly*, 80th sess., 1937, pp. 65–67.

45. Eugene W. Weesner to Thomas Slick, 9 May 1940, *U.S. ex. rel. Marks v. Brooks*, National Archives, Chicago.

46. *Fort Wayne News-Sentinel*, 15 Aug. 1939; Elmer Winters to John Collier, undated, OIA LR 43361, 3 Nov. 1944; William Zimmerman, Jr., to Elmer Winters, 2 Dec. 1944, RG 75, 41706-1937-066; Marks interview, 11 Oct. 1991.

Chapter 9

1. Claimant Exhibit 7, Indian Claims Commission Docket 124, RG 279.

2. Oliver Godfroy, interview with the author, 7 Aug. 1977.

3. Alison R. Bernstein, *American Indians and World War II, Toward a New Era in Indian Affairs* (Norman: University of Oklahoma Press, 1991), 40.

4. James S. Olson and Raymond Wilson, *Native Americans in the Twentieth Century* (Urbana: University of Illinois Press, 1984), 131–33.

5. Ibid., 137.

6. Ibid.

7. Frank Tom-Pee-Saw to Harold Ickes, 23 Aug. 1943, RG 75, 41706-1937-066, OIA LR 34991, National Archives, Washington, D.C.; James A. Clifton, *The Prairie People: Continuity and Change in Potawatomi Indian Culture, 1665–1965* (Lawrence: The Regents Press of Kansas, 1977), 430–31.

8. Godfroy Council Minutes, Miami Nation Tribal Archives (hereafter cited as MNTA).

9. Ibid., 19.

10. Plaintiff's Exhibit "A," RG 279, Docket 124.

11. Robert M. Pennington to Peggy Keltner, 19 Oct. 1970, Tribal Operations File, Department of the Interior, Washington, D.C.

12. Olson and Wilson, *Native Americans in the Twentieth Century*, 137, 140.

13. Ibid., 139–40.

14. Erminie Wheeler-Voegelin, *Miami, Wea, and Eel-River Indians of Southern Indiana* (New York: Garland Publishing Co., 1974).

15. Carl F. Voegelin, *Shawnee Stems and the Jacob P. Dunn Miami Dictionary*, Indiana Historical Society *Prehistory Research Series*, vol. 1, nos. 3, 5, 8, 9, 10 (Indianapolis: Indiana Historical Society, 1938–40).

16. Bert Anson, *The Miami Indians* (Norman: University of Oklahoma Press, 1970), 284–85.

17. Carmen Ryan to Mrs. [Mary] Jones, 25 Nov. 1966, to Louis Bruce, Commissioner of Indian Affairs, 5 Sept. 1970, and to President Richard Nixon, 29 Jan. 1972, MNTA.

18. Exhibit 7, filed 14 Jan. 1955, Docket 124, RG 279.

19. Ibid., Exhibit 8.

20. Anson, *Miami Indians*, 285, 288; Wilma Victor to Andrew J. Marks, 28 July 1971, RG 48, Records of the Office of the Secretary of the Interior.

21. *Marion Chronicle-Tribune*, 15 Mar. 1961.

22. Ibid., 6 Mar. 1961.

23. Walter Maloney to William F. Hale, 26 Apr. 1961, MNTA.

24. William F. Hale to Ardis Miller, 13 Jan. 1964, ibid.

25. *Fort Wayne News-Sentinel*, 12 Aug. 1964; *Fort Wayne Journal Gazette*, 19 June 1965; *South Bend Tribune*, 2 July 1966; Anson, *Miami Indians*, 287 n.

26. *Peru Tribune*, 24 July 1968; Buford Rolin to the author, 17 Dec. 1986.

27. Anson's book, *Miami Indians*, was dedicated to Hale and Forest D. Olds, chief of the Western Miami tribe. There is no evidence that Anson spoke with any of several well-known Miami leaders who were active with the Miami Nation at the time he was researching the book. Long before the book was published, Hale resigned from his own council and had been denied any role in Miami leadership.

28. Council Minutes, Miami Nation of Indians of Indiana, 19 Apr. 1964, MNTA.

29. Francis Shoemaker, interviews with the author, 9–10 Dec. 1980.

30. Ibid.

31. Carmen Ryan to Mary Callahan, 27 Apr. 1964, MNTA.

32. Memorandum, 29 Oct. 1964, ibid.

33. Testimony of Eva Bossley before the House Subcommittee on Indian Affairs, 14 May 1965, RG 279, Docket 124-A.

34. Forest D. Olds to Sen. Mike Monroney, 12 Mar. 1965, MNTA.

35. Robert Mangan to Mina Brooke, 18 June 1964, Robert Pennington to Carmen Ryan, 28 May, 16 Aug. 1946, ibid.

36. S. 1461, 89th Cong., 1st sess., 9 Mar. 1965, ibid.

37. Statement by Walter Maloney on H.R. 7466 and H.R. 5156, undated 1965, ibid.

38. Mina Brooke to Phileo Nash, 13 Apr. 1965, ibid.

39. Ernest C. Friesen, Jr., to Mrs. Ronald Brooke, 22 Apr. 1966, ibid.

40. Indiana Miami Council Book, 1944–67, ibid.

41. Testimony before Indian Claims Commission, RG 279, Docket 124 D-E-F.

42. Herman and Wyneeta Bundy, interview with the author, 24 Nov. 1980.

43. Phyllis Miley, interview with the author, 13 Oct. 1993.

44. E. Wendell Lamb, Josephine Lamb, and Lawrence W. Schultz, *More Indian Lore* (Winona Lake, Ind.: Light & Life Press, 1968), 232–33; Miley interview.

45. Roger Williams, telephone conversation with the author, 13 Nov. 1990.

46. *Indianapolis Times*, 10 Oct. 1955; Wendell W. Wilkinson, 20 Nov. 1990, to the author.

47. Herman and Wyneeta Bundy interview; Shoemaker interviews.

48. *Indianapolis Times*, 2 Nov. 1962.

49. Donald L. Fixico, *Termination and Relocation: Federal Indian Policy, 1945–1960* (Albuquerque: University of New Mexico Press, 1986), 121–22.

50. "Report on Social and Economic Conditions of the Miami Indians of Indiana and the Miami Tribe of Oklahoma," Associate Solicitor, Indian Commissioner's Reading File, Tribal Relations Branch, Bureau of Indian Affairs, undated, MNTA.

51. Louise Wood to Ruthanna Simms, 10 Mar. 1961, National Anthropological Archives Catalog Item #4806, Smithsonian Institution, Washington, D.C.

52. Attendance List, Coalition of Eastern Native Americans, Washington, D.C., Conference, 7–9 Dec. 1972. List in possession of the author.

53. U.S. Indian Claims Commission, *Final Report* (Washington, D.C.: Government Printing Office, 1979), 57–58; Anson, *Miami Indians*, 287. List in possession of author.

54. *Swimming Turtle, a/k/a Oliver Godfroy v. Board of County Commissioners of Miami County*, 441 Fed. Supp. 368, 374–75 (1975).

55. Ibid.

56. Godfroy interview.

Chapter 10

1. James S. Olson and Raymond Wilson, *Native Americans in the Twentieth Century* (Provo, Utah: Brigham Young University Press, 1984), 159.

2. Alvin M. Josephy, Jr., *The Patriot Chiefs: A Chronicle of American Indian Leadership* (New York: Viking Press, 1961), 346.

3. Olson and Wilson, *Native Americans in the Twentieth Century*, 206.

4. "Report on Terminated and Nonfederally Recognized Indians," American Indian Policy Review Commission (Washington, D.C.: Government Printing Office, 1976), 1695–96.

5. Reid Peyton Chambers, conference on federal acknowledgment, Wellesley College, Wellesley, Mass., 7 Nov. 1991.

6. U.S. Indian Claims Commission, *Final Report* (Washington, D.C.: Government Printing Office, 1979), 21.

7. "Regulations, Guidelines and Policies for Federal Acknowledgment as an American Indian Tribe," *Federal Register*, 5 Sept. 1978, p. 39363. The overall guidelines are in 25 *Code of Federal Regulations*, part 81.

8. I had begun historical research on the Indiana Miami in 1978, spending summers in Indiana and winters in Washington, D.C., alternating research between local records and the National Archives. As I visited different families and conducted interviews over kitchen tables, I began to hear occasional comments about health services and other possible benefits of federal status. Claims meetings were still going on as well, and I did not pay particular attention to modern activities, as my research covered the period before 1940. Shortly after I finished my doctoral work in early 1982, a research organization in Lawrence, Kansas, contacted me and asked if I would be interested in doing a petition with the Miami. By then I had seen the regulations and knew that my work in reconstructing family genealogies, land transfers, and in Miami correspondence and reports in Washington would speed the

petitioning process. By coincidence, the Administration for Native Americans, a branch of community services in the Department of Health, Education and Welfare, was offering a few grants for what they called "status clarification" research for petitioning groups. My first work after completing a Ph.D. was to write a grant that was funded by the Administration for Native Americans.

9. George Pierre Castile's analysis of the expansion and contraction of ethnicity in "Of the Tarascanness of the Tarascans and the Indianness of the Indians" closely matches the Miami experience I am describing. Castile writes, "Only a minimal membership must be maintained to support the necessary structural nucleus that provides continuity for the symbolic identity system. It may aid in understanding the phenomenon of endurance to realize that the identity matrix of a people may have large or small numbers of adherents in actual cooperating contact, depending on the environmental circumstances. This notion, something like the expandability of the segmentary lineage, suggests that during times of persecution a minimal membership is likely to be reached with entire local segments sometimes ceasing to be part of the system, but that the matrix can serve as the focal point for expansion of membership as the ethnic adaptive option becomes more workable and attractive. While persecution can serve to reduce membership temporarily, it also serves, as many have noted, to increase the strength of the identification of the post-persecution membership. As long as a minimal, 'adequate' mechanism survives, suitable for the transmittal of the symbol sets to new members, the enclave persists, though many of its members may not." George Pierre Castile and Gilbert Kushner, eds., *Persistent Peoples: Cultural Enclaves in Perspective* (Tucson: University of Arizona Press, 1981), 184.

10. Hazel Elbert to Lois Hammons, 30 Jan. 1985, Miami Nation Tribal Archives, Peru, Ind. (hereafter cited as MNTA).

11. Ibid.

12. Lynn Forcia to James McClurken, undated 1986, Correspondence, Branch of Acknowledgment and Research, Bureau of Indian Affairs, ibid.

13. The cemetery was transferred in May 1993. Larry Thrush to Miami Nation, 7 June 1993, ibid.

14. *Evansville Courier,* 29 May 1988 Special Report. (This was a twelve-page special section devoted to the whole story.)

15. Harvey Arden, "Who Owns Our Past?," *National Geographic* 175 (Mar. 1989): 388.

16. Annual Report, 1985, Grand Traverse Band of Ottawa and Chippewa Indians, Suttons Bay, Mich., author's copy.

17. *Indianapolis Star,* 7 Jan. 1957; *Indianapolis Times,* 2 Nov. 1962.

18. *Prairie Farmer,* 19 Nov. 1977.

19. *Peru Daily Tribune,* 23 Nov. 1987.

20. Eddie Brown to Raymond White, 12 July 1990, MNTA.

21. "Summary under the Criteria and Evidence for Proposed Finding against Federal Acknowledgment of the Miami Nation of Indians, Inc.," Branch of Acknowledgment and Research, Bureau of Indian Affairs, 11.

22. Ibid.

23. Ibid. Anthropological Report, chart "Geographic Distribution of Miami Subgroups," 2.

24. Ibid.

25. "Indiana Miami General Meetings and Tribal Governance Activities since 1945," pp. 1–12, MNTA.

26. Carmen Ryan correspondence, 19 Mar.–27 Apr. 1970, ibid.

27. Robert Pennington to Carmen Ryan, 28 May 1964, Pennington to Mina Brooke, 19 Aug. 1964, and "Supplementary Documents, Series B, December 18, 1991," ibid.

28. *Indianapolis Star,* 10 June 1992.

29. "Summary Status of Acknowledgment Cases," Branch of Acknowledgment and Research, Bureau of Indian Affairs, 6.

30. Elizabeth S. Grobsmith and Betty R. Ritter, "The Ponca Tribe of Nebraska: The Process of Restoration of a Federally Terminated Tribe," *Human Organization* 51 (Spring 1992): 11.

31. "Summary under the Criteria and Evidence for Proposed Finding against Federal Acknowlegment of the Miami," Anthropological Report, Charts, 2.

32. Ibid.

33. Brian S. Vargas and Jennie Lengacher, "The Needs and Goals of the Miami Indian Nation," Public Opinion Laboratory, Indiana University, Indianapolis, 1987, pp. 12, 27, 29, MNTA.

34. "Historical Report on the Snoqualmie Indian Tribe," Branch of Acknowledgment and Research, Bureau of Indian Affairs, 1993, p. 37.

35. Ibid.

36. Ibid., 15–16, 20, 96–142 (meetings).

37. "Anthropological Report on the Snoqualmie Tribe," Branch of Acknowledgment and Research, Bureau of Indian Affairs, 1993, pp. 64, 72.

38. Ibid., 102–3.

39. "Summary Status of Acknowledgment Cases," 6.

40. *Kokomo Tribune,* 18 July 1990.

41. *Philadelphia Inquirer,* 11 Mar. 1990.

42. Ibid.

43. Sen. Richard G. Lugar floor statement of 5 Mar. 1991, included with correspondence to a constituent.

44. Sen. Richard G. Lugar to Sen. Daniel K. Inouye, 4 Nov. 1991.

45. *Peru Daily Tribune,* 12 Sept. 1992.

46. *Indianapolis News,* 10 Aug. 1993.

47. Charles F. Wilkinson, *American Indians, Time and the Law: Native Societies in a Modern Constitutional Democracy* (New Haven, Conn.: Yale University Press, 1987), 37–38.

48. *Indianapolis Star*, 15 Feb. 1993.

49. *Seattle Post-Intelligencer*, 2 July 1992; Cynthia Brown, "Unrecognized Tribes: The Vanished Native Americans," *The Nation*, 11 Oct. 1993, pp. 384–89.

Afterword

1. Telephone interview with LaMoine Marks, 25 Mar. 1994.

2. Bert Anson, *The Miami Indians* (Norman: University of Oklahoma Press, 1970), 295.

IMPORTANT DATES

■

c. 1654   First European contact with Miami in Wisconsin
c. 1672   Lakota drive portion of the Miami back east of Mississippi
           River from Iowa
   1679   René-Robert Cavelier de La Salle meets Miami along St.
           Joseph River in area of today's South Bend, Indiana
   1687   Iroquois kill large number of Miami near Chicago
   1701   French ratify peace with Iroquois, and Miami move into
           Upper Wabash and Maumee Valleys. Miami begin to settle
           at Kekionga (Fort Wayne)
   1734   Miami raid Chickasaw, allies of the English
   1752   French force destroys Miami village at Pickawillany
           in today's Ohio
   1755   Miami participate in destruction of Maj. Gen. Edward Brad-
           dock's army near Fort Duquesne (Pittsburgh)
   1778   Frances Slocum captured near Wilkes-Barre, Pennsylvania
   1780   Little Turtle destroys La Balme's force near Kekionga
   1787   Northwest Ordinance (Article III protectsIndian rights)
   1790   Miami and other tribes defeat Brig. Gen. Josiah Harmar
   1791   Little Turtle leads Miami and other tribes who inflict a
           devastating defeat on Maj. Gen. Arthur St. Clair and nearly
           the whole standing United States army
   1794   Maj. Gen. Anthony Wayne defeats Miami and other tribes of
           the Old Northwest at Fallen Timbers. Miami leave Kekionga
           for new locations along Upper Wabash, Eel, and
           Mississinewa Rivers

1795	Treaty of Greenville
1800	Indiana Territory formed
1803–09	Miami cede southern third of Indiana in three treaties with William Henry Harrison
1812	Little Turtle dies. Battle of Mississinewa near future Marion, Indiana
1816	Indiana becomes a state
1818	Treaty of St. Mary's. Miami cede "New Purchase," which includes all of central Indiana except for Miami "National Reserve"
1824	C. C. Trowbridge interviews Miami Chiefs Richardville and Le Gros concerning Miami customs and traditions
1826	Treaty of Paradise Springs (Wabash, Indiana) ceding land north of Wabash
1828	Treaty with Eel River Miami who cede Thorntown Reserve near Lebanon
1830	Congress passes Indian Removal Act
1834	Treaty that cedes west side of Miami "National Reserve" and many individual village reserves
1835	White captive Frances Slocum discovered living among Miami
1838	Treaty sets off Meshingomesia Reserve. Miami agree to inspect new lands in Kansas Territory
1840	Miami cede remainder of "National Reserve." Agree to removal of part of tribe. Chief Godfroy dies
1841	Principal Chief Jean Baptiste Richardville dies near Fort Wayne
1846	Removal of half of Miami tribe from Indiana to Kansas Territory
1847	Chief Francis Lafontaine dies. Some Miami return from Kansas
1850	Congress passes joint resolution allowing 101 more Miami to remain in Indiana
1854	Indiana Miami sign treaty in Washington, D.C. Tribal roll made
1859	Tribal Council protests congressional addition of 73 people to tribal rolls
1867	United States attorney general rules Indiana Miami are a recognized tribe under 1854 treaty
1872	Congress legislates allotment of Meshingomesia Reserve
1873	Testimony taken from Miami concerning rights to Meshingomesia Reserve land

1879 Meshingomesia dies
1881 Miami annuities ended. Tribal roll made and 1854 treaty funds distributed
1889 Eel River Miami annuities ended. Roll made. Pimyotamah dies
1891 State of Indiana exempts taxes on Miami treaty lands
1893 Commissioner of Indian Affairs affirms treaty status of Indiana Miami tribal government
1895 Court of Claims awards funds diverted to "bogus Miami." Tribal roll made
1897 Assistant United States Attorney General Willis Van Devanter administratively terminates treaty rights
1901 Tribe loses tax exemption case before Indiana Supreme Court
1903 Miami reunion begun. Continuous meetings to present
1905 Tribal leaders attempt to regain rights. Jacob P. Dunn begins recording Miami language
1909–11 Claims legislation introduced for tribe
1910 Gabriel Godfroy dies. Miami community in Butler Township, Miami County, begins to break up
1911 Thomas Richardville dies near Miami, Oklahoma
1921 Claims legislation introduced
1923 Camillus Bundy calls meeting of all Miami to form new tribal organization
1925 Maconaquah Pageant begins
1928 Legislation introduced on behalf of "Miami Nation" to address all tribal claims
1930s Tribe attempts to regain federal recognition. Fish and game protests
1935 Camillus Bundy dies
1937 Tribe is chartered as "Miami Nation of Indians of the State of Indiana"
1939 Interior Department guides tribal elections. Oklahoma Miami gain federal recognition
1939–41 Claims legislation reintroduced on behalf of Indiana tribe
1942 Tribal council informs President Franklin D. Roosevelt of its support of American war effort
1944 Tax-exempt Meshingomesia church land sold over tribal protest. Miami in Peru area organize to pursue claims
1949 Tribal leaders sign attorney's contract to pursue claims
1958 Indian Claims Commission declares Indiana Miami an "organized entity" having equal standing with Oklahoma Miami in claims cases

1961　Ira Sylvester "Ves" Godfroy, leader of claims, dies

1964　Miami Nation reorganizes. Army Corps of Engineers relocates Miami graveyards

1969　First claims award. New tribal roll made

1972　Second claims award

1977　Swimming Turtle (Oliver Godfroy) wins tax exemption on treaty land

1979　Tribe informs Bureau of Indian Affairs it will petition for federal recognition. Third claims award

1983　Tribe establishes an office. Junior council begins

1984　Petition for federal recognition submitted

1990　Bureau of Indian Affairs preliminary finding against recognition

1991　Tribe moves into new headquarters, establishes day care, archives, and bingo

1992　Bureau of Indian Affairs final determination against recognition. Tribe sues federal government

1993　Judge rules Miami treaty of 1854 valid, but that six-year statute of limitations applies to lawsuit. Chief Francis Shoemaker retires. Raymond O. White, Jr., named chief

1994　Chief Raymond White dies. Tribe loses second motion of legal case

BIBLIOGRAPHY

■

MANUSCRIPT MATERIALS

Chicago, Illinois. National Archives. Records of U.S. Circuit Court,
 Seventh District.
Indianapolis, Indiana. Indiana Historical Society.
 A. A. Cole Papers, M586.
 Census of the U.S., Agricultural Schedules, Indiana, 1850–1880.
Indianapolis, Indiana. Indiana State Library.
 Jacob P. Dunn Papers.
Peru, Indiana. Archives of the Miami Nation of Indians of Indiana.
 Peru High School. Yearbooks, 1920–40.
 Miami County Historical Society. Hal Phelps Papers.
St. Louis, Missouri. Federal Records Center. Records of U.S. Circuit
 Court, Seventh District.
Wabash, Indiana. Wabash High School, Principal's Office.
 "Non-graduates File."
Wabash County Historical Society.
Washington, D.C. National Archives.
 Records of the Bureau of the Census (Record Group 29).
  Seventh through Fourteenth Censuses, Population Schedules,
   Indiana, 1850–1920.
  Twelfth Census of the United States, 1900. Indian
   Population, Indiana.
  Thirteenth Census of the United States, 1910. Indian
   Population, Indiana.

Records of the Bureau of Indian Affairs (Record Group 75).
Annuity rolls, Miami Indians of Indiana, 1854, 1855, 1867–81.
Bureau of Indian Affairs Report Book 37.
Bureau of Indian Affairs, Correspondence, Land Division,
Vol. 176.
Carlisle Indian School Student Files.
Census Roll of Miami Indians of Indiana, 1854.
Census List of Miami Indians of Indiana, 1881.
Roll of Miami Indians of Indiana, 1895.
Central Classified Files, 1907–36.
General Service Files.
Miami Claims and Legislation File.
Miami Indians of Indiana.
Miami Attorney Contract File.
Claim of Van Devanter & McDowell.
Commissioner of Indian Affairs. Letters Received, 1881–1907.
_____ . Letters Sent, 1881–1907.
Letterbook, Meshingomesia Reserve.
Letters Received by the Office of Indian Affairs (M234).
Microfilm. Indiana Agency, 1824–50.
Minutes of Conference with Miami Delegation, 23 May–5 June
1854 (T494). Microfilm. 1801–53.
Report of Commission appointed by the Secretary
of the Interior to make partition of the Reserve of
Me-shin-go-me-sia.
Testimony Pursuant to Congressional Legislation of 1 June 1872.
Records of the Indian Claims Commission (Record Group 279).
Docket 124, 124-A, 124 D-E-F.
Washington, D.C. Department of the Interior.
Branch of Acknowledgment and Research Files.
Indian Commissioner's Reading File, Tribal Relations Branch.
Records of the Office of the Secretary of Interior.
Tribal Operations File.
Washington, D.C. Smithsonian Institution. National Anthropological
Archives. Albert S. Gatschet Papers.

CONGRESSIONAL DOCUMENTS

House Executive Document 23, 49th Cong. 1st Sess., Serial 2392.
6 Jan. 1886.
Sen. Doc. 164, 26th Cong. 1st Sess. 10 Feb. 1840.
Annual Report, Commissioner of Indian Affairs, 1840.

LEGISLATION

Acts of Indiana General Assembly, 80th Sess., 1937.
Statutes at Large of the United States of America, 1789–1873. 17 vols.
Washington, D.C.: Government Printing Office, 1850–73.

COURT CASES AND OPINIONS

Board of Commissioners of Miami County v. Godfroy, 60 N.E. 610 (1901).
Board of Commissioners of Allen County v. Simons, 28 N.E. 420 (1891).
Charles Z. Bondy v. Aetna Life Ins. Co., No. 310, Northern District of
　Indiana, South Bend Division (1944).
Godfroy v. Poe. Miami County (Ind.) Circuit Court, Spring Sess. (1855).
Godfroy v. Loveland. Miami County (Ind.) Circuit Court, Fall Sess. (1859).
Godfroy v. Soames. Northern District of Indiana, South Bend
　Division (1943).
Me-shin-go-me-sia v. State, 36 Ind. 310 (1871).
Opinions of the Attorney General. Washington, D.C.: Government
　Printing Office.
The State, ex. rel. Godfroy v. The Board of Commissioners of Miami County,
　43 Ind. 497 (1878).
*Swimming Turtle a.k.a. Oliver Godfroy v. Board of Commissioners of Miami
　County*, 441 F. Supp. 368 (1975).
U.S. Court of Claims, Appeal No. 2-59, 15 July 1960.
U.S. ex. rel. Marks v. Brooks, 32 F. Supp. 422 (1940).
Wau-pe-man-qua v. Aldrich, 28 F. 489 (1886).

UNPUBLISHED MATERIALS

Holsinger, M. Paul. "Willis Van Devanter: The Early Years,
　1859–1911." Ph.D. diss., University of Denver, 1964.
Rafert, Stewart J. "The Hidden Community: The Miami Indians of
　Indiana, 1846–1940." Ph.D. diss., University of Delaware, 1982.
＿＿＿＿ . Individual Survey Forms, Indiana Miami enrollees of 1846, 1854,
　1881, 1889, and 1895.
Rose, Mark. "A Nineteenth Century Miami House on the Mississinewa."
　Honors thesis, Ball State University, 1979.
Schultz, Lawrence W. "Godfroy Family Genealogy." Miami County
　Historical Society, Peru, Ind.

INDIANA COUNTY RECORDS

Grant County. Auditor's Office. Property Transfer Books.
＿＿＿＿ . Clerk's Office. Marriage Record Books.

_____ . Health Department. Register of Births, Register of Deaths.

_____ . Recorder's Office. Deed Records, Miscellaneous Records, Mortgage Records, Sheriff's Decree Records.

Miami County. Auditor's Office. Property Transfer Books.

_____ . Clerk's Office. Circuit Court Order Books, Criminal Fee Books, Guardianship Record Books, Marriage Record Books, Will Inventory Records.

_____ . Health Department. Register of Births, Register of Deaths.

_____ . Maconaquah School District. Butler Township High School Records.

_____ . Recorder's Office. Deed Records, Chattel Mortgage Records, Mortgage Records.

Wabash County. Auditor's Office. Property Transfer Books.

_____ . Clerk's Office. Circuit Court Order Books, Guardianship Record Dockets, Marriage Record Books, Register of Wills.

_____ . Health Department. Register of Births, Record of Dangerous Diseases, Register of Deaths.

_____ . Recorder's Office. Deed Records, Chattel Mortgage Records, Miscellaneous Records, Mortgage Records.

NEWSPAPERS

Congressional Globe. 46 vols. Washington, D.C., 1834–73.

Fort Wayne Journal-Gazette.

Fort Wayne News-Sentinel.

Huntington Press.

Huntington Herald-Press.

Indianapolis Journal.

Indianapolis News.

Indianapolis Star.

Indianapolis Times.

Marion News-Tribune.

Marion Chronicle-Tribune.

Miami County Sentinel.

Peru Tribune.

Peru Daily Tribune.

Philadelphia Inquirer.

Seattle Post-Intelligencer.

Wabash Weekly Intelligencer.

BOOKS AND ARTICLES

American State Papers: Indian Affairs. 2 vols. Washington, D.C.: Gales and Seaton, 1832–34.

Anson, Bert. "Chief Francis Lafontaine and the Miami Emigration from Indiana." *Indiana Magazine of History* 60 (Sept. 1964): 241–68.

_____. *The Miami Indians.* Norman: University of Oklahoma Press, 1970.

Baird, W. David. *The Quapaw Indians: A History of the Downstream People.* Norman: University of Oklahoma Press, 1980.

Barnhart, John D., ed. *Henry Hamilton and George Rogers Clark in the American Revolution.* Crawfordsville, Ind.: R. E. Banta, 1951.

Barnhart, John D., and Dorothy L. Riker. *Indiana to 1816: The Colonial Period.* Indianapolis: Indiana Historical Society, 1971.

Bemis, Samuel Flagg. *Jay's Treaty: A Study in Commerce and Diplomacy.* New Haven: Yale University Press, 1962.

Berthrong, Donald. *Indians of Northern Indiana and Southwestern Michigan.* New York: Garland Publishing, 1974.

Billington, Ray Allen. *Westward Expansion: A History of the American Frontier.* New York: Macmillan Publishing Co., 1949.

Blair, Emma Helen. *The Indian Tribes of the Upper Mississippi Valley and Region of the Great Lakes.* 2 vols. Cleveland: Arthur H. Clark Co., 1911.

Brice, Wallace A. *History of Fort Wayne.* Fort Wayne, Ind.: D.W. Jones and Son, 1868.

Brown, Cynthia. "The Vanished Native Americans." *The Nation* 275, no. 11 (October 1993): 384–89.

Carter, Clarence E., ed. *The Territorial Papers of the United States.* 27 vols. Washington, D.C.: Government Printing Office, 1934–69.

Carter, Harvey Lewis, *The Life and Times of Little Turtle: First Sagamore of the Wabash.* Urbana: University of Illinois Press, 1987.

Chindahl, George Leonard. *History of the Circus in America.* Caldwell, Idaho: Caxton Printers, 1959.

Clifton, James A. *The Prairie People: Continuity and Change in Potawatomi Indian Culture, 1665–1965.* Lawrence: Regents Press of Kansas, 1977.

Crosby, Alfred W., Jr. *The Columbian Exchange: Biological and Cultural Consequences of 1492.* Westport, Conn.: Greenwood Pub. Co., 1972.

Danhof, Clarence H. "Farm-Making Costs and the 'Safety Valve': 1850–1860." *Journal of Political Economy* 49 (June 1941): 317–59.

Decisions Relating to the Public Lands. Vol. 25. Washington, D.C.: Government Printing Office, 1898.

Dillon, John B. *The National Decline of the Miami Indians.* Vol. 1, no. 4 of Indiana Historical Society *Publications.* Indianapolis: The Bowen-Merrill Co., 1897.

Dobyns, Henry F. *Their Number Become Thinned: Native American Population Dynamics in Eastern North America.* Knoxville: University of Tennessee Press in cooperation with the Newberry Library Center for the History of the American Indian, 1983.

Dorian, Nancy C. *Language Death: The Life Cycle of a Scottish Gaelic Dialect.* Philadelphia: University of Pennsylvania Press, 1981.

Dunn, Caroline. *Jacob P. Dunn: His Miami Language Studies and Indian Manuscript Collection.* Vol. 1, no. 2 of *Prehistory Research Series.* Indianapolis: Indiana Historical Society, 1937.

Dunn, Jacob P. *Indiana and the Indianans: A History of Aboriginal and Territorial Indiana and the Century of Statehood.* 5 vols. Chicago and New York: American Historical Society, 1919.

___. *True Indian Stories: With Glossary of Indiana Indian Names.* Indianapolis: Sentinel Printing Co., 1909.

Edmunds, R. David. *The Potawatomis: Keepers of the Fire.* Norman: University of Oklahoma Press, 1978.

___. *Tecumseh and the Quest for Indian Leadership.* Boston: Little, Brown, 1984.

Esarey, Logan, ed. *Messages and Letters of William Henry Harrison.* 2 vols. Indianapolis: Indiana Historical Commission, 1922.

Fixico, Donald L. *Termination and Relocation: Federal Indian Policy, 1945–1960.* Albuquerque: University of New Mexico Press, 1986.

The French, the Indians, and George Rogers Clark in the Illinois Country: Proceedings of an Indiana American Revolution Bicentennial Symposium. Indianapolis: Indiana Historical Society, 1977.

Gilmore, Melvin R. *Uses of Plants by the Indians of the Missouri River Region.* Lincoln: University of Nebraska Press, 1977.

Glenn, Elizabeth J., B. K. Swartz, Jr., and Russell E. Lewis. *Archaeological Reports, Number 14.* Muncie, Ind.: Ball State University, 1977.

Godfroy, Gabriel. "An Indian Story." *Indiana Magazine of History* 1 (1905): 19–21.

Goebel, Dorothy Burne. *William Henry Harrison, A Political Biography.* Indianapolis: Historical Bureau of the Indiana Library and Historical Department, 1926.

Grand Traverse Ottawa and Chippewa Tribe. Suttons Bay, Mich. Annual Report, 1985.

Grobsmith, Elizabeth S., and Beth R. Ritter. "The Ponca Tribe of Nebraska: The Process of Restoration of a Federally Terminated Tribe." *Human Organization* 51, no. 1 (spring 1992).

Hagan, William T. *American Indians.* Chicago: University of Chicago Press, 1979.

Hauser, Raymond E. "The *Berdache* and the Illinois Indian Tribe during the Last Half of the Seventeenth Century." *Ethnohistory* 37, no. 1 (winter 1989): 45–65.

Herman, Bernard. *The Stolen House.* Charlottesville: University Press of Virginia, 1992.

Hicks, Ronald, ed. *Native American Cultures in Indiana: Proceedings of the First Minnetrista Council for Great Lakes Native American Studies.* Muncie, Ind.: Minnetrista Cultural Center and Ball State University, 1992.

History of St. Joseph County, Indiana. Chicago: Charles C. Chapman & Co., 1880.

Horsman, Reginald. *Expansion and American Indian Policy, 1783–1812.* East Lansing: Michigan State University Press, 1967.

Houck, Louis, ed. *The Spanish Regime in Missouri.* 2 vols. Chicago: R. R. Donnelley, 1909.

Hoxie, Frederick E., ed. *Indians in American History: An Introduction.* Arlington Heights, Ill.: Harlan Davidson, Inc., 1988.

Hundley, Will M. *Squawtown: My Boyhood among the Last Miami Indians.* Caldwell, Idaho: The Caxton Printers, Ltd., 1939.

Hurt, R. Douglas. *Indian Agriculture in America: Prehistory to the Present.* Lawrence: University Press of Kansas, 1987.

Hyde, George E. *Indians of the Woodlands, from Prehistoric Times to 1725.* Norman: University of Oklahoma Press, 1962.

Illinois State Historical Library *Collections.*

Indians and a Changing Frontier: The Art of George Winter. Indianapolis: Indiana Historical Society, 1993.

Iverson, Peter. *Carlos Montezuma and the Changing World of American Indians.* Albuquerque: University of New Mexico Press, 1982.

Jaenen, Cornelius J. *Friend and Foe: Aspects of French-American Cultural Contact in the Sixteenth and Seventeenth Centuries.* New York: Columbia University Press, 1976.

Josephy, Alvin M., Jr. *The Patriot Chiefs: A Chronicle of American Indian Leadership.* New York: Viking Press, 1961.

The Journals and Indian Paintings of George Winter, 1837–1839. Indianapolis: Indiana Historical Society, 1948.

Joys, Joanne Carol. *The Wild Animal Trainer in America.* Boulder, Colo.: Pruett Publishing Co., 1983.

Kappler, Charles J., ed. *Indian Affairs: Laws and Treaties.* 2d ed. 2 vols. Washington, D.C.: Government Printing Office, 1904.

Kellogg, Louise Phelps. *The French Régime in Wisconsin and the Northwest.* New York: Cooper Square Publishers, 1968.

Kinietz, W. Vernon. *The Indians of the Western Great Lakes, 1615–1760.* Ann Arbor: University of Michigan Press, 1965.

Kinnaird, Lawrence, ed. *Spain in the Mississippi Valley, 1765–1794: Translations of Materials from the Spanish Archives in the Bancroft Library.* 3 vols. Washington, D.C.: Government Printing Office, 1946.

Lamb, E. Wendell, Josephine Lamb, and Lawrence W. Schultz. *More Indian Lore*. Winona Lake, Ind.: Light and Life Press, 1968.

Lang, Elfrieda. "An Analysis of Northern Indiana's Population in 1850." *Indiana Magazine of History* 49 (March 1953): 17–60.

McKee, Irving. *The Trail of Death: Letters of Benjamin Marie Petit*. Vol. 14, no. 1 of Indiana Historicial Society *Publications*. Indianapolis: Indiana Historical Society, 1941.

Meginness, John F. *Biography of Frances Slocum, the Lost Sister of Wyoming*. Williamsport, Pa.: Heller Bros.' Printing House, 1891. Reprint, New York: Garland Publishing Co., 1975.

Miami County Historical Bulletin. Vol. 14, no. 7 (July 1988).

Michigan Pioneer and Historical Society. *Historical Collections*. 40 vols. Lansing, 1877–1929.

Miner, H. Craig, and William E. Unrau. *The End of Indian Kansas: A Study of Cultural Revolution, 1854–1871*. Lawrence: Regents Press of Kansas, 1978.

Mooney, James. *The Aboriginal Population of America North of Mexico*. Vol. 80, no. 7 of Smithsonian *Miscellaneous Collections*. Washington, D.C.: Smithsonian Institution, 1928.

Morris, Richard B., ed. *Encyclopedia of American History*. New York: Harper and Row, 1970.

Nieberding, Velma. *The History of Ottawa County*. Marceline, Mo.: Walsworth Pub. Co., 1983.

Olson, James S., and Raymond Wilson. *Native Americans in the Twentieth Century*. Provo, Utah: Brigham Young University Press, 1984.

Peckham, Howard H. *Pontiac and the Indian Uprising*. Princeton, N.J.: Princeton University Press, 1947.

Poinsatte, Charles R. *Fort Wayne during the Canal Era, 1828–1855: A Study of a Western Community in the Middle Period of American History*. Indianapolis: Indiana Historical Bureau, 1969.

Prucha, Francis Paul. *American Indian Policy in the Formative Years: The Indian Trade and Intercourse Acts, 1780–1834*. Cambridge, Mass.: Harvard University Press, 1962.

Quaife, M. M. *Fort Wayne in 1790*. Vol. 7, no. 7 of Indiana Historical Society *Publications*. Indianapolis: Indiana Historical Society, 1921.

Quimby, George Irving. *Indian Life in the Upper Great Lakes, 11,000 B.C. to A.D. 1800*. Chicago: University of Chicago Press, 1960.

Report on Terminated and Nonfederally Recognized Indians: Final Report to the American Indian Policy Review Commission. Washington, D.C.: Government Printing Office, 1976.

Resnick, Daniel. "Indian Country: Proud People Preserve Their Heritage and Tribal Hunting Grounds." *Prairie Farmer*, 19 November 1977.

Ritzenthaler, Robert E., and Pat Ritzenthaler. *The Woodland Indians of the Western Great Lakes*. Garden City, N.Y.: Natural History Press, 1970.

Robertson, Nellie A., and Dorothy Riker, eds. *The John Tipton Papers*. 3 vols. Indianapolis: Indiana Historical Bureau, 1942.

Royce, Charles C., comp. *Indian Land Cessions in the United States*. New York: Arno Press and the New York Times, 1971.

Satz, Ronald N. *American Indian Policy in the Jacksonian Era*. Lincoln: University of Nebraska Press, 1975.

Schoolcraft, Henry Rowe. *Information Respecting the History Condition and Prospects of the Indian Tribes of the United States*. 6 vols. Philadelphia: J. B. Lippincott, 1853–57.

Sheehan, Bernard W. *Seeds of Extinction: Jeffersonian Philanthropy and the American Indian*. Chapel Hill: University of North Carolina Press, 1973.

Stewart, George R. *American Place-Names: A Concise and Selective Dictionary for the Continental United States of America*. New York: Oxford University Press, 1970.

Sword, Wiley. *President Washington's Indian War: The Struggle for the Old Northwest, 1790–1795*. Norman: University of Oklahoma Press, 1985.

Tanner, Helen Hornbeck. *Atlas of Great Lakes Indian History*. Norman: Published for the Newberry Library by the University of Oklahoma Press, 1987.

Taylor, Robert M., Jr., ed. *The Northwest Ordinance, 1787: A Bicentennial Handbook*. Indianapolis: Indiana Historical Society, 1987.

Thornbrough, Gayle, ed. *Letter Book of the Indian Agency at Fort Wayne, 1809–1815*. Vol. 21 of Indiana Historical Society *Publications*. Indianapolis: Indiana Historical Society, 1961.

———. ed. *Outpost on the Wabash, 1787–1791*. Vol. 19 of Indiana Historical Society *Publications*. Indianapolis: Indiana Historical Society, 1957.

Thwaites, Rueben Gold, ed. *Early Western Travels, 1748–1846*. 32 vols. Cleveland: Arthur H. Clark Co., 1904–07.

———. ed. *Jesuit Relations and Allied Documents*. 73 vols. Cleveland: Burrows Brothers Co., 1896–1901.

Trennert, Robert A., Jr. *Indian Traders on the Middle Border: The House of Ewing, 1827–54*. Lincoln: University of Nebraska Press, 1981.

Trigger, Bruce, ed. *Northeast*. Vol. 15 of *Handbook of North American Indians*. Washington, D.C.: Smithsonian Institution, 1978.

Trowbridge, C. C. *Meearmeear Traditions*. Ed. Vernon Kinietz. Ann Arbor: University of Michigan Press, 1938.

U.S. Bureau of the Census. *Statistics of Population, Ninth Census of the United States*. Table 3. Washington, D.C.: Government Printing Office, 1872.

U.S. Indian Claims Commission. *Final Report*. Washington, D.C.: Government Printing Office, 1979.

Vargus, Brian S., Jennie Lengacher, and Sheila Sego. "Needs and Goals of the Miami Indian Nation." Public Opinion Research Laboratory, Indiana University. Indianapolis, 1987.

Voegelin, Carl F. *Shawnee Stems and the Jacob P. Dunn Miami Dictionary*. Vol. 1, nos. 3, 5, 8, 9, and 10 of *Prehistory Research Series*. Indianapolis: Indiana Historical Society, 1938–40.

Vogel, Virgil J. *American Indian Medicine*. Vol. 95 of Civilization of the American Indian Series. Norman: University of Oklahoma Press, 1970.

Volney, C. F. *A View of the Climate and Soil of the United States of America*. London: Printed for J. Johnson, 1804.

Wallace, Anthony F. C. *The Death and Rebirth of the Seneca*. New York: Alfred A. Knopf, 1970.

Washburn, Wilcomb, ed. *History of Indian-White Relations*. Vol. 4 of *Handbook of North American Indians*. Washington, D.C.: Smithsonian Institution, 1988.

Weslager, C. A. *The Delaware Indian Westward Migration*. Wallingford, Pa.: Middle Atlantic Press, 1978.

———. *The Delaware Indians: A History*. New Brunswick, N.J.: Rutgers University Press, 1989.

Wheeler-Voegelin, Erminie, Emily J. Blasingham, and Dorothy R. Libby. *Miami, Wea, and Eel-River Indians of Southern Indiana*. New York: Garland Publishing Inc., 1974.

White, Richard. *The Middle Ground: Indians, Empires, and Republics in the Great Lakes Region, 1650–1815*. New York: Cambridge University Press, 1991.

Wilkinson, Charles. *American Indians, Time and the Law: Native Societies in a Modern Constitutional Democracy*. New Haven, Conn.: Yale University Press, 1987.

Winger, Otho. *The Frances Slocum Trail*. North Manchester, Ind.: The News-Journal, 1943.

Collections of the State Historical Society of Wisconsin. 31 vols. Madison, 1855–1931.

Zitkala-Sa, "Why I Am a Pagan." *Atlantic Monthly* 90 (1902): 801–3.

INTERVIEWS

(by author unless otherwise indicated)

Bundy, Herman and Wyneeta. 24 November 1980.

Bossley, Eva and Swan Hunter. 10 August 1978.

Boyer, Chris and Paul Galbreath, Jr. 10 February 1992.
Godfroy, Oliver. 7 August 1977.
Marks, LaMoine. 6 July 1979. 24–25 August 1989.
    7 November 1989. 25 July, 11 October,
    11 November 1991.
    ———. Telephone interview. 25 March 1994.
Miley, Phyllis. 13 October 1993.
Shoemaker, Francis. 9–10 December 1980.
Siders, Lora. 9 July 1985.
Wadsworth, Sarah. Interview by Jacob P. Dunn.
    10 October 1909. 14 January 1911.

PERSONAL COMMUNICATIONS

Rolin, Buford. 17 December 1986.
Chambers, Reid. 7 November 1991.
Shoemaker, Francis. 6 July 1985.
Walker, Rebecca. 17 May 1990.
Williams, Roger. 13 November 1990.

AUTHOR'S DOCUMENTS

Attendance List, Eastern Indian Conference, 1972.
Ryan, Carmen to author, 20 August 1983.
    Wilkinson, Wendell, U.S. Army Corps of Engineers, Louisville
        District, to author. 20 November 1990

INDEX

■